THE
ESSENTIAL
MAIMONIDES

THE ESSENTIAL MAIMONIDES

TRANSLATIONS OF THE RAMBAM

Avraham Yaakov Finkel

JASON ARONSON INC.
Northvale, New Jersey
London

This book was set in 11 pt. Palacio by Aerotype Inc., Amherst, NH.

First Jason Aronson Inc. edition—1996

10 9 8 7 6 5 4 3

Library of Congress Cataloging-in-Publication Data

Maimonides, Moses, 1135-1204.
   [Selections. English. 1996]
   The essential Maimonides : translations of the Rambam / Avraham
Yaakov Finkel.
     p. cm.
   Includes index.
   ISBN 1-56821-464-2 (alk. paper)
   1. Rabbinical literature—Translations into English. 2. Judaism—
Apologetic works—Early works to 1800. 3. Islam—Controversial
literature—Early works to 1800. 4. Jews—Yemen—Early works to
1800. 5. Martyrdom (Judaism)—Early works to 1800. 6. Mishnah—
Criticism, interpretation, etc. 7. Ethics, Jewish—Early works to
1800. I. Finkel, Avraham Yaakov. II. Title.
BM545.A2513 1996
296.1'72—dc20

                                              96-4766

Manufactured in the United States of America. Jason Aronson Inc. offers books and cassettes. For information and catalog write to Jason Aronson Inc., 230 Livingston Street, Northvale, New Jersey 07647.

Dedicated to the memory of my father and teacher
HeChaver Reb Yehoshua Mattisyahu Finkel ע״ה
Beloved by my mother תבל״ח, five generations of his offspring,
and a host of students and friends.
He embodied the teachings of the Rambam
each day of his fruitful life.
10 Nissan, 5753/1993
תנצבה

Contents

INTRODUCTION   XI

PART 1—IGGERES TEIMAN, THE LETTER TO THE JEWS OF YEMEN 1

Rambam's Introduction   3
Words of Consolation   6
Encouraging Words   14
Refuting Moslem Claims   20
The Coming of Mashiach   29
The False Mashiach   39
Epilogue   49

PART 2—MAAMAN KIDDUSH HASHEM, DISCOURSE
ON MARTYRDOM   51

A Misleading Answer   53
The Gravity of Maligning a Jew   57
The Importance of Every Mitzvah   62
Discussion of Kiddush Hashem   66

PART 3—COMMENTARY ON THE MISHNAH   79

Translator's Introduction   81
The Written and the Oral Torah   83
The Power of Prophecy   86
The Transmission of the Oral Torah   99
Categories of the Oral Torah   101
Dissenting Opinions   111
The Structure of the Mishnah   113
Expounding the Mishnah   131

Following the Completion of the Talmud   144
Discussion about the Commentary of the Mishnah   146
Appendix   148

**PART 4 — SHEMONAH PERAKIM, THE EIGHT CHAPTERS,
AN INTRODUCTION TO ETHICS OF THE FATHERS**   **165**

Introduction   167
Chapter One. The Human Soul and its Powers   169
Chapter Two. The Source of Virtue and Vice   174
Chapter Three. Diseases of the Soul   177
Chapter Four. Curing the Soul   179
Chapter Five. The Ultimate Goal   189
Chapter Six. The True Saint   194
Chapter Seven. Barriers To Hashem   198
Chapter Eight. Man's Nature   202

**PART 5 — PEREK CHELEK, DISCOURSE ON THE WORLD
TO COME**   **217**

Discourse   219
Commentary on Mishnah 1   235
Thirteen Principles of Faith   237
The Basis of our Faith   245

GLOSSARY   **246**
INDEX   **251**

Acknowledgments

First and foremost, I would like to express my deep gratitude to Hashem Yisbarach for enabling me to be instrumental in making the wisdom inherent in the fundamental teachings of the Rambam accessible to a wide audience of English-speaking readers.

I am thankful to Rabbi Yaakov Shnaidman, Rosh Yeshivah of Yeshivath Beth Moshe of Scranton who suggested the idea of creating the present translation, and to Rabbi Shmuel Flam of Yeshivath Beth Moshe for his valued assistance.

I am indebted to my friend Mr. Arthur Kurzweil, vice-president of Jason Aronson Inc. and the motivating force of this outstanding publishing company, for producing this volume. With vision and boldness he disseminates a large number of oustanding works of Torah and tradition to the thinking Jewish public. In a sense, this makes him a true *marbitz Torah* (one who teaches Torah to the multitudes).

Many thanks to Mr. Anthony Rubin for meticulously copyediting this book, to Judie Tulli for creating the artistic and distinctive cover design, and to the entire dedicated staff of Jason Aronson Inc., for their unfailing courtesy and cooperation whenever called upon.

Most importantly, I want to express my sincere gratitude to my dear wife, Suri, for her encouragement, enthusiasm, and sage advice, always given with a smile.

Introduction

Rabbi Moshe ben Maimon (Maimonides), better known as Rambam (the acronym of his name) is universally recognized as the greatest codifier of Torah law and the foremost Jewish thinker. His influence remains unabated until the present time. The committed leader of his generation, he made the study of *Torah She'be'al Peh* (the Oral Torah) accessible to the masses and enunciated the principles that form the bedrock of *hashkafah*, the Torah viewpoint. A compassionate leader of his fellow Jews, he commiserated with their suffering and offered them sage guidance and encouragement. He wrote the classic *Guide for the Perplexed* for students of philosophy who were bewildered by seeming contradictions between the teachings of the Torah and prevailing secular philosophical theory. The greatest testimony to the unsurpassed genius of the Rambam is the fact that today, as in the past, his works are avidly studied by scholars, laymen and students as indispensable aids to understanding Torah law and the Torah outlook on life.

THE TIMES

After the decline of the great Talmudic centers of Babylonia in the 10th century, Jewish culture began to flourish in Spain and North Africa under the benevolent rule of the Moslem caliphs. The next two centuries were the Golden Age of Spanish Jewry, an epoch during which Torah scholarship rose to extraordinary heights. This is exemplified by the towering figures of that time such as the scholar-statesmen Chisdai ibn Shaprut (c.915–c.990) and Shmuel HaNagid (933-1055), as well as the brilliant poet-philosopher Shlomoh ibn Gabirol (1021-1050). Other spiritual giants of that epoch were Rabbi Bachya ibn Pakudah (c.1000–c.1065), author of *Chovot HaLevavot*, (Duties of the Heart), the seminal work on Torah ethics, and the illustrious Talmudist Rabbi Yitzchak Alfasi (the Rif,

1013–1103). His successor as *rosh yeshivah* (dean) of the Talmudic academy of Lucena was the young Rabbi Yosef ibn Migash (1077–1141), who in turn became the inspiration of the young Moshe ben Maimon (Maimonides). Other famous personalities of that time were the poet Rabbi Yehudah HaLevi (c.1080–c.1145), author of the philosophical book *The Kuzari,* and the great Torah commentator Rabbi Avraham Ibn Ezra (1089–1164).

The Golden Age was a period during which Sephardic Jewry reached unprecedented levels of learning, morality and observance of Torah. It was a time when the Jewish community enjoyed a spiritual climate of love of Torah learning and unquestioning respect of its scholars.

The Golden Age began to wane, however, when the Almohads, a fanatical Moslem sect from northern Africa, invaded southern Spain. They took the city Cordova in 1148, and drove out the reigning Almoravids with much violence and bloodshed. Abd-al-Mu'min, the implacable leader of the Almohads, offered the Jews under his control the sad choice of conversion to Islam, exile, or a martyr's death. Many Jews pretended to accept Islam while inwardly remaining faithful to the beliefs of their ancestors. Others fled to foreign countries like France or Italy, or settled in northern Christian Spain. Many escaped to northern Africa, Egypt and Asia Minor. Some died a martyr's death.

It was during those dismal days that there emerged one man who lit up the gloom and darkness and spread soothing balm on the wounded souls of his fellow Jews. That man was Rabbi Moshe ben Maimon, Maimonides.

THE MAN

Rabbi Moshe ben Maimon was born on the eve of Passover in 1135, in Cordova, a thriving center of Jewish life during the Sephardic Golden Age in Spain. He was a scion of a prominent rabbinical family that traced its ancestry to Rabbi Yehudah HaNassi, the compiler of the Mishnah, and further back to King David. His principal mentor was his father, Rabbi Maimon ben Yosef, the *dayan* (religious judge) of Cordova, from whom he received a wide-ranging proficiency in the Talmud. He also received a thorough understanding of the fundamentals of mathematics, astronomy, and philosophy.

When young Moshe was only thirteen years old, his tranquil adolescent life was disrupted by the conquest of Cordova by the Almohads, an extremist militant Moslem sect from Morocco. When the Almohads forced the Jews to convert to Islam, under the banner of the ancient Moslem doctrine, "The Koran or the Sword," Rabbi Maimon and his family went into exile to Andalusia and from there to Christian northern Spain. After wandering from place to place for almost twelve years, the Maimon family left Spain for the city of Fez in North Africa. After a brief stay in Jerusalem, they finally made their home in Fostat, a suburb of Cairo, Egypt, in 1165.

Shortly before arriving in Egypt, Rambam's father died. While Rambam devoted himself to Torah study, his younger brother David, a dealer in diamonds and precious stones, supported the entire family. However, tragedy struck. In 1169, on one of his business trips, David perished when his ship went down in the Indian Ocean, and with him the family fortune was lost. Shattered by the calamity, Rambam fell ill and was bedridden for an entire year. The burden of sustaining both his family and that of his brother now fell on Rambam's shoulders. Unwilling to derive benefit from his vast Torah knowledge, he took up the study of medicine. Before long, he earned a reputation as an outstanding healer and was appointed physician to the Court of Sultan Saladin in Cairo. Recognizing his phenomenal knowledge, wisdom, and strength of character, the Jews of Egypt appointed Rambam as chief rabbi of Cairo and head of all Egyptian Jewry. As his fame spread, he became the leading authority of his generation.

Despite his busy schedule as Court physician, he found the time to write his famous books, letters and discourses, and oversee the religious affairs of the Egyptian Jewish community. He also responded to halachic questions and answered requests for guidance that were pouring in from the far reaches of the Jewish world.

The Jewish communities of that time were battered by turbulent currents and grave crises. Rambam tackled all problems with a blend of firmness, compassion and understanding for human frailties. In addition to addressing the external threat of forced conversions to Islam, he brought an end to the internal strife with the Karaites, a Jewish sect that denied the divine origin and the validity of the Oral Law. He spoke out forcefully against Karaite doctrines, proving them to be fraudulent. At the same time, he lovingly invited individual Karaites to return to authentic Judaism. As a result, many Karaites joined the traditional Jewish community where they were welcomed and accepted. He advocated a tolerant attitude toward Jews who had been forced into apostasy, and who professed to be Moslems while secretly adhering to Judaism.

He used his influence with the Sultan to secure goodwill and security not only for the Jews of Egypt, but also for the Jewish community in Eretz Yisrael. Ever since the Crusaders captured Jerusalem in 1099, Jews had been banned from that city. However, after seizing Jerusalem from the Christians in 1187, Saladin permitted the Jews to return there, thanks in a large measure to behind-the-scenes lobbying by the Rambam.

The Rambam passed away in his seventieth year, on the 20th Tevet, 4965/1204. His death was mourned by Jews the world over. In Egypt three days of mourning were observed by both Jews and Moslems. In Jerusalem the news prompted an outbreak of weeping and lamenting, and at a special service the *Tochachah* (Leviticus 26 or Deuteronomy 29), the chapter of dreadful curses, was read. His remains were brought to Tiberias and interred in a tomb that is visited by thousands of devotees year after year. His incomparable greatness as a scholar, thinker and humanitarian is best summed up in the famous dictum inscribed on his tomb, *MiMoshe ad Moshe lo kom keMoshe*, "From Moshe (Moses) till Moshe (Rambam), no one arose like Moshe (Rambam)."

RAMBAM'S WRITINGS
PEIRUSH HAMISHNAYOT – COMMENTARY ON THE *MISHNAH*

While only twenty-three years old and a wandering refugee, the Rambam wrote his Commentary on the *Mishnah*, known as *Peirush HaMishnayot*. The *Mishnah*, which is the earliest portion of the Talmud, had been compiled and edited by Rabbi Yehudah Hanassi (the Prince). Written in an extremely concise style, wherein every word and literary nuance is laden with meaning, it forms the basis of all later Talmudic writings. By itself, the *Mishnah* text is extremely difficult to understand. Maimonides wrote the first clear commentary on this work. He completed it in 1168 after seven years, and it was published under the Arabic title of *Kitab as-Siraj*, in Hebrew, *Sefer Ha'orah* (The Book of Light), but it is universally known as *Peirush*

HaMishnayot, (Commentary on the *Mishnah*). The Rambam's purpose in writing this work was to enable people who are not capable of studying the *Gemara*, to understand the *Mishnah*. Rather than explaining the literal meaning of the text, he provides a summary and analyzes the gist of the *Mishnah*, defining difficult terms at the end, and adding the final halachic decision of the subject at hand.

Rambam's Commentary on the *Mishnah* was written in Arabic and translated into Hebrew by Rabbi Yehudah ben Shlomoh al-Charizi. It is printed in the standard Vilna edition of the Talmud, in the back of each tractate. The Introduction is in the back of tractate *Berachot*.

Mishneh Torah

Rambam's *magnum opus* is the monumental *Mishneh Torah*, (the words mean repetition of the law), an all-encompassing work in which he extracted every legal decision and law from the Talmud and the writings of the *Geonim*, codified and analyzed them, and arranged them all into 14 systematic volumes. He completed it in 1180, after ten years of painstaking labor. The book is also called *Yad HaChazakah*. The word *yad* has the numeric value of 14, alluding to the 14 volumes of this work. For short, it is generally called the *Yad*, or simply, "the Rambam." It was written in a lucid and concise Hebrew and is the first comprehensive codification of all Torah Laws. It includes both the laws of immediate relevance, such as the laws of *Shabbat, kashrut* and family purity, and those pertaining to the Messianic Age, such as the laws of the Temple service and sacrifices. Yet, *Mishneh Torah* is not a dry, legalistic book of statutes and ordinances. Its rulings are interspersed with ethical insights and philosophical teachings that infuse it with vitality and spirituality. Vast in scope, it has never been equalled or surpassed by any other work. This awe-inspiring compendium attests to the Rambam's breathtaking range and depth of knowledge and clear, penetrating thinking. In his concern for brevity Maimonides omitted the source of each decision. This gave rise to numerous commentaries that attempt to identify the sources on which his rulings are based.

In his introduction the Rambam states the aim of *Mishneh Torah* to be "to make the Oral Law accessible to everyone, to the point where every *mitzvah* will be plain to understand to young and old, so that they will have to consult no other book."

Mishneh Torah immediately gained immense popularity. It became the most authoritative text on *halachah*, and over the years more than 325 commentaries were written on it. Today, as in the past, every Talmudic discussion or discourse invariably will involve seeking a solution to a "difficult Rambam."

Its first section, *Sefer Hamada*, (Book of Knowledge), comprises a synopsis of the fundamental beliefs of Judaism. The concluding section, *Hilchot Melachim*, (Laws of Kings), deals with the Rambam's views on the coming of *Mashiach*, and the establishment of the Kingdom of God here on earth, "when the Jews will be great sages and know hidden matters, attaining knowledge to the full extent of human potential, as it says, 'The world will be filled with the knowledge of God as water covers the sea (Isaiah 11:9).' "

Moreh Nevuchim, **Guide for the Perplexed**

Rambam's third major work is *Moreh Nevuchim*, (The Guide for the Perplexed). Written in Arabic under the title, *Dalalat al Hairin*, it was translated into Hebrew by Rabbi Shmuel ibn Tibbon. In this book the Rambam addresses people who are baffled by seeming contradictions between the teachings of the Torah and Aristotelian philosophy. He demonstrates that the inconsistencies can be reconciled, and that there is no conflict if the fundamentals of both are properly understood and interpreted.

Although the Rambam respected Aristotle's philosophy, he differed with him on many issues. Thus, for example, he proved the Biblical account of Creation and refuted Aristotle's theory of the Eternity of the Universe. He also sharply disagreed with Aristotle on the principle of Free Will, arguing that man is endowed with free determination. He devotes a chapter to the notion that man is a microcosm, a miniature reflection of the universe, and explains at great length that such Biblical terms as the "eyes" or "hand" of God are anthropomorphisms that are used figuratively. Rambam proves God's existence, discusses prophecy, Divine Providence, the purpose of Creation and many other philosophical themes.

The Guide for the Perplexed has greatly influenced the thinking of the philosophers of the world and established Maimonides as the foremost of all Jewish philosophers.

FIVE GREAT DISCOURSES AND LETTERS

Each of the five discourses and letters offered in the present volume is a celebrated treatise of timeless relevance. Taken together they comprise, in capsule form, the full range of the Rambam's views on God, Torah, man, and the world. In addition to answering questions on crucial issues relating to our faith, they provide an insight into the mindset of Maimonides, the prodigious genius and compassionate leader of the Jewish people.

1. *Iggeret Teiman* (Letter to Yemen)

Maimonides did not only produce great scholarly works. When circumstances demanded it he could write moving letters of encouragement to simple Jews suffering from tyranny in faraway countries, bolstering their faith with easy-to-understand expositions and concepts. *Iggeret Teiman,* written in 1172, is such a letter.

The letter is Rambam's response to an inquiry from Rabbi Yaakov ben Netanel Fayumi, the leader of the Jewish community of Yemen on the southern tip of the Arab peninsula. At that time, the Jews in that far-off country were plagued by harrowing misfortunes and confronted a dreadful dilemma. A fanatical Shi'ite Moslem rebel had risen to power and forced the Jews of Yemen to convert to Islam. The alternative was death or expulsion. At the same time, a Jewish apostate who had become a missionary for Islam was trying to win converts among the Yemenite Jews by spouting spurious Scriptural proofs to confirm the authenticity of Mohammed's message. Adding to the confusion, a man purporting to be *Mashiach* appeared on the scene, duping the unlearned masses and gaining a large following among them. Bewildered by these multiple assaults on their beliefs, many Yemenite Jews tried to calculate the date of the coming of *Mashiach* by means of astrology.

Maimonides, who personally had experienced the ordeals of reigious persecution and the threat of forced conversion, sent his reply in the form of the *Letter to the Jews of Yemen.* With great sensitivity he addressed each of the problems facing that hapless community. Mincing no words, he pointed out the patent falsehood of Christian and Islamic doctrine, the futility of astrology, and the absurdity of the apostate missionary's so-called proofs. Replying to the claims of the false messiah, he ended his letter with a discussion of the characteristics of the true *Mashiach*, and the criteria by which *Mashiach* can be recognized.

At the Rambam's request, *Iggeret Teiman* was read in public gatherings in every town and hamlet. Its inspiring words had a tremendous impact on the Jews of Yemen. Infused with hope and pride in their heritage, they resolved to remain faithful to Judaism and ignore the arguments of missionaries and the "miracles" of fraudulent messiahs.

It is interesting to note that through the centuries, from the time of Maimonides until the present, the Jews of Yemen, despite ceaseless persecution and harassment, staunchly have clung to the faith of their fathers and are known for their scrupulous observance of the Torah and all *mitzvot*.

2. *Maamar Kiddush Hashem* (Discourse on Martyrdom)

The *Discourse on Martyrdom* is the Rambam's reply to a query by a Jew from Morocco. The Jews of that region were forced to convert to Islam by the ruling Almohad Moslem sect, the same regime that had forced the Rambam to leave Spain and find refuge in Egypt. The questioner, who publicly professed Islam, had asked a Talmudic scholar whether he should clandestinely observe as many *mitzvot* as he could. The scholar replied that any *mitzvah* a converted Jew performed or any prayer he uttered constituted a sinful act.

Shocked by the scholar's misinterpretation of the law, Maimonides wrote his *Discourse on Martyrdom* in 1165, offering instruction and counsel on the proper course one should follow when confronted with religious coercion. This letter is much more than a response to one individual caught in a difficult situation. It is a timeless document that has provided guidance and succor during the countless persecutions and forced conversions the Jewish people have endured in its long exile, including the Holocaust.

The *Letter to Yemen* and the *Discourse on Martyrdom* are two classic examples of the Rambam's deep love of the Jewish people, his erudition, sagacity, and statesmanship. It is in these letters that the Rambam's extraordinary personality comes to the fore. One marvels at his humility, his kindness, and his wit. The reader smiles at the scathing sarcasm with which Maimonides unmasks impostors, deflates pompous ignoramuses and assorted perverters of the truth. Like *Moshe Rabbeinu*, the Rambam winces at the pain each

Jew is suffering. With deep compassion he does his utmost to alleviate their torment. Like a father, he gently soothes our pain, encourages us, and inspires us with hope and a sense of pride. Through the clarity of his writing the Rambam springs to life, exuding such warmth that one is spellbound by his words.

3. Introduction to the Commentary on the Mishnah

This treatise is much more than the name implies, because rather than a mere introduction, it is a work of great importance in its own right. In it the Rambam clarifies the chain of transmission of the Oral Law as it came down through the ages from Moses to Rabbi Yehudah HaNassi, the compiler of the *Mishnah*. The Rambam conveys the proper perspective needed for the study of the *Mishnah*, and emphasizes that *halachah* (Jewish law) is not determined by prophetic inspiration but rather by analysis of the Written Law according to a set of prescribed rules.

This leads to a detailed discussion of the phenomenon of prophecy and the ways we can distinguish a true prophet from an impostor.

After giving an outline of the six Orders of the *Mishnah* and the subjects treated in the various tractates, Maimonides explains the origin of halachic disagreements. He then turns his attention to the seemingly bizarre *Aggadic* tales that sometimes are found in the Talmud, explaining that these stories are in fact allegories that conceal profound concepts that cannot be spelled out in simple language. This leads to a very enlightening philosophical discussion about the purpose of the creation of man and the ideals he should pursue.

Rambam then lists all the tractates of the Talmud and concludes by stating his aim in writing the commentary on the *Mishnah*.

4. *Shemonah Perakim* (The Eight Chapters)

Shemonah Perakim, (The Eight Chapters), the fourth treatise featured in the present volume, is one of the all-time great works on Jewish ethics, psychology, and philosophy. This treatise is actually the Rambam's introduction to tractate *Avot*. In its eight chapters he discusses the nature of the soul, its sicknesses and cures, focusing on the ideal of the "golden mean." He deals with the various degrees of prophecy, the qualifications of a prophet, and the impediments that interfere with prophecy. He devotes several sections to the spurious theory of predestination, contending that man is endowed with a free will. This is followed by a wide-ranging discussion of the question that has baffled all thinkers: How can God's omniscience be reconciled with man's freedom of will? If God has foreknowledge, how can an individual have freedom of action? *The Eight Chapters* concludes by providing a glimpse into the world of metaphysics, touching on such esoteric subjects as the essence of God and knowledge of God.

The Eight Chapters was written in Arabic and translated into Hebrew by Rabbi Shmuel ibn Tibbon. The Hebrew text can be found in the standard Vilna edition of the Talmud, before tractate *Avot* and immediately following tractate *Eduyot*.

5. Discourse on the World to Come

In the fifth treatise rendered into English in this volume Maimonides delves into the basic tenets of Judaism. In this discourse which is his commentary to *Sanhedrin* 10:1, (*Perek Chelek*) he concentrates on such fundamental beliefs as the existence of God, His unity and incorporeality. He deals with prophecy, with reward and punishment, with the Messianic Age, and the resuscitation of the dead during the days of *Mashiach*. He maintains that the ultimate reward is the World to Come, and concludes the treatise by formulating the famous Thirteen Principles of Faith. A summary of these fundamentals was stated succinctly in the famous *Ani maamin* prayer, and set to poetic verse in the popular hymn *Yigdal*.

Maimonides wrote most of his works in Arabic, because Arabic was the language spoken by the Jewish community of his time, and he wanted to reach as large a readership as possible. In translating his works I have tried to give a faithful rendering of the Hebrew text while maintaining an informal, conversational tone. In cases where a literal translation would distort the meaning of the text I used the appropriate idiom to convey the thought behind the words.

FIRST EDITIONS

Peirush HaMishnayot, Rambam's Commentary on the *Mishnah*

The first printed edition of the *Mishnah,* published in Naples in 1492, contains Rambam's commentary. Retranslated from the Arabic into Hebrew by Rabbi Yosef Kafich, Jerusalem, 1964.

Mishneh Torah also called *Yad Hachazakah,* first published in Rome before 1480; Soncino, 1490.

Iggeret Teiman, Letter to Yemen, Basel, 1629; Vilna, 1835; Warsaw, 1837.

Maamar Kiddush Hashem, Discourse on Martyrdom, Breslau, 1937.

Moreh Nevuchim, Guide for the Perplexed, Rome, before 1480; Venice, 1551; Sabionetta, 1553.

OTHER WORKS BY THE RAMBAM:

Sefer Hamitzvot, Book of the Commandments, traces the 613 Torah laws. Constantinople, 1510; Venice, 1544.

Maamar Techiat HaMeitim, on the resurrection of the dead, Venice, 1546.

Milot HaHegayon, on the terminology of logic, Venice, 1552.

Responsa, Constantinople 1536, Jerusalem, 1934.

A number of medical treatises.

•1•

Iggeres Teiman
The Letter to the Jews
of Yemen

Rambam's Introduction

By Moshe son of Rabbi Maimon, the Judge,
son of Rabbi Yosef,
son of Rabbi Yitzchak,
son of Rabbi Ovadiah, the Judge.
To strengthen the hands that are slack;
and make firm tottering knees!

To the holy, wise, congenial, and distinguished scholar, Rabbi Yaakov al-Fayumi, son of the distinguished Rabbi Nesanel al-Fayumi, to all the communal leaders and scholars of the communities of Yemen: may Hashem, the Rock, keep and protect them. Amen. Selah.

PRAISING THE YEMENITE COMMUNITY

Stems attest to the integrity of their roots, and streams bear witness to the excellence of their springs. So too, has a faithful twig sprouted out of a root of truth. A mighty river has flowed out of the wellspring of kindness in the land of Yemen to water all gardens and make blossoms flourish.[1] It flows leisurely to quench the thirst of every weary and thirsty wanderer in the wilderness. It satisfies the needs of all travelers on the roads and distant islands. So the message was heralded throughout Spain and beyond from one end of heaven to the other, *"All who are thirsty, come for water."*[2] Unanimously, all wayfarers reported that they had found in the land of Yemen a beautiful, luscious garden. They found a rich pasture where every shriveled creature becomes fat, a dependable grazing-

---

[1]These sentences are meant to praise both Rabbi Yaakov Al-Fayumi and his father.

[2]Ref. to *Yeshayah* 55:1.

ground for their shepherds. The [Jews of Yemen] share their bread with the poor; they welcome the rich and offer them hospitality. Caravans from Sheba count on them;[3] they stretch out their hands to every voyager. Their homes are wide open. Everyone finds there tranquility and solace from sorrow and sighs.[4] They study the Torah all day and follow in the path of Rav Ashi.[5] They pursue justice and maintain their synagogues in good repair. They restore the principles of the Torah to their former glory. With kind words they bring back to Hashem those who have strayed, and fulfill all mitzvos meticulously. There is no breach and no defection, and no wailing in their streets.[6]

Blessed is Hashem for not depriving the distant isles (Yemen) of Jews who observe the Torah and keep its law, as He promised in His goodness and mercy through His servant Yeshayah. You [the Yemenite Jewish community] are the people that [Yeshayah] had in mind when he announced, *"From the end of the earth we hear singing"* (Yeshayah 24:16). May Hashem help you to fulfill the laws and precepts of the Torah, to heed justice and righteousness, to guard His mitzvos and decrees, and to uphold His covenant. Amen.

When your esteemed letter reached us in Egypt,[7] everyone was delighted to hear of it and enjoyed reading it. It told us that you are servants of Hashem who are standing in His Sanctuary and camping under His banner. You pursue the study of the Torah, love its laws, and wait at its doors.[8] May Hashem reveal its hidden treasures to you and fill your hearts with its riches. May its words be a lamp to your feet and a light for your path.

DENIES LAVISH PRAISES

Beloved friends, you state that you heard fellow Jews in the lands of our exile—may God protect them—praise me, extol me, and rate me

---

[3]Ref. to *Iyov* 6:19.

[4]Ref. to *Yeshayah* 35:10.

[5]Rav Ashi was a leading Amora, (Talmudic authority), who together with Ravina, compiled and edited the Talmud. For almost sixty years he led the yeshivah of Masa Mechasya, near Sura in Babylonia.

[6]Ref. to Tehillim 144:14.

[7]In 1172, when the Rambam wrote the Iggeres Teiman, he was the chief rabbi of Cairo and spiritual leader of all Egyptian Jewry.

[8]Ref. to Mishlei 8:34.

as a towering scholar. They only said this out of love for me and spoke this way out of the goodness of their hearts and their kindness. Let me give you the facts. Do not listen to anyone else.

I am one of the humblest of scholars of Spain whose prestige was lowered in exile. Although I always study the teachings of the Torah, I did not reach the level of learning of my ancestors because evil days and hard times came upon us. We have not lived in tranquility. We were exhausted but were given no rest. I have pursued the reapers in their paths and gathered ears of grain, both the solid and the full ones, as well as the shriveled and the thin ones. Only recently have I found a home.[9] Were it not for the help of Hashem, I would not have attained the small amount of knowledge that I gathered and from which I continually draw.

Concerning my dear friend and student Rabbi Shlomoh Cohen who, according to your letter, praised me exceedingly, he exaggerates out of his great love for me.

May Zion and Jerusalem be rebuilt and become a flourishing garden. May Hashem return it to us in good health and happiness.

[The rhymed preface was written in Hebrew. The remainder of the Letter to Yemen was written in Arabic and translated into Hebrew by Rabbi Shmuel ibn Tibbon, in 1210. A second translation was written by Rabbi Nachum Ma'arabi (of the Maghreb)[10] and appeared in Basel, Switzerland, in 1629.]

Regarding the subject matter of your letter about which you asked for a response, I thought it best to reply in Arabic so that all—men, women, and children alike—should be able to read and understand it. The answer is of primary concern to your entire community.

---

[9]Fleeing from persecution, the Rambam left his native Spain, traveled to Fez, Morocco, to Eretz Yisrael, and at last settled in Egypt.

[10]The Maghreb is a region in NW Africa, consisting mainly of Morocco, Algeria, and Tunisia (compare with the Hebrew *ma'ariv*, "west"); it usually means just Morocco.

Words of Consolation

BEMOANING THE FATE OF THE YEMENITE JEWS

You write that the rebel leader in Yemen[1] forced the Jews to convert to Islam. He compelled the inhabitants of all the places under his control to abandon their religion. This is just as the Berber leader has done in the lands of the Maghreb.[2] This news has appalled us and has caused our entire community to tremble and shudder. And with good right, for these are indeed bad tidings, and both ears of anyone who hears about it will tingle.[3] Yes, our hearts are faint and our minds are confused because of these dreadful calamities, which brought forced conversion on our people in the two ends of the world, the East and the West.[4] The Jewish people are caught in the middle and are under attack from both sides.[5]

It was a vision of this dreadful time that inspired the prophet to plead and pray for us, stating, *"I said, 'O Lord God, stop! How will Yaakov survive? He is so small'"* (Amos 7:5). This persecution should not cause one whose faith in Hashem is strong to come to doubt or one who believes in Moshe to waver. There can be no doubt that these are the pangs of the Age of Mashiach about which the Sages begged Hashem that they be spared from suffering. The prophets trembled when they foresaw them. As it is stated, *"My mind is confused, I shudder in panic. The twilight that I longed for has turned to terror"* (Yeshayah 21:4). Hashem Himself in the Torah exclaims His sympathy for those who will experience the times preceding

---

[1]His name is Abd el-Nabi ibn Mahdi. In c. 1170 he conquered Yemen and forced all Jews to convert to Islam.

[2]The Berber Almohads (from 1150–1180), forced the Jews of Morocco to convert to Islam.

[3]Ref. to Shmuel I 3:11.

[4]Yemen and Morocco.

[5]Ref. to *Yehoshua* 8:22.

Mashiach, stating, *"Alas, who can survive God's devastation!"* (Bamidbar 24:23).

You write that the minds of some people have become clouded. As uncertainty grips their hearts, their faith begins to waver, and their hope falters. Others have not lost faith and have neither weakened nor become fearful.

Regarding this matter, we have a Divine prophecy by Daniel. He foretold that as a result of the long stay in exile and the continuous persecutions, many would forsake our faith as doubt entered their minds and made them go astray. The primary reason for this breakdown is that they witnessed our weakness in contrast to the power of our oppressors and their mastery over us. Others would not be plagued by doubts. Their belief would remain firm and unshaken. This is expressed in the verse, *"Many will be purified and purged and refined; the wicked will act wickedly and none of the wicked will understand; but the knowledgeable will understand"* (Daniel 12:10). Daniel also prophesied that even these knowledgeable people and men of understanding who would have put up with milder misfortunes and remained steadfast in their faith in God and His servant Moshe, would give way to disbelief and would stray when they were made to endure harsher and more severe afflictions. Only a few of them would remain pure in faith, as it is stated, *"Some of the knowledgeable will stumble, that they may be refined and purged and whitened until the time of the end, for an interval still remains until the appointed time"* (Daniel 11:35).

TWO STRATEGIES

And now, dear brothers, it is essential that you pay attention and listen to what I am about to present to you. Teach it to your wives and children, so their faith, which has been weakened by misgivings, may be strengthened. May their souls be bolstered by the unshakable truth. May Hashem save us and all of you from religious doubt!

Bear in mind that our Torah is the true Divine Teaching that was given to us through Moshe, the master of both the early and the later prophets. By means of His Torah, God has distinguished us from the rest of mankind. As it says, *"It was only with your ancestors that Hashem developed a closeness. He loved them and therefore chose you, their descendants, from among all nations—as is now the case"* (Devarim 10:15). This did not happen because we were worthy of it. Rather, it was an act of Divine kindness, because our forefathers recognized Hashem and worshipped Him. As it says, *"It was not because you had greater numbers than all the other nations that Hashem preferred you . . . It was because of Hashem's love for you, and because He was keeping the oath He made to your fathers"* (Devarim 7:7).

Hashem made us special through His laws and decrees. The other nations recognize our superiority because we are guided by His rules and statutes. As it says, *"[The nations will say,] 'What nation is so great that they have such righteous rules and laws' "* (Devarim 4:8). As a result, the nations of the world became terribly envious of us. Because of the Torah, all the kings of the earth stirred up hatred and jealousy against us. Their real intention is to make war against Hashem, but no one can oppose the Almighty. Ever since the time of the Giving of the Torah, every non-Jewish king, no matter how he rose to power, has made it his first objective to destroy the Torah. Amalek, Sisera, Sancheriv, Nebuchadnezzar, Titus, Hadrian, and many others like them tried to overturn our religion by force, by violence, and by the sword. [The nations who want to annihilate us through violence] are one of two groups whose aim is to defeat the Divine will.

The second group consists of the brightest and most educated among the nations, such as the Syrians, Persians, and Greeks. They also attempt to tear down our religion and wipe out our Torah [but they do it] by means of arguments they offer and questions they dream up. They try to demolish the Torah and to erase its last trace with their writings. The tyrants tried to do the same with their wars.

Neither the one nor the other will succeed. Hashem proclaimed through the prophet Yeshayah, that He will destroy the armaments of any despot or oppressor who intends to destroy our Torah and abolish our religion by weapons of war. In the same way, whenever a disputant will argue to undermine our religion, he will lose the debate. His theory will be exploded and refuted. This thought is expressed in the following verse, *"No weapon formed against you will succeed, and every tongue that contends with you at law you will defeat. Such is the lot of the servants of Hashem, such is their triumph through Me—declares Hashem"* (Yeshayah 54:17).

Although advocates of both strategies (compulsory conversion and conversion through argumentation) realized that [Judaism] is a structure that cannot easily be demolished, they made a concerted effort to tear down its solid foundations. They are only increasing their toil and pain while the structure remains as strong as ever. Hashem, who is the Truth, mocks and ridicules them, because, with their feeble intelligence they try to reach an unattainable goal. Observing their attempt to wreck the true faith and watching Hashem ridicule them, David was inspired to say, *"[About those that say:] 'Let us break the cords of their yoke, shake off their ropes from us!' He who is enthroned in heaven laughs; Hashem mocks at them"* (Tehillim 2:3). Both groups have troubled and tormented us without letup throughout the era of our independence and during part of the period of our exile.

After that, a new sect arose that made our lives miserable by combining the approaches of the two groups: brute force and persuasion. It believed that this method would be more effective in wiping out the last vestige of the Jewish nation. It, therefore, conceived a plan to claim Divine revelation and establish a new religion, contrary to our God-given Torah. It declared publicly that both revelations were given by God. It meant to raise doubts and sow confusion. The new religion claimed to believe in the same God but to be the recipients of a new set of commandments. Thereby it hoped to destroy our Torah.

The first ne who devised this plan was Jeshu the Nazarene, may his bones be crushed. He was a Jew because his mother was Jewish although his father was a gentile. Our law states that a child born of a Jewish woman and a gentile or a slave is a kosher Jew. We only call him a *mamzer* (illegitimate child) in a manner of speaking. He led people to believe that he was sent by Hashem to explain bewildering passages in the Torah, and that he was the Mashiach who was predicted by each and every prophet. He interpreted the Torah in a way that would invalidate it completely, do away with all its mitzvos, and sanction all its prohibitions. The Sages guessed his purpose before his fame spread among the people, and condemned him to receive the punishment he deserved. Daniel predicted his emergence when he spoke of the downfall of a renegade and heretic who would arise in Yisrael. He spoke of one who would attempt to destroy the Torah and boast of having prophetic powers, of being able to perform miracles and who would declare himself as Mashiach, as it says, *"The lawless sons of your people will assert themselves to claim prophecy, but they will fail"* (Daniel 11:14).

Long after he lived, the descendants of Eisav created a religion and traced its origins to him. He did not establish a new faith, and did not actually do any harm to Yisrael, since neither the community as a whole nor any individuals were shaken in their beliefs because of him. His flaws were obvious to everyone. He fell into our hands and his fate is known to all.

After him, the Madman (Mohammed) arose. He followed in his forerunner's footsteps and attempted to convert us. He had the added ambition of pursuing political power, seeking to subjugate the people under his rule, and he originated his well-known religion [of Islam].

THE SUPERIORITY OF THE TORAH

These men had one purpose: to place their false religions on the same level with our Divine faith. Only a child who knows nothing about either religion would equate our God-given faith to man-made theories. Our religion is as different from other religions as a living, thinking human being differs from a wooden, metal, or stone statue that looks like a man. On the surface and in its shape, form, and appearance the statue looks exactly like man. The simple-minded person who knows nothing of Divine wisdom or of the art of sculpture thinks that it is made the same way man is made; he does not understand the inner workings of both. A knowledgeable person, who knows the inner nature of both, knows that the internal structure of the statue does not manifest any skillful workmanship at all. The inner parts of man are the true wonders that reveal the wisdom of the Creator: the nerves extending into the muscles that allow man to move his limbs at will; the attachment of ligaments, how they cling to bone, and the manner in which they grow; the connection of bones and joints; blood vessels that pulsate and those that do not and how they branch out; the placement of man's organs overlapping one another; how every part of the body has its proper composition, form, and place.

Similarly, a person unfamiliar with the Holy Scriptures' secret meaning and the commandments' deeper significance may think that our religion has something in common with, or is comparable to, the spurious manmade faith. He is misled. Both in Judaism and in the false religion there are things that you may not do and things that you must do; both in Judaism and the false religion there are various forms of worship. The Torah provides many positive and negative commandments, punishments, and rewards, and so does the fraudulent, manmade religion.

But if he knew the deeper meaning of the commandments, he would realize that the God-given Torah is true. It is the essence of Divine wisdom. Every commandment and prohibition moves man closer to perfection and removes the barriers that prevent him from attaining excellence. Through these commandments, both the broad masses and the individual will be able to reach moral and intellectual refinement, each according to his ability and perception. Through the mitzvos, the community of God becomes elevated, reaching a twofold perfection. By the first perfection, I mean living in this world under the most pleasant and gratifying conditions. The second perfection is the attainment of intellectual heights for each person according to his ability.

The other religions that resemble our religion really have no deeper meaning. They are only stories and imaginary tales in which the founder is trying to glorify himself, stating that he is as great as so-and-so. The Sages saw through the deception. They saw the entire religion as a farce and a joke, just as people laugh at a monkey who apes the actions of men.

PROOFS FROM THE PROPHETS

Hashem made it known to us through Daniel that something like this would happen in the future. He revealed to us that in the future, a person would arise who would announce a religion similar to the true one. He would speak haughtily. He would claim through prophetic powers that the prophetic spirit had given him a scripture, that God had spoken to him, that he had replied to Him, and many other claims such as these. Daniel had a vision of a horn that grew and became long and strong. In it, he prophesied the rise of the Arabic kingdom, the emergence of the Madman (Mohammed), and how he would triumph over the kingdoms of Syria, Persia, and Greece. This is clearly shown in verses that can be understood by everyone. This interpretation is borne out by historical facts. The verses cannot be explained any other way. Daniel says, *"While I was gazing upon these horns, a new little horn sprouted up among them; three of the older horns were uprooted to make room for it. . . . There were eyes in this horn like those of a man, and a mouth that spoke arrogantly"* (Daniel 7:8).

Now consider how marvelously fitting this allegory is. Daniel says that he saw a little horn sprouting. As he was wondering about its length and that it uprooted three horns, he noticed that this horn had eyes like those of a man and a mouth that spoke arrogantly. Clearly this refers to the person who will establish a religion that will resemble Hashem's Torah and who will claim to be a prophet. Daniel lets us know that this person wants to destroy, abolish, and alter our Torah. He states, *"He will think of changing times and laws. They will be delivered into his power for a time, times, and half a time"* (Daniel 7:25).

Hashem informed Daniel that He would destroy this religion in spite of its greatness and the great length of its reign, together with the remnants of the nations that preceded it.

The three groups that tried to wipe us out: that is to say, the one that tried to overwhelm us with the sword, the second that sought to defeat us by arguments, and the third that founded a religion similar to ours, will perish in the end.

Although they will seem to be powerful and victorious for a while, their power will not last and their triumph will not endure. Hashem so ordained it. He promised us from time immemorial that whenever Jews are forced to convert or any evil decree is issued against us, He will in the end remove and abolish it. David saw, through Divine Spirit, the future of the Jewish people. He saw heathen nations oppress us, rule over us, persecute us, and try to force us into apostasy, but they were not able to annihilate us. He exclaimed in the name of Yisrael, *"Since my youth they have often assailed me, let Yisrael now declare; since my youth they have often assailed me, but they have never overcome me"* (Tehillim 129:1,2).

PARALLELS IN HISTORY

My brothers, you all know that in the time of the wicked Nebuchadnezzar, the Jews were forced to worship idols. Only Daniel, Chananaiah, Mishael, and Azariah were spared.[6] Yet ultimately,

---

[6]In the third chapter of Daniel, we are told that these three men refused to bow down to an idol. They were thrown into a fiery furnace and miraculously, they came out unscathed.

Hashem crushed Nebuchadnezzar and abolished his laws, and the religion of truth was restored.

During the second Temple, when the wicked Greek kingdom came to power, the Greeks instituted brutal and harsh measures against Yisrael in order to destroy the Torah. They forced the Jews to desecrate the Shabbos and prohibited the observance of *bris milah* (circumcision). Every Jew was compelled to write on his garment the words, "We have no portion in Hashem, the God of Yisrael." He also had to etch this phrase on the horn of his ox and then to plow with it. These decrees were in force for about fifty-two years. After this time, Hashem demolished both their regime and their laws.

The Sages often refer to persecutions. We find, "Once the wicked Greek rulers forced the Jews to abandon their faith," and, "they issued such and such decree." After a while, Hashem would nullify and cancel the decree and obliterate the nation that issued it. Noting this historic pattern prompted the Sages of blessed memory to say, "Persecutions do not last" (Kesuvos 3b).

Hashem promised Yaakov that his offspring would outlive the nations who enslaved and oppressed them. They would survive and rise again while the tyrants would fade away, as it is written, *"Your descendants will be like the dust of the earth"* (Bereishis 28:14). Although Yaakov's descendants will be degraded and stepped on like dust, eventually, they will win and emerge triumphant. In a metaphoric sense we can say, just as the dust finally settles on he who steps on it and exists long after he has perished, [so will Yisrael outlive their tormentors.]

Yeshayah foretold in Divine prophecy that while the Jewish people are in exile, any nation that wishes to overpower and oppress them will be successful. In the end Hashem will help the Jewish people. He will remove their affliction and pain. Yeshayah says, *"A harsh prophecy has been announced to me: 'The betrayer is betraying, the ravager ravaging. Advance, Elam! Lay siege Media! I will put an end to all her sighing' "* (Yeshayah 21:2).

Encouraging Words

Hashem has assured us through his prophets that Yisrael will never be destroyed and we will never stop being His treasured nation. Just as it is unthinkable for Hashem to cease to exist, so is it impossible for Yisrael to be destroyed and annihilated. As it says, *"For I am Hashem—I have not changed; and you the children of Jacob—have not ceased to be"* (Malachi 3:6). He announced and confirmed to us that it is inconceivable that He will reject us entirely, even if we anger Him by violating His commandments. As it is written, *"Thus says Hashem, 'If the heavens above could be measured, and the foundations of the earth could be fathomed, only then would I reject all the offspring of Yisrael for all that they have done—declares Hashem' "* (Yirmiyah 31:37).

Indeed, the very same promise has been made to us in the Torah through Moshe our teacher: *"Thus even when they are in their enemies' land, I will not grow so disgusted with them nor so tired of them that I would destroy them and break My covenant with them, for I am Hashem their God"* (Vayikra 26:44).

Dear brothers, be strong and brave. Place your trust in these true Scriptures. Don't be disheartened by the persecutions that continually befall you. Don't be frightened by the power of our enemy and the helplessness of our people. These trials are meant to test you and to prove your faith and your love of Hashem. The God-fearing Torah scholars of the pure and untainted lineage of Yaakov will remain faithful to the true religion in times like these. About these the prophet states, *"And among the remnant are those whom Hashem will call"* (Yoel 3:5). The prophet makes it clear that they are only a few individuals. They are the men whose ancestors stood at Mount Sinai and heard Hashem's words, entered into the covenant of Hashem, and took upon themselves to do and obey. They said, *"We will do and obey all that Hashem has declared"* (Shemos 24:7). They obligated not only themselves but also their descendants, as we read, *"That which has been revealed applies to us and our children forever"* (Devarim 29:28). Hashem assured us, like a man who vouches for his neighbor—and we certainly can rely on His guarantee—that not only all those who stood at Mount Sinai [when Hashem gave the Torah] believe in the prophecy of Moshe our Teacher and in the laws he transmitted to us. Their descendants likewise would do so, until the end of time. Hashem said, *"I will come to you in a thick cloud, so that all the people will hear when I speak to you. They will then believe in you forever"* (Shemos 19:9).

It follows, therefore, that anyone who rejects the religion that was given at this Revelation at Sinai is not a descendant of the people who witnessed it. In the same vein, our Sages of blessed memory stated that whoever harbors doubts about the Divine prophecy is not a descendant of the people who were present at Mount Sinai (*Nedarim* 20a). May Hashem save me and you from doubt. May He keep away from all of us the thoughts that lead to skepticism and failure.

ADVICE FOR THE YEMENITE JEWS

And so, dear brothers who are scattered through the far reaches of [Yemen], you should encourage one another. Let the elders hearten the youth and the leaders inspire the masses. Convince your community of the immutable and unalterable truth. Proclaim loudly that our faith will never fail and will never be destroyed. Announce publicly [the principles of our religion]:

> The Holy One Blessed is He is One. There is no other unity like His.[1]
>
> Moshe is His prophet who spoke with Him, he is the master of all prophets, and he is superior to all other prophets. He perceived the Godly surpassing every other prophet whether he preceded him or arose afterwards.[2]
>
> The entire Torah, starting from the verse *"In the beginning"* (Bereishis 1:1), until the verse *"before the eyes of all Yisrael"* (Devarim 34:12), was transmitted by Hashem to Moshe, as it says, *"With him I speak mouth to mouth"* (Bamidbar 12:8).[3]

---

[1] The second of the Rambam's Thirteen Principles of the Jewish faith.

[2] The seventh principle of the Rambam's Thirteen Principles of the Jewish faith.

[3] The eighth principle of the Rambam's Thirteen Principles of the Jewish faith.

[The Torah] will neither be revoked nor altered, nothing can ever be added or subtracted from it. Never will Hashem give another Torah or a new positive or negative commandment.[4]

Keep in mind that Hashem commanded us to remember and never to forget, the Revelation on Mount Sinai. He instructed us to teach this event to our children so that they will grow up with this lesson etched in their minds. As it is written, *"Only take heed and watch yourself very carefully, so that you do not forget the things that your eyes saw. Do not let [this memory] leave your hearts, all the days of your lives. Teach your children and children's children about the day that you stood before Hashem at Chorev"* (Devarim 4:9-10).

It is essential, my dear brothers, that you impress on your children's minds this momentous Stand at Sinai. Proclaim at mass meetings its overriding significance. Stress that it is the cornerstone of our faith and the proof of its truthfulness. Accentuate the pivotal importance of this event, as Hashem did in the verse, *"You might inquire about times long past, going back to the time that Hashem created man on earth, and from one end of the heavens to the other. See if anything as great as this has ever happened, or if the like has ever been heard"* (Devarim 4:32).

THE PURPOSE OF THE REVELATION AT SINAI

Remember, my fellow Jews, the fact that [the Torah is of Divine origin] is attested to by the best possible evidence. Never before or since has an entire nation heard the Divine word or witnessed His glory with their own eyes. The purpose of this was to implant the faith firmly in us so that nothing can shake it, and to give us conviction that will uphold us so that we will not slip[5] in these trying times of recurring persecution and forced conversion, when our enemy will have gained the upper hand. As it is stated, *"For Hashem has come in order to test you, and in order that the fear of Him may be on your faces, so that you will not sin"* (Shemos 20:17). The verse explains that the reason Hashem revealed Himself to the Jewish people was in order to enable them to withstand all trials until the

---

[4]The ninth principle of the Rambam's Thirteen Principles of the Jewish faith.

[5]Tehillim 37:31.

end of time. They will not be swayed and not be led astray. You, dear brothers, keep the faith, stay on course, and remain true to your belief.

FORCED APOSTASY PREDICTED IN THE TORAH

King Shlomoh compared the Jewish people to a woman of matchless grace and flawless beauty. He stated, *"Every part of you is beautiful, my beloved, there is no blemish in you"* (Shir Hashirim 4:7). By contrast, he describes the followers of other religions and philosophies who want to lure us and convert us to their creed as worthless men. They seduce virtuous women in order to satisfy their depraved lust. This is exactly what they are doing to us when they beguile and ensnare us in their web of deceit and falsehood. These nations try to lead the Jewish people astray by contending that their religion is better than the Jewish faith. Yisrael says to them in rebuttal, *"Why do you take hold of me? Have you anything to show like 'the encirclement of the two camps?'"* (Shir Hashirim 7:1). The meaning of this metaphor is, "Show me something, as magnificent as the Revelation on Sinai in which the camp of Yisrael faced the camp of the Divine Presence. Then we will accept your teaching."

This thought is allegorically expressed in the verses, *"[The Gentile nations say to Yisrael:[6]] 'Turn away, turn away [from Hashem], Shulamis! Turn away, turn away, that we may gaze upon you, [we shall choose nobility for you].' [But Yisrael replies:] 'What can you bestow on Shulamis that can equal* mecholas hamachanaim *[literally, the encirclement of the two camps]?'"* (Shir Hashirim 7:1).

Now, the name *Shulamis* signifies "the nation whose faith in Hashem is perfect."[7] The expression *mecholas hamachanaim* signifies "the encirclement of the two camps." This alludes to the joy of the Stand at Sinai, which was shared by both the camp of Yisrael and the camp of Hashem. As we see in the following verses: *"Moshe led the people out of the camp toward the Divine Presence. They stood transfixed at the foot of the mountain."* (Shemos 19:17), and *"Hashem's chariots are myriads upon myriads, thousands upon thousands; Hashem is among them as in Sinai in holiness"* (Tehillim 68:18).

---

[6]Commentary between brackets is Rashi's interpretation of this verse.

[7]From the root *shalem,* "perfect."

Now pay close attention to the fitting imagery and the deeper meaning of the verse [in Shir Hashirim]. Note that the phrase *turn away* is repeated four times. This alludes to the four empires that will try to force us to abandon our faith. Incidentally, we are living today under the domination of the fourth and last empire.

In the Torah, Hashem foretold that while [we are in exile, the nations of the world] would compel us to embrace their religion. As it says, *"There you will serve Gods that men have made"* (Devarim 4:28). However, this will not happen all over the world; we will never be completely cut off from the Torah. Hashem gave us His assurance. He stated, *"[The Torah] will not be forgotten by their descendants"* (Devarim 31:21). Yeshayah, the harbinger of our nation's redemption, already declared that the Divine guarantee of our survival as a nation is the permanence of the Torah among us. As it is written," *'And as for Me, this is My covenant with them,' said Hashem. 'My spirit that is upon you and My words that I have placed in your mouth shall not be absent from your mouth, nor out of the mouth of your children nor from the mouth of your children's children' said Hashem, 'from now on, for all time' "* (Yeshayah 59:21).

OUR RESPONSE

With pride, our nation speaks to Hashem of the dreadful oppression and persecution it has suffered. We state, *"It is for Your sake that we are killed all day long, that we are regarded as sheep to be led to slaughter"* (Tehillim 44:23). The Sages comment that the phrase, "It is for Your sake that we are killed all day long," refers to the generation that suffers forced apostasy (*Midrash Shir Hashirim* 1:3).

We should rejoice in the fact that we have suffered misfortune, lost our wealth and possessions, and were driven into exile. All these hardships are a source of distinction and honor in the eyes of Hashem. Whatever losses we suffered through these disasters are counted as a burnt offering on the altar. The following verse[8] expresses this thought: *"Dedicate yourselves to Hashem today, . . . that He may bestow a blessing on you"* (Shemos 32:29).

[Those who are being pressured into converting] should run away and remain faithful to Hashem. They should flee into the

---

[8]As translated by Targum Onkelos.

desert and hide in uninhabited places. They should give no thought to being separated from family and friends or being concerned with loss of income. Such deprivations are only a small sacrifice and a trifle [we can offer] to the King of kings, the Holy One, Blessed is He, Ruler of the universe, whose Name is glorious and awesome, Hashem your God. He can be trusted to give you a rich reward in this world and in the world to come.

Many pious and pure-hearted people, who seek the truth and pursue it, follow the practice of [leaving home and family]. They leave [society] behind. They advance from the far reaches of the world to the place where the word of Hashem is manifest. They make their way to the homes of the pious sages. They want to gain a deeper understanding of the Torah and earn a rich reward from Hashem. How much more so is one obligated to leave his homeland and his family, if it means preserving the Torah in its entirety.

Sometimes when a man cannot earn a livelihood in one country, he becomes disgusted with it, he feels cramped and fenced in, and he moves to another country. Surely, when a Jew is prevented from observing the Torah and the Divine faith, he should run away to another place. If he finds it impossible to leave at the present, he should not gradually backslide, lapse into sin and feel free to desecrate the Shabbos and eat forbidden foods. He should not think that he is exempt from observing the laws of the Torah. Whether he likes it or not, every descendant of Yaakov, as well as his children and children's offspring, is forever and inescapably bound to the Torah. Furthermore, a violator will be punished for every negative commandment he transgresses. Let no one think that since he was forced to commit some major sins he can freely and with impunity violate the commandments with the lesser penalties. *Yerovam ben Nevat,* may his bones be crushed, was punished, not only for erecting the two golden calves that he worshipped and enticed Yisrael to worship, he was also punished for his failure to observe the mitzvah of building a *sukkah* on *Sukkos.* This is one of the fundamental principles of the Torah and our religion. Master it, and apply it to your own situation.

Refuting Moslem Claims

THE FALLACY OF MOSLEM ARGUMENTS

In your letter you mention that the apostate introduced doubt in the minds of several people. He claimed that a number of verses in the Torah allude to the Madman [Mohammed].

With the verse, *"I will bless him (Yishmael), and make him fruitful, increasing his numbers* bimeod meod — *very greatly"* (Bereishis 17:20), Moslem apologists contend that *bimeod meod,* which sounds like Muchammad, is an allusion to Mohammed. They also contend that the numeric value of both *bimeod meod* and Muchammad is 92.

They argue that the verse, *"He appeared from Mount Paran"* (Devarim 33:2), alludes to Mohammed [since Mount Paran is a reference to Yishmael, son of Avraham, and ancestor of the Arab nation, who lived in the wilderness of Paran].

They also believe that the passage, *"Hashem your God will raise up for you a prophet from among you, from your brothers, like myself"* (Devarim 18:15), and the promise to Yishmael, *"I will make him into a great nation"* (Bereishis 17:20), refer to Mohammed.

These arguments have been bandied about so much that everyone is sick and tired of them. To say that they are absolutely unsound is an understatement. To use these verses as proofs is ludicrous and outrageous. Such statements do not confuse anyone, not even the gullible masses.

The apostates who amuse themselves by concocting these "scriptural proofs" do not believe a word of them. They do not even entertain any doubts about their veracity. Their purpose in quoting these verses is to creep into the good graces of the Moslems and ingratiate themselves with them by showing that they are believers. Even knowledgeable Moslems do not believe these proofs. In trying to support the statement of the Koran that the Madman [Mohammed] is mentioned in the Torah, they don't rely on or accept these arguments. Clearly these proofs are worthless.

The Moslems, when they could not find a single usable proof in the Torah—even by inference or hint—were forced to say that we revised and edited the Torah, deleting every mention of the name [Mohammed] from it. They could not find a more tenable argument in support of the Koran, even though it is absolutely absurd and does not hold water.

It is obvious to one and all [that nothing was deleted from the Torah], for the following reasons: First, the Torah was translated into Aramaic, Persian, Greek, and Latin hundreds of years before the emergence of the *pasul*, the "Defective One" [Mohammed]. Second, the Torah text has been transmitted from generation to generation, both in the East and the West. There has never been found the slightest difference in the text, not even in the vocalization. There exists not even a variation between a *kametz chataf* and a *shuruk*.[1] The Moslems only used this feeble argument, because they could not find any inference to Mohammed in the Torah.

YITZCHAK IS HEIR TO AVRAHAM'S BLESSING

As for the true meaning of the verse, *"I will make of him (Yishmael) a great nation"* (Bereishis 17:20); the word "great" does not denote greatness in wisdom and prophecy. It only refers to vastness in numbers. Similarly, the Torah describes idol worshipers as, *"nations greater and more populous than you"* (Devarim 4:38).

What of the promise to Yishmael, *"[I will increase his number]* bimeod meod—*very greatly,"* (Bereishis 17:20)? If this Scripture intended to predict that Mohammed would descend from Yishmael it would have said, "I will bless him *bimeod meod*—very greatly." A very weak argument could then be made to interpret this to mean, "I will bless him by making Mohammed (which sounds like *bimeod meod*) one of his descendants." But since the phrase *bimeod meod* follows after *"I will increase his number,"* it is clear that this is intended only as a superlative, as if to say, "exceedingly numerous."

Hashem clearly explained to Avraham that all Divine promises regarding blessings and commandments to be given to his offspring

---

[1] Two similar sounding vowels.

and their separateness from the nations refer only to Yitzchak's descendants, not to the other one [Yishmael]. Yishmael's blessing comes only as an adjunct and is secondary to Yitzchak's blessing. This is evident in the passage, *"Also I will make the son of the slave-woman into a nation, for he is your child"* (Bereishis 21:13). This passage clearly places Yitzchak in first place, making the other one (Yishmael) inferior. In addition, the Torah expressly spells it out, *"It is through Yitzchak that there will be called for you a lineage"* (Bereishis 21:12). Even if we were to concede that Yishmael's offspring would be very great in numbers, they would still not be renowned and acclaimed for their qualities of righteousness and human perfection. On the other hand, Yitzchak's descendants will be celebrated for their righteousness. This is implied in the expression *yikarei lecha*—"will be called for you." This expression signifies fame and renown, as in *"veyikarei vahem shemi*—In them may my name be called" (Bereishis 48:16), meaning, "May my name become famous through them."

Regarding the blessings, Hashem specifically sets forth that these were given to Avraham. Included in this blessing was that the covenant and the Torah would exist in his descendants. Hashem put it into these words, *"To you and your descendants I will give the land where you are now living as a foreigner. The whole land of Canaan shall be your eternal heritage, and I will be a God to your descendants"* (Bereishis 17:8). Hashem singled out Yitzchak. Yishmael was excluded from all the blessings.

He then specifically selected Yitzchak for a covenant, eliminating Yishmael, as it says, *"But My covenant I will maintain with Yitzchak"* (Bereishis 17:20). Hashem then bestowed a blessing on Yishmael, stating, *"I will bless him and make him fruitful,"* (Bereishis 17:20). The process of the transmission of the blessings is later clarified by Yitzchak when he passed on Avraham's blessings to Yaakov, leaving out Eisav. Yitzchak phrased his blessing to Yaakov in the following terms, *"May He grant the blessing of Avraham to you and your offspring"* (Bereishis 28:4).

It is now abundantly clear that the pledges Hashem made to Avraham and his descendants would be fulfilled exclusively first in Yitzchak and then in Yaakov, Yitzchak's son. This is confirmed by a passage that states, *"He is ever mindful of His covenant . . . that He made with Avraham, swore to Yitzchak, and confirmed in a decree for Yaakov, for Yisrael, as an eternal covenant* (Tehillim 105:8,9).

POINT BY POINT REFUTATION OF MOSLEM ALLEGATIONS

Let me point out that the idea the Moslems have adopted that the name Mohammed occurs in the Torah—a notion that was dreamed up by the apostates—is senseless. They claim that the phrase *bimeod meod* alludes to Muchammad. But the name that is used in the Koran and the "Gospels"[2] is Achmed. And of course, the numeric value of *bimeod meod*—92—is not the same as that of Achmed, which is 53.

With regard to the so-called proof of *"hofia me'har Paran*—He appeared from Mount Paran" (Devarim 33:1), *hofia*—"he appeared" is written in the past tense. If it would have read *"yofia*—He **will** appear," the Moslem spokesman might have used the passage to taunt us and lend credence to his belief, but the word *"hofia*—He **appeared,"** points to an event that happened in the past. In fact, it refers to the Giving of the Torah on Mount Sinai. It is telling us that when Hashem revealed Himself on Mount Sinai, He did not plummet down from heaven like a barrage of hailstones; he came down gently from higher mountaintops to lower mountaintops until He descended on Mount Sinai, as it says, *"Hashem came from Sinai; He shone upon them from Seir; He appeared from Mount Paran. From the holy myriads, He brought a law of fire to them from His right Hand"* (Devarim 33:2). This interpretation is indisputable to anyone with an open mind.

Notice how unerringly accurate is the choice of words in the text. Hashem's descent on Paran, which is a more distant mountain, is described with the vague term of *hofia*, "He appeared," while His emergence on Mount Seir, which is closer, is characterized with the more clear-cut verb *zarach*, "He shone." Mount Sinai was His final destination, the place where His glory came to rest. As we read, *"Hashem's glory rested on Mount Sinai"* (Shemos 24:16). And so, with regard to Mount Sinai we find the plainest and most explicit phraseology, "Hashem **came** from Sinai."

It is noteworthy that Devorah portrays the Revelation on Mount Sinai in much the same way. She, too, is telling us that Hashem's glory came down gently from mountain to mountain. Devorah expresses it this way: *"Hashem, when You came forth from*

---

[2]The Rambam uses the word *avon galui*—"an open sin," as a play on the Greek word *evangelion*, which means "good tidings" or gospels.

Seir, Advanced from the country of Edom, The earth trembled; The heavens dripped, Yea, the clouds dripped water" (Shofetim 5:4).

The Sages (*Avodah Zarah* 2b) offer a beautiful allegorical interpretation of this verse. They say that initially, Hashem sent a messenger to the Edomites to offer them the Torah, but they rejected it. Then He offered it to the Yishmaelites but they, too, rejected it. Finally, He sent Moshe Rabbeinu to us and we readily accepted the Torah, exclaiming, *"We will do and obey all that Hashem has declared"* (Shemos 24:7). Now all this took place **before** the Giving of the Torah, as is evident in the words "He came," "He shone," and "He appeared," which are all in the past tense, and do not presage future events.[3]

DISCUSSION OF PROPHECY

There still remains the proof they derive from the passage, *"Hashem your God will raise up for you a prophet from among you, from your brothers,* kamoni — *like myself; him you shall obey"* (Devarim 18:15). In your letter you mention that [the word *kamoni* — like myself — in] this verse raised uncertainty in the minds of some of the people. [They claim that the Torah is foretelling the arrival of a prophet as great as Moshe]. Others cast off their doubts, as they realize that the Torah speaks of a prophet "from among you, from your brothers," [which Mohammed obviously is not]. [This leads me to believe that] were it not for the phrase *"from among you, from among your brothers,"* they would have considered this verse a valid proof. Please concentrate and pay very close attention to what I am about to tell you:

You must understand that you cannot simply take a word or a phrase out of context and use it to prove a point. You must consider the background clauses, both those that lead up to the statement and those that follow it. In other words, before using a fragment of a verse to bolster your argument, you must look at the entire verse and the paragraph in which that verse is found. Only then can you grasp the meaning of that phrase. Only then can you use that phrase to prove your hypothesis. A statement that is detached from its surrounding clauses cannot be advanced as proof. For if it were permissible to bring proof from passages taken out of context, you

---

[3]Whereas the Moslems falsely maintain that it alludes to Mohammed, who was born almost 2,000 years after the Giving of the Torah.

could say that Hashem has forbidden us to obey any prophet. After all, it is written, *"Do not heed the words of that prophet"* (Devarim 13:4). What's more [following this logic], you could say that Hashem commands us to worship idols—Hashem forbid—for it says in the Torah, *"You shall serve other Gods and bow to them"* (Devarim 11:16). Many other such examples can be cited. This demonstrates the idiocy of such proofs and establishes the rule that you cannot adduce any proof whatsoever from a word or phrase unless you understand the context of that word.

Now, take the present verse, *"a prophet from among you, from your brothers, like myself."* Consider the context;

> Let there not be found among you one who passes his son or daughter through fire, an augur, a soothsayer, a diviner, one who practices witchcraft, who uses incantations, who consults mediums and oracles, or who attempts to communicate with the dead (Devarim 18:10,11). You must be totally faithful to Hashem your God. The nations that you are driving out listen to astrologers and stick-diviners, but what Hashem has given you is totally different. Hashem your God will raise up for you a prophet from among you, from your brothers, like myself, and it is to him that you must listen (Devarim 18:13,15).

The paragraph begins by warning us against becoming involved with sorcerers, soothsayers, and the like. In other words, [don't involve yourselves] with people who perform occult practices by means of which the gentiles think they can predict future events. In warning us against engaging in such practices, Hashem tells us that the gentiles think that these procedures are effective in forecasting the future. But we should not use such means to ascertain what the future holds. We are to learn these things from a prophet whom He will raise up for us to inform us of what lies ahead. This prophet will foretell the future without resorting to sorcery, black magic, astrology, or other occult practices.

The Torah goes on to tell us that finding out what the future holds will not require any effort on our part. Every prophet that Hashem will send us will come *from among you.* Thus, you will not have to travel great distances, journeying from town to town, before you can find him. Next, the Torah tells you another thing: in addition to being close to you and among you, he will also be one of your brothers. He will be a Jew. Therefore, the attribute of Divine prophecy will be restricted to the Jewish people. To emphasize this point the words *like myself* have been added. You might mistakenly infer that *from your brothers,* also includes [a prophet who is a descendant] of Eisav or Yishmael. Such a mistake could easily be made. We do read that when Moshe sent envoys to the king of Edom [a descendant of Eisav] he addressed him as "brother," stating, *"Thus says your brother Yisrael . . ."* (Bamidbar 20:14). To preclude this error it was necessary to add the clause, *"like myself,"* meaning "a Jew."

To contend that the phrase "like myself" implies that a prophet will arise who will be as great as Moshe is impossible, for we read, *"Never again did there arise in Yisrael a prophet like Moshe"* (Devarim 34:10).

THE TRUE AND THE FALSE PROPHET

It should be absolutely clear that the prophet who will arise will not issue any new commandments or create innovations in the Torah. He will not resort to occult practices, but we will be able to ask him about future events, the way the gentiles consult astrologers and fortunetellers. An example of this is when young Shaul went to ask the prophet Shmuel where he could find his father's donkeys that had gone astray (Shmuel I 9:3–14).

The reason we do not believe the prophecies of Zeid and Amar is not because they are not Jewish. Many people have this erroneous idea because they infer this from the phrase, *"a prophet from among you, from your brothers."* After all, *Iyov* and his friends Tzofer, Bildad, Elifaz, and Elihu received prophecy, even though they were not Jewish. On the other hand, Chananiah ben Azur, a Jew, was a false prophet. A prophet should be believed because of what he preaches, not for reasons of lineage.

It is an established fact that Moshe Rabbeinu is the supreme prophet. When we heard the Divine Voice speak to him we believed in him and his prophecy. We said to him, *"You approach Hashem our God, and listen to all He says"* (Devarim 8:24). Moshe told us that there are no commandments left in heaven to be given. There exists neither another faith nor another Torah beside the one we received. He said, *"It is not in heaven, so [that you should] say, "Who shall go up to heaven and bring it to us so that we can hear it and keep it?"* (Devarim

30:12). He warned us neither to add nor to subtract from the Torah, saying, *"Do not add to it and do not subtract from it"* (Devarim 13:1). Further, in Hashem's Name, he required us, our children, and children's children to believe in this Torah until the end of time. This is evident in the following verse, *"Hidden things concern Hashem our God, but that which has been revealed applies to us and our children forever. [We must therefore] keep all the words of the Torah* (Devarim 29:28).

If a prophet ever appears, regardless of his lineage, who says that one of the commandments of the Torah has been abrogated, he contradicts and denies what Moshe said: that the Torah applies "to us and our children forever." Therefore, we must denounce him. If we have the power to do so, we must put him to death. We must disregard any miracles he might perform, just as we pay no attention to a prophet who tells us to worship other gods. As we read, *"Even if the miracle or sign comes true, do not listen to the words of that prophet or dreamer"* (Devarim 13:3,4). Since Moshe told us never to worship other gods, we know with certainty that the "miracles" he performed in the name of the foreign deity are nothing but trickery and magic. Since Moshe told us explicitly that the Torah will last forever, we know that any prophet who claims that it is valid for only a set length of time is a false prophet. He is contradicting Moshe Rabbeinu. Consequently, we should not even ask him to corroborate his message through a sign or miracle. If he did perform a miracle we should ignore and dismiss it. We must realize that our belief in Moshe was not based on the miracles he performed. Therefore, we do not have to compare the miracles of this "prophet" to the miracles of Moshe. We believe in Moshe with complete, everlasting, and unshakable trust because we heard the Revelation just as he heard it. This is expressed in the verse, *"They will believe in you forever"* (Shemos 19:9).

This makes us and Moshe like two witnesses who testify that they observed an event. Each witness knows with certainty that both his own and his partner's testimony is true. No further proof of their veracity is needed.

The same is true in our case. We, the community of Yisrael, were convinced of the trustworthiness of Moshe Rabbeinu, because we ourselves were there when Hashem spoke at Mount Sinai. When Moshe performed miracles it was only because the situation demanded it, as is evident from the Torah verses. This important principle has been widely ignored and most people do not rely on it any longer. Therefore, [it should be reiterated that] our belief in Moshe Rabbeinu is far greater than our trust in miracles. Shlomoh had this in mind when he wrote, *"Have you anything to show like the encirclement of the two camps?"* (Shir Hashirim 4:1). In a figurative sense, Yisrael is saying to the nation, "Can you show us anything as magnificent as the Revelation on Sinai?"

Therefore, if a Jewish or even a non-Jewish prophet urges people to follow the Jewish faith without adding or subtracting from it, as Yeshayah, Yirmiyah, and others like them did, we should demand that he perform a miracle. If he does, we believe in him, and recognize him as a prophet. But if he fails, and one of his predictions remains unfulfilled, he must be put to death. We believe him if he gives a sign, even though he might be an impostor. Hashem told us in the Torah that if two witnesses testify in a case, we bring in a verdict on the basis of their testimony. Although we cannot be absolutely sure their testimony is true, we give the witnesses the benefit of the doubt and rely on their reputation of honesty, even though we cannot be absolutely sure whether their testimony is true. So too, the Torah states, if a prophet predicts the future or performs a miracle and his prediction comes true, we accept him, even though we cannot say with certainty that he is a true prophet. At the same time, we are told explicitly the major factor that disqualifies a prophet: if he says anything that contradicts the prophecy of Moshe Rabbeinu.

The entire subject of prophecy has been thoroughly and extensively discussed in our Introduction to the Commentary on the Mishnah.[4] There you will find a detailed analysis of this important principle that forms the cornerstone of the Torah and is the pillar of our faith. You should realize that not only is it forbidden to add to or subtract from the Torah, but even the Oral Law that was handed down by the Sages from one generation to the next may not be altered.

---

[4]See pages 86–98.

The Coming of Mashiach—
The Messiah

CALCULATIONS OF THE DATE OF REDEMPTION

Your letter mentions the calculations that *Rabbeinu Saadiah Gaon*[1] made for the date of the coming of Mashiach. You should be aware that no human being will ever be able to determine the exact date [of Mashiach's coming], as Daniel stated, *"For these words are secret and sealed to the time of the end"* (Daniel 12:9). Nevertheless, many theories were suggested by a few scholars who thought that they had discovered the date. This was predicted by Daniel, *"Many will run far and wide and opinions will increase"* (Daniel 12:4). In other words, there will be much speculation about it. Furthermore, Hashem informed us through His prophets that many people will calculate the time of the coming of Mashiach; the date will pass and nothing will happen. We are warned against yielding to doubt and misgivings because of these miscalculations. We are urged not to be disillusioned if these computations do not come to fruition. We are told: The longer the delay, the more intensely you should hope. As it says, *"For there is yet a prophecy for a set term, it declares of the end and does not lie. Even if it tarries wait for it still; for it will surely come, without delay"* (Chavakuk 2:3).

Even the date of the end of the Egyptian exile was not exactly known. This gave rise to various interpretations. Hashem, however, clearly spelled it out, stating, *"They will be enslaved and oppressed for four hundred years"* (Bereishis 15:13). Some thought that the period of 400 years began when Yaakov arrived in Egypt. Others counted it from the beginning of Yisrael's enslavement, which

---

[1]Rabbeinu Saadiah Gaon (892–942 C.E.), one of the foremost personalities in Jewish history. He wrote Emunos Vedeyos (in Arabic), a seminal philosophical work.

happened seventy years later. Others figured it from the time of the *Bris Bein Habesarim* (The Covenant of the Halves), when this prophecy was given to Avraham. As our Sages taught us, 400 years after this Covenant, and thirty years before Moshe appeared on the scene, a group of the Children of Yisrael [from the tribe of Ephraim] left Egypt. They thought that the predicted end of the exile had arrived. However, the Egyptians captured and killed them and increased the workload of the Hebrew slaves [who remained in Egypt]. David alluded to these men who miscalculated and left Egypt, in the verse, *"Like the Ephraimite bowmen who turned back in the day of battle"* (Tehillim 78:9).

The end of the Egyptian exile came 400 years after the birth of Yitzchak the heir of Avraham, as it is written, *"It is through Yitzchak that you will gain posterity"* (Bereishis 21:12). About him it was said, *"Your descendants will be foreigners in a land that is not theirs. They will be enslaved and oppressed for four hundred years"* (Bereishis 15:13). During this exile, they would rule over them, enslave them, and wear them down. The 400 years refer only to exile and not to the years of enslavement. This was misunderstood until the great prophet (Moshe) came. When the Exodus took place exactly 400 years after the birth of Yitzchak, it became clear. Now, if so much uncertainty surrounded the end of the Egyptian exile [the duration of which was known], then surely the end of this long exile is shrouded in obscurity. Its long duration has appalled and dismayed the prophets to the point that one of them exclaimed in utter amazement, *"Will You be angry with us forever, prolong Your wrath for all generations?"* (Tehillim 85:6). Yeshayah, too, alluded to the seeming endlessness of this exile. He stated, *"They shall be gathered in a dungeon as prisoners are gathered; They shall be locked up in a prison. But after many days they shall be released"* (Yeshayah 24:22).

Daniel declared the date of the final redemption a deep secret. Our Sages have discouraged the calculation of the time of the coming of Mashiach. They feared that the masses may be confused and led astray when the predicted time arrives and Mashiach does not come. This led our Sages to say, "May the people that calculate the final redemption meet with adversity" (Sanhedrin 97b).

Although making calculations of the time of redemption is forbidden, we must judge Rabbeinu Saadiah Gaon favorably. The Jews of his time were influenced by many distorted ideologies. If not for [Rabbeinu Saadiah's] work of explaining the perplexing portions of the Torah and strengthening their faltering faith with the power of his word and his pen, they would have abandoned the Torah altogether. He sincerely believed that by means of Messianic calculations he could rally the Jewish public, encourage them, and inspire them with hope. Whatever he did was done for the sake of heaven. Since he had only the purest of motives, we should not fault him for engaging in Messianic calculations.

THE RAMBAM REJECTS ASTROLOGY

I notice that you have a liking for astrology, and you find meaning in the constellations and conjunctions of planets. You should reject such thoughts and banish such concepts from your minds. Cleanse your mind of these worthless ideas like you wash dirt from your clothes. Accomplished non-Jewish scholars, and certainly Jewish scholars, do not consider astrology a genuine science. Its theories can easily be disproved by rational arguments, but this is not the place to go into them.

Before Moshe rose to prominence, the astrologers had unanimously predicted that the Jewish nation would never be released from slavery or attain its independence. Just when the astrologers thought the Jewish people had reached the bottom of degradation, destiny shone brightly on Yisrael. The most illustrious human being (Moshe) was born among them. Just when the astrologers unanimously foretold that Egypt would enjoy a period of wholesome climate, prosperity, and tranquility, the plagues struck. Speaking of these failed forecasts, Yeshayah says, *"Where indeed are your sages? Let them tell you; let them discover what the God of Hosts has planned against Egypt"* (Yeshayah 19:12).

The same thing happened to the kingdom of Nebuchadnezzar. When all the astrologers, scholars, and wise men unanimously agreed that his reign marked the beginning of a long period of supremacy, his empire collapsed and vanished from the scene. This was foretold by Hashem through Yeshayah. [Yeshayah] ridiculed their scholars and wise men who boasted of their wisdom. He mocked the government that took pride in its outstanding scholars. Said Yeshayah, *"You are helpless despite all your art. Let them stand up and help you now, the astrologers, the star-gazers, who announce, month by month, whatever will come upon you* (Yeshayah 47:13).

The same situation will prevail in the days of Mashiach, may he soon come. The gentiles believe that our people will never become an independent nation nor will they ever be released from the subservient condition they are in. All the astrologers and sorcerers will share this opinion. Hashem will give lie to their thoughts and discredit their false views by revealing the Mashiach. Yeshayah said this prophecy

> [It is I] Who annuls the omens of diviners, and makes fools of the augurs; Who turns sages back, and makes nonsense of their knowledge; Who confirms the word of My servant, and fulfills the prediction of My messengers. It is I Who says of Jerusalem, "It shall be inhabited," and of the towns of Judah, "They shall be rebuilt; and their ruins I will restore." [Yeshayah 44:25,26]

[Therefore,] do not pay any attention to astrological theories that deal with the conjunction of the stars in the greater or smaller constellations.

DISPROVES ASTROLOGERS' ALLEGATIONS

You write that science is at a low ebb and research is nonexistent in your country (Yemen). You attribute this to the influence of the constellations in the earthly trigon [of the zodiac].[2] Please understand that this lack of learning is prevalent not only in your country. Disrespect of sages and poor standards of education are widespread throughout Yisrael today. A Divine prophecy predicts this, stating, *"Truly, I shall further baffle that people with bafflement upon bafflement; and the wisdom of its wise shall fail, and the prudence of its prudent shall vanish"* (Yeshayah 29:14). This situation is not due to the earthly or the fiery trigon. This can be proved by the fact that King Shlomoh lived during the earthly trigon. Yet he is described as *"the wisest of all men"*

---

[2]The zodiac is an imaginary belt encircling the heavens. It is divided into twelve parts, called signs of the zodiac or *mazalos* that correspond to twelve constellations bearing the same name (Aries, Taurus, Gemini, etc., or in Hebrew, *T'leh, Shor, Te'omim, Sartan, Aryeh, Besulah, Moznayim, Akrov, Keshes, G'di, D'li, Dagim*). The zodiac is also divided into four quarters, called trigons, each consisting of three signs. The four trigons represent earth, water, air, and fire. Astrologers believe that the influence of the earthly trigon causes a decrease in the pursuit of knowledge.

(Melachim I 8:11). In the same way our Father, Avraham, who is called the Pillar of the World, discovered the First Cause of all Creation. He taught it to all the scholars, and proclaimed the fundamental principle of the Unity of God to all mankind. Furthermore, Avraham, Yitzchak, and Yaakov carried the Throne of Glory in their hearts: they attained a true understanding of the Essence of the *Shechinah* (glory of Hashem). The Sages said, "The Patriarchs are the chariots [of the Shechinah]", which the Midrash (*Bereishis Rabbah* 82:7) derives from the verse, *"Hashem rose up from upon him"* (Bereishis 35:13). Yet the three Patriarchs lived during the earthly trigon.

Let me explain. There is a small conjunction[3] in which Saturn and Jupiter come together. This happens once in about twenty solar years. This conjunction repeats itself twelve times in each trigon so that they conjunct in each trigon for 240 years. Then they move into the next trigon in what is called the medium conjunction. According to this calculation, an interval of 960 years will elapse between the first and second conjunction of two planets in the same point of the zodiac. This is called the great conjunction. It extends for 960 years, from the first until the second meeting of Saturn and Jupiter in the constellation Aries. By counting back, you will understand all that I have said about Avraham, Yitzchak, and Yaakov, as well as David and Shlomoh living during the earthly trigon. My aim in explaining all this is to convince you to dismiss any thought you might have that the trigon can influence human affairs.

You also wrote that some people calculated that at some future point all seven planets will come together in one of the constellations of the zodiac. This just is not true. There will never be a meeting of the seven planets, neither in the next conjunction nor in any future ones. This calculation was made by an ignorant person, which is evident from another statement of his, that you quote, to the effect that there will be a flood of air and dust.

You must recognize that these and similar statements are nothing but lies and deceptions. Do not believe such things just because they are in a book; the liar shrinks no more from deceiving with his pen than he does with his mouth. Fools and the uneducated will take a written statement at face value. But one must demand proof before he can believe a theory.

---

[3]In astronomy, conjunction means the position of two planets when they are in the same longitude.

A blind person relies on a sighted man for direction and follows his guidance. A sick person will follow his doctor's orders and advice. It is essential for people at large to place their trust in the prophets who were men of true insight and rely on them when they are taught the truth or falsehood of a given teaching. In the absence of prophets [people should look for guidance] from the Sages who study and analyze wisdom and doctrines day and night, and can distinguish between the truth and that which is false.

I want to impress on you that anything you heard or read on the subject of astrology and related fields is untrue. The author of such statements is either a fool, a clown, or one who tries to destroy the Torah and tear down its protective walls. Don't you recognize the audacity of these individuals who say that there will be a flood of air and dust? They might as well say, there will be a deluge of fire. Their prediction is meant to mislead and seduce people into believing that the deluge in the time of Noach was caused merely by a convergence of water. They claim that it was not sent as a punishment by the True Judge for the many sins of the world's population, contrary to the teachings of the Torah. If you follow their reasoning, Sedom and the other cities were not destroyed because of their lack of belief and the wickedness of their inhabitants. This is a direct denial of the Torah, which says, *"I will go down and see, if they have acted according to the outcry that has reached Me; I will destroy them"* (Bereishis 18:21). Whatever happens in the world by the Hand of Hashem, they say is the outcome of the conjunctions of the planets.

They advance these theories because they want to undermine the principles of our faith and unleash their animal lusts and cravings, like beasts and ostriches. Hashem warned us in the Torah against this view. He said that, "If you make Me angry you will be struck with disaster because of your transgressions. But if you attribute these disasters to chance rather than to your sinful conduct, then I will increase your calamities more and more." This is spelled out in the Chapter of Reproof, where it says, *"If you are keri to Me . . . then I will be-keri to you with a vengeance"* (Vayikra 26:27, 28). The word *keri* means "something that is unplanned, that happens by chance; by accident." Thus the meaning of the verse is: "If you treat My acts as an accident . . . then I will increase this kind of 'accident' with a vengeance, bringing yet another sevenfold increase in your punishment for your sins."

The above remarks make it abundantly clear that the coming of Mashiach is in no way influenced by the orbits of the stars.

It should be noted that one of the brilliant scholars in Andalusia, Spain, wrote a book, in which he calculated by means of astrology, the date of the final redemption and predicted the coming of Mashiach in a certain year. Every one of our pious scholars sneered at his words, belittled his scheme, and ostracized him for what he had done in foretelling the future. But reality dealt him a more severe blow than we could have. At the very time Mashiach was supposed to make his appearance [by his reckoning], a rebel leader rose up in the Maghreb who issued an order for everyone to convert. The rebel takeover ruined the reputation of the practitioners of astrology. The hardships our people suffered in the Exile caused them to turn to pseudo-sciences that do not have a shred of evidence to back them up.

WORDS OF ENCOURAGEMENT

Now, dear brothers, *"be strong and of good courage, all you who wait for Hashem"* (Tehillim 31:25). Strengthen one another. Implant in everyone's heart the faith in the coming of the Redeemer, may he soon appear. *"Strengthen the hands that are slack and make firm tottering knees"* (Yeshayah 35:3). Remember, Hashem has let us know through Yeshayah, the herald of Yisrael, that the prolonged affliction of the exile will lead many people to believe that He has abandoned us and turned away from us—God forbid. In light of that, He assured us that He will never abandon us or forget us. As it says, *"Zion says, 'Hashem has forsaken me, Hashem has forgotten me.' "* The prophecy continues, *"Can a woman forget her baby, or disown the child of her womb? Though she might forget, I never could forget you"* (Yeshayah 49:14,15). Hashem has already related a similar message through the first prophet (Moshe), stating, *"For Hashem your God is a compassionate God. He will not fail you nor will He let you perish; He will not forget the covenant with the fathers which He swore to them"* (Devarim 4:31). Also, *"Hashem will bring back your remnants and have mercy on you. Hashem your God will once again gather you from among all the nations where He scattered you"* (Devarim 30:3).

Dear brothers, it is one of the cornerstones of the Jewish faith that a Redeemer will arise who is a descendant of Shlomoh. He will gather in our scattered ones, take away our humiliation, publicize the true religion, and wipe out those who flout His commands. Hashem promised this in the Torah. *"I see it, but not now; I perceive it, but not in the near future. A star[4] shall go forth from Yaakov, and a staff shall arise in Yisrael, crushing all of Moab's princes, and dominating all of Shes's descendants. Edom shall be demolished, and his enemy Seir destroyed, but Yisrael shall be triumphant"* (Bamidbar 24:17,18). The time of his arrival will be a period of great calamity for the Jewish people. As it is written, *"He will have seen that their power is gone, and none is left to set free or take captive"* (Devarim 32:36). Only then Hashem will identify Mashiach, and He will fulfill the promises He made. The prophet, horrified by the vision of the time the Redeemer will appear, exclaimed, *"Who can endure the day of his coming, and who can hold out when he appears?"* (Malachi 3:2). This is the correct view that you must believe about this subject.

We know from the prophecies of Daniel and Yeshayah, and from the words of our Sages, that Mashiach will come after the Roman and Arab empires have swept across the world. This is the case today. No one can doubt this or deny it. Only after Daniel spoke of the Arab empire and the rise of Mohammed, did he speak of the coming of Mashiach, which will take place afterward. Yeshayah, too, declared in his vision that the arrival of Mashiach is linked to the appearance of the Madman [Mohammed]. He says, *"He will see mounted men, horsemen in pairs, riders on donkeys, riders on camels, and he will listen closely, most attentively"* (Yeshayah 21:7). Now the rider on the donkey is Mashiach, who is described as *"humble, riding on a donkey"* (Zechariah 9:9). He will come soon after the rise of the man riding a camel. That is, the Arab empire. The phrase "horsemen in pairs" refers to the bond between the two empires Edom and Yishmael. The same interpretation applies to Daniel's dream of the statue and the beasts.[5] You can plainly see this by simply reading the verses.

THE RAMBAM'S AMAZING FAMILY TRADITION

The exact date of the coming of Mashiach cannot be known. But I have in my possession a great and amazing tradition that I received

---

[4]This is a messianic prophecy.

[5]The Rambam is referring to Daniel, chapters 2 and 7.

from my father. He received it from his father and his grandfather, going back to our ancestors who went into exile at the time of the destruction of Jerusalem. As it says, *"and the exiles of Jerusalem that are in Spain"* (*Ovadiah* 1:20).

This tradition is that Bilam's sayings contain a hint of the future restoration of prophecy in Yisrael. There are many instances where a verse in the Torah, in addition to its simple meaning, also contains an allusion to something else. For example, we find that Yaakov, speaking to his sons, said, *"R'du—Go down there [to Egypt]"* (*Bereishis* 42:2). *R'du* has the numeric value of 210, which is an allusion to the 210 years the children of Yisrael would be exiled in Egypt. So too, *venoshantem*, in the verse, *"When you have children and grandchildren,* venoshantem—*and have been established for a long time in the land"* (*Devarim* 4:25), foretells in a hidden way how long the Jewish people would live in Eretz Yisrael. From the time they entered the land until the exile in the days of King Yehoyakim is a total of 840 years. This is the numeric value of *venoshantem*. Many similar examples can be cited.

The family tradition that I received is based on this system of scriptural interpretation [by means of *remez*—hidden allusion]. The tradition is based on Bilam's oracle, *"Ka'eis—at this point in time—it is said of Yaakov and of Yisrael: 'What God is doing' "* (*Bamidbar* 23:23). This contains a concealed allusion regarding the restoration of prophecy in Yisrael. [Based on another translation of *ka'eis,* which means "equal to the time"] the verse means that after the passage of a period equal to the time that elapsed since the six days of Creation, prophecy would be restored in Yisrael. Prophets will once again foretell *"what God is doing."* Bilam made this prediction in the fortieth year after the Exodus, which was the year 2488 of Creation. According to this equation, prophecy will be restored in Yisrael in the year 4976[6] of Creation. It is true beyond doubt that the restoration of prophecy is the first phase of the coming of Mashiach. As it is stated, *"After that I will pour out My spirit on all flesh; your sons and daughters shall prophesy"* (*Yoel* 3:1).

This is the most dependable of all the calculations that have been made about the coming of Mashiach. Although I have spoken

---

[6]Two times 2488 equals 4976. The year 4976 of Creation corresponds with 1216 c.e. It should be remembered that the Rambam wrote the Letter to Yemen in 1172.

out against making such calculations and strongly opposed the publicizing of the date of his arrival, I have done this in order to keep people from [falling into despair], thinking that his coming is in the distant future. I have mentioned this to you earlier. Blessed is Hashem Who knows [the truth].

You mention in your letter that ours is the time [of the coming of Mashiach] about which Yirmiyah prophesied, *"It is a time of trouble for Yaakov, but he shall be delivered from it"* (Yirmiyah 30:7). This is not correct. This verse definitely refers to the wars of Gog and Magog, which will take place some time after the appearance of Mashiach.

The various signs you mention are very flimsy. They are not attributed to our Sages and were not given by them. Some of them are proverbs and allegories that have nothing to do with this subject.

The False Mashiach

You write about a certain man who makes the rounds of the cities of Yemen, claiming to be Mashiach. Let me assure you that I am not surprised at him. Without a doubt, the man is insane. You cannot blame a sick person for an illness that is not his own doing. Neither am I shocked at the masses who believe in him. They were captivated by him due to their broken spirit and their ignorance of both the illustrious character of Mashiach and the place where he will appear. However, I am astonished that you, a Torah scholar who is well-versed in the Talmud and its commentaries, came under his spell. Don't you know, dear brother, that Mashiach is a prophet of the highest order who ranks higher than any other prophet with the exception of Moshe Rabbeinu? Don't you know that a person who falsely pretends to be a prophet must be put to death for having assumed this great title, just as a person who prophesied in the name of idols must be executed? The Torah states, *"If a prophet presumptuously makes a declaration in My name when I have not commanded him to do so, or if he speaks in the name of other gods, then that prophet shall die"* (Devarim 18:20). What stronger proof is there that he is a liar than his laying claim to the title of Mashiach?

I am really puzzled by your remark about this man; that he is known to be a serene person who has some wisdom. Do you really think these qualities make him Mashiach? You were convinced by him because you have not given any thought to the grandeur of Mashiach, nor to how and where he would appear, and by what specific sign he can be identified. Mashiach will be more sublime and more revered than any other prophet, except Moshe Rabbeinu. The marks of distinction Hashem has given him are even greater than those of Moshe Rabbeinu. Mashiach is described in the following terms: *"His delight shall be in the fear of God; he shall not judge by what his eyes behold, nor decide by what his ears perceive"* (Yeshayah 11:3), and *"The spirit of God shall rest upon him: a spirit of wisdom and insight, a spirit of counsel and valor, a spirit of devotion and reverence for God"* (Yeshayah 11:2). *"Justice shall be the girdle of his loins and faithfulness the girdle of his waist"* (Yeshayah 11:5). Hashem called him six special names in this verse: *"For a child has been born to us, a son has been given us, and authority has settled on his shoulders. He has been named Wondrous One, Adviser, Great, Strong, Eternal Father, Peaceable Ruler"* (Yeshayah 9:5). The name Great is meant as a superlative: to tell you that he is superior to any human being.

We know that one of the basic conditions for a prophet is that he possess limitless knowledge and wisdom. Only to such an individual will Hashem grant the power of prophecy. It is a fundamental belief that prophecy is granted only to a man who is wise, strong, and wealthy. The Sages explain that strong means the ability to subdue one's cravings. Wealthy means rich in knowledge. If we do not believe a man's claim to prophecy unless he is a scholar of eminent stature, then surely we must not believe an ignoramus who claims that he is Mashiach. This person is an illiterate know-nothing. This is apparent from the command he issued to the people to donate all their money to the poor. Whoever obeyed him is a fool, for this man acted against the laws of the Torah. According to the Torah, one should give away only part of his money to charity, not all of it. It says, *"But of all that anyone owns, be it man or beast or land of his holding, nothing that he has consecrated for Hashem may be sold or redeemed"* (Vayikra 27:28). The Sages of the Talmud interpret the phrase *"of all that anyone owns"* to mean, "part of what he owns, but not all that he owns." Based on this passage, they placed a limit on how much you should give to charity. They stated, "Whoever wants to be liberal should not give away more than one fifth of his possessions" (*Kesuvos* 50a). No doubt, the same insanity that motivated this man to claim that he is Mashiach prompted him to order his followers to give all their possessions to the needy. As a result, the rich will become poor and the poor will become rich. By his law, the newly rich then would have to return the money they received to the newly needy. The money would then move around in a vicious cycle, which is the height of stupidity.

CHARACTERISTICS OF THE TRUE MASHIACH

Regarding the question of how and where Mashiach will appear; we know he will make his first appearance in Eretz Yisrael. As it says, *"Suddenly he will come to His temple"* (Malachi 3:1). But no one will know how he will arise until it actually happens. Mashiach will not be a known person that can be identified beforehand as the son of so-and-so of such-and-such family. The signs and wonders he will perform will be proof that he is the true Mashiach. We are told by Hashem regarding Mashiach's person, *"Behold, a man called Tzemach (Sprout) shall sprout forth from the place where he is"* (Zechariah 6:12). Similarly, Yeshayah said that he will arrive without anyone knowing anything about either his father, mother, or family: *"For he shot up like a sapling, like a root out of dry ground"* (Yeshayah 53:2).

After making his appearance in Eretz Yisrael and gathering the entire Jewish people in Jerusalem and the surrounding country-side, the news will spread to the East and the West until it reaches Yemen and the Jews beyond in India. This has been prophesied by Yeshayah, *"Go, swift messengers to a nation tall and of glossy skin, to a people awesome from their beginning onward; a nation that is sturdy and treads down, whose land rivers divide . . . To the place where the name of Hashem of Hosts abides, to Mount Zion"* (Yeshayah 18:2, 7).

The qualities of Mashiach are described by all the prophets from Moshe to Malachi. You can gather this information from the twenty-four books of *Tanach*. His most outstanding characteristic is that the news of his coming will appall and terrify all the kings of the world. Their kingdoms will collapse. Their attempts to defy him by military force or otherwise will utterly fail. Overwhelmed by the miracles they are witnessing, they will stare open-mouthed at the wonders he performs. Yeshayah portrays the subservience of the kings to Mashiach in the verse, *"Kings will be silenced because of him, for they will see what has not been told them, will behold what they never have heard"* (Yeshayah 52:15). He will kill whomever he wants by word of his mouth. No one can escape or be saved, as it says, *"He will strike down a land with the rod of his mouth, and slay the wicked with the breath of his lips"* (Yeshayah 11:4). Worldwide upheavals and wars, ranging from East to West will not come to an end at the beginning of the reign of Mashiach, but only after the wars of Gog and Magog. This was foretold by Yechezkel (Yechezkel 38, 39).

THE FALSE MASHIACH IS INSANE

I do not believe that the man who has appeared in your country has any of these qualifications. The Christians falsely attribute great miracles to *oso ha'ish* — "that man" [the founder of their religion], such as reviving the dead. Even if we conceded this for the sake of argument, we could not accept their argument that Jeshu is Mashiach. We can show them a thousand proofs in *Tanach* that he is not, even from their point of view. Indeed, would anyone lay claim to this title unless he wanted to make himself a laughingstock?

To summarize, if this man had made his claim willfully and scornfully, he would deserve to die a thousand times. I tend to believe that he became mentally unbalanced and lost his mind. Let me offer you advice that will benefit both you and him: Lock him up until the gentiles find out about it, and pass the word around that he is crazy. Afterwards you can release him, and he will be safe. For if the gentiles hear that you locked him up because he claims to be Mashiach, they will realize that you believe him insane, and you will escape the anger of the gentiles. But if you delay until the gentiles find out about it by themselves, they will believe that he is trying to rebel. They will kill him, and you might provoke their anger against your community, God forbid.

SUBMIT TO OPPRESSION

Dear brothers, because of our many sins Hashem has cast us among this nation, the Arabs, who are treating us badly. They pass laws designed to cause us distress and make us despised. The Torah foretold: *"Our enemies will judge us"* (Devarim 32:31). Never has there been a nation that hated, humiliated, and loathed us as much as this one. So bad is our lot that when David had a divinely inspired vision of the troubles that would happen to Yisrael, he bemoaned and lamented the suffering of the Jewish nation at the hands of the Arabs. He prayed on their behalf, saying, *"Woe is me, that I live with Meshech, that I dwell among the clans of Kedar"* (Tehillim 120:5). Note how the verse sets apart Kedar from the other children of Yishmael. This is done because as everyone knows, the Madman is a descendant of the people of Kedar. Daniel, too, when speaking of our degradation and poverty associated with the Arab empire, may it soon be defeated, said, *"It hurled some stars of the [heavenly] host to the ground and trampled them"* (Daniel 8:10). We suffered unbearable oppression and had to endure their lies and defamations. Yet, we acted like David as he describes himself in the verse, *"But I am like a deaf man, who does not hear, like a dumb man who does not open his mouth"* (Tehillim 38:14). We followed the admonition of our Sages who told us to bear the deceit and the falsehood of Yishmael in silence. They found an allusion for this attitude in the names of Yishmael's sons, *"Mishma, Dumah and Massa"* (Bereishis 25:14). They homiletically interpreted these names to mean, "Listen *(sh'ma)*, be silent *(dom)* and endure *(massa)."* All of us, both old and young, agreed to put up with their tyranny. As Yeshayah told us, *"I offered my back to the floggers, and my cheeks to those who tore out my hair; I did not hide my face from insult and spittle"* (Yeshayah 50:6). In spite of that, we cannot escape their constant abuse and harassment. Much as we try to appease them, they continue to persecute and molest us. As David said, *"I am all peace, but when I speak, they are for war"* (Tehillim 120:7). Surely, if we stir up trouble and challenge the government with unfounded allegations, we endanger ourselves and risk our lives.

OTHER IMPOSTORS

I want to tell you that when the Moslem empire began to rise,[1] a man appeared on the other side of the river who pretended to be Mashiach. As proof, he performed a "miracle" by going to sleep afflicted with leprosy and waking up healthy. He inspired an exodus of tens of thousands of Jews. But his mission ended in failure and his plans collapsed. His followers returned to Isfahan[2] and the Jews of Isfahan suffered troubles because of him.

A similar incident occurred forty-eight years ago in the Maghreb, in the city of Fez.[3] A person declared himself the herald and messenger of Mashiach. He announced that Mashiach himself would arrive that very year. His prediction did not materialize, and the result was renewed persecutions of the Jews. I heard this from a person who was there and witnessed the entire episode.

About ten years before this incident,[4] a man in Cordova, Spain claimed to be Mashiach. This brought that Jewish community to the brink of destruction.

---

[1] The religion of Islam was established in 622 C.E.

[2] Isfahan is a city in west central Iran, former capital of Persia.

[3] Fez is a city in north east Morocco. This incident happened in 1127, forty-five years before the Rambam wrote the Iggeres Teiman in 1172.

[4] In 1117.

Thirty years before his emergence,[5] a man in France pretended to be Mashiach and performed so-called miracles. But the French killed him, and along with him they slew many in the Jewish community.

[The text of the above accounts of the emergence and fall of various impostors is found in the standard translations of the Iggeres Teiman from the Arabic by R. Shmuel ibn Tibbon, R. Nachum Maghrabi, and R. Avraham Halevi ben Chasdai of Barcelona. The Rambam's original Arabic text is said to contain a much more detailed version of these reports. This original, full Arabic text was translated into Hebrew by Dr. Jacob Mann in 1928.]

I will now brie³y tell you the events that happened at the beginning of the rise of the Arab empire, which will be helpful to you. In one of these episodes, tens of thousands of Jews marched from the East beyond Isfahan, led by a man who pretended to be Mashiach.[6] They were carrying weapons and drawn swords. They killed everyone who tried to stop them. They ultimately reached the vicinity of Baghdad. This happened in the beginning of the reign of the Omayyad dynasty.[7]

The Sultan then said to the Jews of his kingdom, "Let your rabbis go out to this crowd and determine whether he is indeed the one you are anticipating (Mashiach). If so, we will make a peace treaty with you and abide by any conditions you may set. But if it is untrue, I will kill them." When the rabbis met these Jews, they were told, "We come from the other side of the river." Then the rabbis asked them, "Who incited you to make this revolution?" They replied, "This man here, a descendant of David, whom we know to be a pious and upright man. We found out that he went to sleep a leper and arose the next morning cured and healthy." They thought this was one of the characteristics of Mashiach that is alluded to in the verse, *"plagued, smitten and afflicted by Hashem"* (Yeshayah 53:4). The rabbis explained to them that this interpretation was wrong, and that he lacked many, if not all, of the qualities of Mashiach. The rabbis told them, "Brothers, since you are still close to your home-

---

[5] In 1087.

[6] The Rambam is referring to the false Mashiach Abu Isi Ovadiah from Isfahan, Persia who lived during the reign of Caliph Abd al Malach (659–705).

[7] The Omayyad dynasty ruled the Islamic empire from 661 to 750. They spread Islam over a large region.

land, you can go back. If you stay here, you will perish. You will also invalidate the words of Moshe by misleading the people into thinking that Mashiach has appeared and has been vanquished. The truth is that there is no prophet among you, nor do you have a sign to substantiate your leader's claims." In the end, the Jews were convinced by the rabbis. The Sultan gave them a gift of thousands of dinars to induce them to return home. But after they had returned home, he imposed a fine on them to recover the vast amount of money he had given to them. He began to harass them. He ordered them to mark their clothing with the word "cursed," and to attach an iron bar to their backs and one to their chests. Ever since, the communities of Khorasan and Isfahan suffered the trials of the harsh exile. Report of this incident came to me by word of mouth.

The following episode I researched. I can vouch for its authenticity, because it happened not long ago. About fifty years ago,[8] Rabbi Moshe Dar'i, a pious and upright man, an outstanding Torah scholar came from Dara[9] to Andalusia to study under Rabbi Yosef Halevi Ibn Migash[10] of whom you surely have heard. Later he left for Fez, in the center of the Maghreb. People flocked to him because of his piety, his virtue and his learning. He told them that Mashiach had come, and that Hashem had revealed this to him in a dream. He did not pretend to be Mashiach, as this lunatic did, he only declared that Mashiach had already appeared. Many people became his followers and believed him implicitly. My father and master admonished the people not to follow him, and ordered them to leave him. Only a few obeyed my father. Most, or to be exact, almost all of them, remained faithful to Rabbi Moshe. Finally, he foretold things that actually came true. He would say to the crowd, "Tomorrow such will happen," and it did happen precisely as he predicted. Once he predicted a heavy rain for the coming week, and that the raindrops would be blood. This was thought to be a sign of the coming of Mashiach, as indicated in the verse, *"I will set portents in the sky and on earth, blood and fire and pillars of smoke"* (Yoel 3:3). This took place in the month of Marcheshvan. A very heavy rain did

---

[8] In 1122, fifty years before the Rambam wrote Iggeres Teiman in 1172.

[9] Dara is a town in Morocco.

[10] Rabbi Yosef Halevi ibn Migash, known as Ri Migash (1077–1141). He studied under the Rif (Rabbi Yitzchak Alfasi) and became his successor. As rosh yeshivah of Lucena, Spain, Rabbi Yosef taught Rabbi Maimon, father of the Rambam.

indeed fall during that week. The raindrops were reddish and muddy, as if mixed with clay. This miracle proved to everyone that he was undoubtedly a prophet. This occurrence is not inconsistent with the doctrine of the Torah. Prophecy, as I explained, will return to Yisrael before the coming of Mashiach.

After the majority of the people had faith in him, he foretold that Mashiach would come that same year, on the night of Pesach. He advised the people to sell their property and buy things on credit from the Moslems, paying ten dinars for something that is worth one. This they did. Pesach came and nothing happened. The people were impoverished, since most of them had sold their possessions very ·cheaply, and were heavily burdened by debt. The gentiles and their slaves would have killed him [Rabbi Moshe Dar'i] were they able to find him. Since this Moslem country no longer offered him shelter, he left for Eretz Yisrael where he died, may his memory be blessed.[11] I was told by eyewitnesses that when he left [the Maghreb] he predicted both important and trivial things that actually happened later to the Jews of the Maghreb.

My father told me that about fifteen or twenty years before this incident,[12] some respectable people in Cordova,[13] the capital of Andalusia, who believed in astrology came to the conclusion that Mashiach would arrive that year. They sought a revelation in a dream, night after night, in order to find out whether Mashiach would be a native of their region. In the end, they chose a pious and virtuous person named Ibn Aryeh who had been teaching the people. He performed miracles and foretold the future, just as Al Dari did, until he won over the hearts of the people. When the elders and the rabbis of our community heard this, they assembled in the synagogue and had Ibn Aryeh brought there. They flogged him and imposed a fine on him. They also put him under a ban because he stood idly by and permitted people to use his name. He should have restrained them and reprimanded them for transgress-

---

[11] Rabbi Moshe Dar'i was held in high regard when he moved to Eretz Yisrael after this incident. The Rambam mentions him respectfully in one of his responsa (Kovetz, Volume 1:26).

[12] Sometime between 1102 and 1107.

[13] Rabbi Maimon, the Rambam's father lived in Cordova with his family. When the Rambam was 13 years old, the city fell to the fanatical Almohad Moslem sect. The family wandered from place to place for almost twelve years, and finally settled in Cairo, Egypt.

ing Torah law. They did the same thing to his followers. It was only with great difficulty that the Jews were saved from the gentiles.

About forty years before the incident of Ibn Aryeh in Andalusia, a man of Linon,[14] a large city in France with a Jewish population numbering tens of thousands of families, proclaimed himself Mashiach. On a clear night, he went out into the field, climbed to the top of a high tree, and skipped and jumped from tree to tree as though he were sailing through the sky. He claimed that, according to Daniel, this feat proved that he was Mashiach, as it says, *"One like a human being came with the clouds of heaven, and he was given dominion, glory, and a kingdom"* (Daniel 7:13, 14).

The large crowd which witnessed the miracle became his devoted followers. When the French found out about it they pillaged the city and slew the impostor together with many of his followers. Some of his adherents believe, however, that he is hiding somewhere until this very day.

[End of translation of the detailed account that is omitted in the standard translations, but appears in the original Arabic text.]

CONCLUSION

These incidents[15] were predicted by our prophets. They informed us, as I have told you, that when the time of the coming of the true Mashiach approaches, the number of people who pretend to be Mashiach will increase. Their claims will not be substantiated nor will they be borne out. They will perish and so will many of their followers. Shlomoh was inspired by *ruach hakodesh* (Divine spirit). He foresaw that the long duration of the exile would induce some of our people to take action to end it before the time of redemption comes. As a result, they would perish or meet with disaster. He, therefore, admonished the Jewish people against taking matters into their own hands. He put them under oath, stating, in a figurative sense, *"I adjure you, O maidens of Yerushalayim, by the gazelles or by the hinds of the field: Do not wake or rouse love until it is desired!"* (Shir Hashirim 3:5). Now, dear brothers and friends, accept this oath upon yourselves and do not arouse love until it is desired.

---

[14] Presumably this is Lyons, France.

[15] Of false messiahs arising in various places at various times.

May Hashem Who created the world with the attribute of Mercy remember us and gather us when He gathers in the dispersed of His exile to the Land of His Inheritance. Then may we behold the sweetness of Hashem and contemplate in His Sanctuary. May He take us out from the Valley of the Shadow of Death into which He has placed us. May He remove darkness from our eyes and gloom from our hearts. May He fulfill in our days and in your days the prophecy, *"The people that walked in darkness have seen a brilliant light, on those who dwelt in a land of gloom, light has dawned"* (Yeshayah 9:1). May He in His fury spread darkness on all our oppressors. May He illuminate our pitch-blackness, as He promised us, *"Behold! Darkness shall cover the earth, and thick clouds the nations; but upon you Hashem will shine, and His Glory be seen over you"* (Yeshayah 60:2).

Epilogue

Greetings to you, my dear friend, master of the sciences, storehouse of wisdom,[1] to all our learned colleagues, and to all the people of the country (Yemen). May there be peace as the light that shines; an abundance of peace until the moon is no more. Amen.

I request that you send a copy of this letter to every community, to its rabbis and members, to strengthen their faith and make them stand staunch and steadfast. Read it privately and at public gatherings. Thereby, you will lead the many to righteousness. Be extremely careful and cautious lest its contents fall into the hands of an evil person who would publicize them to the Moslems. This would bring misfortune in its wake, may Hashem in His mercy spare us from it. When I was writing the letter, I was very afraid of that. However, I realized that the mitzvah of leading the many to righteousness is something that one should not fear. In addition, I am sending this letter as a, *"secret of Hashem to those who fear Him"*[2] (Tehillim 25:14). Besides, the Sages gave us an assurance, which they in turn received from the prophets "persons engaged in doing a mitzvah will not suffer harm" (*Pesachim* 8a). Certainly, there is no mitzvah that is more important than this.

Peace upon all Yisrael. Amen.

---

[1]This is Rabbi Yaakov al-Fayumi, who was a learned rosh yeshivah in Yemen. The final paragraphs were written in Hebrew by the Rambam.

[2]In other words, since you are a God-fearing man you will guard the letter and treat it discreetly.

•2•

Maamar Kiddush Hashem Discourse on Martyrdom

A Misleading Answer

A contemporary of mine inquired about how he should act during these times of persecution,[1] in which he is forced to acknowledge "that man"[2] [Mohammed] as God's messenger and a true prophet. He directed his question at someone whom he calls a sage and who [himself] was not affected by the persecutions that wreaked havoc on many of the Jewish communities, may Hashem end them soon. He asked whether he should make the confession in order to save his life; and that he be able to raise his children so that they will not be lost among the gentiles. Or does the Torah of Moshe demand that he die and not accept their creed. We must also take into consideration that this confession may eventually cause him to abandon the observance of all the mitzvos.

The man whom he asked his question gave a weak and pointless answer, a reply that was repulsive both in meaning and language. He made statements that are utterly meaningless, as even unlearned women can realize.

Although his reply is long-winded, weak, and tedious, I thought I would respond to his every point. However, I took pity on the gift Hashem bestowed on us, by that I mean [the power of] speech, as it says in the Torah, *"Who gives man speech? . . . Is it not I, Hashem?"* One should use words more sparingly than money. Indeed, the Wise Man (Shlomoh) has denounced [people who] talk much and say things of little substance, stating, *"Just as dreams come with much brooding, so does a fool's voice come with much speech"* (Koheles 5:2). In the same way, you see what Iyov's friends said

---

[1] The Almohads, a fanatical Moslem sect that rose to power in Morocco and Spain (1130–1223), forced the Jewish population of these regions to choose between Islam and exile.

[2] The Rambam is very reluctant to mention the name of the founder of Islam. Here he uses the term *oso ish*, "that man," the same expression used in referring to the founder of Christianity. In Iggeres Teiman he uses the appellation *hameshuga* — the madman, instead of *oso ish*.

when he talked on and on, *"Is a multitude of words unanswerable? Must a talkative person be right?"* (Iyov 11:2), *"Iyov does not speak with knowledge; his words lack understanding"* (Iyov 34:35). Many other examples can be cited.

Since I am thoroughly familiar with this situation,[3] and I do not want to burden you with the ignorance of this man, I think it is worthwhile to mention the thrust of what he said and omit that which does not deserve an answer. Although, on reflection, nothing he said is worthy of a reply.

He states at the outset that whoever acknowledges that [Mohammed] is a [divine] messenger has thereby automatically renounced his belief in Hashem, the God of Yisrael. He proves his assertion by citing the saying of our Sages, *"Whoever acknowledges idolatry is considered as if he denied the entire Torah"* (*Nedarim* 28a). In making this analogy, he does not differentiate between a person who voluntarily accepts idolatry, like Yerovam and his clique, and one who says under duress that someone is a prophet, because he fears death by the sword.

When I read this first statement of his, I said to myself, "It is not right for me to attack him before reading all he has to say, in compliance with the words of Shlomoh, *"To answer a man before hearing him out is foolish and disgraceful"* (Koheles 18:13).

When I scanned his words a bit more, I noticed that he said the following, *"Whoever makes this confession is a gentile, even if he observes the entire Torah privately and publicly."* Evidently, this "intelligent" individual [who does not differentiate between one who confessed voluntarily and one who confessed under duress] sees no difference between a person who does not observe Shabbos because he is afraid of the sword and one who does not observe it because he does not want to.

Then I read, *"If one of the forced converts enters one of their houses of worship, even if he does not utter a word, and then goes home and says his prayer there, this prayer counts as an added sin and transgression."* He brings proof from the comments of our Sages on the verse, *"For My people have done a twofold wrong"* (Yirmiyah 2:13) [which the Sages explain to mean] *"they bowed to the idol and then bowed to the Beis*

---

[3]When the Rambam was 13 years old, his father and the entire family fled Cordova after the city fell to the Almohads. They wandered from place to place for about twelve years, until they settled in Cairo, in 1165.

Hamikdash" (Shir Hashirim Rabbah 1:6). This [would-be] "Bible commentator" makes no distinction between a heretic who willingly bowed to an idol and then in order to defile the *Bais Hamikdash* bowed to it, and one who enters a mosque under duress, pretends to promote the magnificence of their God, and does not utter a single word opposed to our religion.

Likewise, he said that "Whoever acknowledges that this man [Mohammed] is a prophet, although compelled to do so, is a wicked person and is disqualified by the Torah from serving as a witness, as it says, *"Do not join forces with a wicked person to be a corrupt witness"* (Shemos 23:1), [which the Talmud expounds to mean], *"do not make a wicked man a witness"* (*Bava Kamma* 72b).

Even as I read his blasphemous insults and his inane and foolish long-winded chatter, I said to myself, it still is not right to criticize him before I read the rest of his writing. It might be as Shlomoh said, *"The end of a matter is better than the beginning of it"* (Koheles 7:8).

However the end of his discourse says "Even heretics and Christians would choose death rather than acknowledge that [Mohammed] has divine mission." When I read this I was utterly shocked and amazed. I wondered, *"Is there no God in Yisrael"* (Melachim II 1,3). ["Do the Jewish people lack their own laws? Can we derive the proper way to act from the gentiles?"] If an idol worshiper burns his son or his daughter to his idol, should we say that we too should set ourselves on fire in the service of Hashem? Woe for such a question, and woe for the answer!

Seeing that he started out by bringing proofs for his arguments that had no bearing on the subject and ended up by approving the views of heretics and Christians, I thought it appropriate to apply this verse to him, *"His talk begins as silliness and ends as disastrous madness"* (Koheles 10:13).

No one has the right to speak and deliver sermons in public before he has gone over his speech two, three, and four times and then reviewed it thoroughly. The Sages derived this from Scriptural verse, *"Then He saw it and gauged it; He measured it and probed it."* And afterward, *"He said to man"* (Iyov 28:27). This is what a person needs to do before he speaks. But the things a person writes down with his own hand and inscribes in a book, he should review a thousand times, if possible. This man did nothing of the kind. He recorded all these important ideas in a document, but did not prepare a first draft or edit it. He considered his statements beyond doubt. They did not need to be checked. He handed them to someone who brought them to every city and province. He brought darkness into the hearts of the people, as it says *"He sent darkness, and it was very dark"* (Tehillim 105:28).

The Gravity of Maligning a Jew

I will now begin to outline the magnitude of the error that this poor creature committed, and the [damage] he caused through his ignorance. He meant to do good, but instead he caused harm [by making statements] that are not substantiated. His long, drawn out prose demonstrates self-love of his own style of writing.

It is well known from the commentaries of our Sages that in Moshe's time, before the Exodus, the people of Yisrael had gone astray and broken the covenant of *bris milah*. None except for the tribe of Levi, were circumcised (*Shemos Rabbah* 19:6). [This situation prevailed] until the mitzvah of *Pesach* was announced. Hashem said to Moseh *"No uncircumcised may eat it"* (Shemos 12:43). He then told them to perform the *milah*—circumcision. Our Rabbis give an account of the procedure: Moshe did the circumcision, Yehoshua performed the *periah*, and Aharon did the *metzitzah.*[1] Then they piled the foreskins in heaps. The blood of *milah* became mixed with the blood of the *korban Pesach* (the paschal lamb), and this made them worthy to be redeemed. This is the meaning of Hashem's message to *Yechezkel*, *"When I passed by you and saw you wallowing in your blood, I said to you, 'Live by your blood;' yea, I said to you, 'Live by your blood'"* (Yechezkel 16:6). Our Sages remark that [the Jewish people] had become debased with incest, as it is described [in the chapter[2] that begins with] *"Once there were two women, daughters of one mother"* (Yechezkel 23:2).

Although they were perverted to such an extent, when Moshe said, *"But they will not believe me"* (Shemos 4:1), Hashem admonishes him saying, "Moshe, they are believers, children of believers; believers, for it says, *'and the people believed'* (Shemos 14:31); sons of

---

[1]*periah*—revealing the corona and *metzitzah*—sucking the blood are essential parts of the *milah*.

[2]In this chapter, Yechezkel describes in detail the depraved conduct of the kingdoms of Yehudah and Yisrael.

believers, for it says, 'He [Avraham] believed in Hashem, and He counted it as righteousness' (Bereishis 15:6). But you [Moshe] will end up not believing, as it says, 'You did not have enough faith in Me to sanctify Me'" (Bamidbar 20:12). As a matter of fact, [Moshe] was punished immediately, as the Rabbis expounded, "He who suspects the innocent is punished physically. From where is this derived? From Moshe."[3]

In the same vein, in Eliyahu's days, they all willfully worshiped idols, except for *"the seven thousand—every knee that has not knelt to Baal and every mouth that has not kissed him"* (Melachim I 19:18). Nevertheless, when [Eliyahu] accused Yisrael at *Chorev*, he was taken to task for it, as can be gathered from the verse, "[Hashem said to him], *'Why are you here Eliyahu?'* He replied, *'I am moved by zeal for Hashem, the God of Hosts, for the Israelites have forsaken Your covenant, torn down Your altars, and put Your prophets to the sword. I alone am left, and they are out to take my life"* (Melachim I 19:9, 10).

[The Sages interpret this verse as a dialogue between Hashem and Eliyahu. Eliyahu: They have forsaken Your covenant.]

> *HASHEM:* Is it your covenant by any chance?
> *ELIYAHU:* They also tore down Your altars.
> *HASHEM:* Were they your altars perhaps?
> *ELIYAHU:* They put Your prophets to the sword.
> *HASHEM:* But you are still alive!
> *ELIYAHU:* I alone am left, and they are out to take my life.
> *HASHEM:* Instead of accusing Yisrael, shouldn't you rather denounce the gentile nations? They maintain a house of debauchery, a house of idol worship, and you indict Yisrael! *"Forsake the cities of Aroer"* (Yeshayah 17:2). *"Go back by the way you came, and on to the wilderness of Damascus"* (Melachim I 19:15). This is all explained by the Rabbis in Midrash Chazisa (*Shir Hashirim Rabbah* 1:6).

Likewise, in Yeshayah's days, the Jewish people were deeply steeped in sin, as it says, "Ah, sinful nation! People laden with iniquity! (Yeshayah 1:4). They worshiped idols, as it says, *"Behind the door and doorpost you have directed your thoughts"* (Yeshayah 57:8). There were also murderers among them, as it says, *"Alas, she has become a harlot, the faithful city that was filled with justice, where righteousness dwelt—*

---

[3]The Torah relates that immediately after Moshe made this comment, his hand was struck with leprosy.

but now murderers" (Yeshayah 1:21). They also desecrated God's Name, saying, *"Eat and drink for tomorrow we shall die"* (Yeshayah 22:13). They treated Hashem's mitzvos with contempt, saying, *"Leave the way! Get off the path! Let us hear no more about the Holy One of Yisrael"* (Yeshayah 30:11).

In spite of all this, when Yeshayah said *"And I live among a people of unclean lips,"* he was punished immediately, as it says *"one of the seraphs flew over to me with a live coal . . . He touched it to my lips and declared, 'Now that this has touched your lips, your guilt shall depart and your sin purged away'"* (Yeshayah 6:5-7). According to the Sages, his sin was not forgiven until Menashe killed him (Sanhedrin 103b).

When the angel appeared and pleaded unfavorably against Yehoshua the son of Yehotzadak because his sons had married women who were unsuitable to be the wives of priests, Hashem distanced himself from the angel as it is written, *"Hashem rebuke you, O Satan, may Hashem Who has chosen Jerusalem rebuke you! For this is a brand plucked from the fire"* (Zechariah 3:2).

This is the kind of punishment that has been meted out to the pillars of the world—Moshe, Eliyahu, Yeshayah, and the ministering angels—for speaking just a few disparaging words about the Jewish people. You can imagine [what will happen to] the least among the lowly if he unleashes his tongue and speaks out against Jewish communities, rabbis and their students, priests and Levites, calling them sinners, evildoers, disqualified to testify as witnesses, and heretics who deny Hashem the God of Yisrael. Remember, the writer recorded these [slanderous remarks] in his own handwriting! Just think what his punishment will be! [The forced converts] did not rebel against God to seek pleasure and enjoyment. They did not abandon the Jewish religion to attain status and mundane delights. *"For they have fled before swords, before the whetted sword, before the bow that was drawn, before the stress of war"* (Yeshayah 21:15). This man did not realize that these were not willful transgressors. Hashem will not abandon or forsake them, *"for he did not scorn, He did not spurn the plea of the poor"* (Tehillim 22:25). Concerning such people the Torah says, *"[Yitzchak] smelled the fragrance of his (Yaakov's) clothes"* (Bereishis 27:27). Said the Sages, "Instead of reading *begadav* (his clothes), read *bogdav*[4] (those that deceive him)" [*Bereishis Rabbah* 65].

---

[4]The word *begadav* (his clothes) has the same letters as *bogdav* (his deception); and the verse ends "and he (Yitzchak) blessed him." The

Whatever this man said are things he dreamed up. During one of the persecutions in which the great rabbis were killed, Rabbi Meir was arrested. People who knew him said, "You are Meir, aren't you?" and he replied, "No, I am not." Pointing at the meat of a pig they ordered, "Eat this if you are not a Jew." He answered, "I'll be glad to eat it," and made believe he was eating but in fact did not (*Avodah Zarah* 16b–18). No doubt, in the view of this "humble" person who knows the true meaning of the Torah,[5] Rabbi Meir who worshipped Hashem secretly is considered a gentile, since in his responsum he writes that whoever acts publicly like a gentile while secretly behaving like a Jew is a gentile.

There is also the famous story of how Rabbi Eliezer was seized by heretics, whose offense is worse than idolatry. The heretics— may Hashem cut them down—ridicule all religion and say such things as, "Believers are fools!" "Students of religion are crazy!" They deny prophecy entirely. Rabbi Eliezer was a famous scholar in the sciences. They asked him, "How can you have reached such a high level of scholarship and still believe in religion?" He answered them, appearing to have adopted their creed, whereas he really had in mind the true faith and no other.

This story is told in the Midrash (*Koheles Rabbah* 1:8) as follows:

> It happened that Rabbi Eliezer was seized [by heretics] in order to convert him to heresy. The general brought him to the capital and said, "How is it that an old man like you spends his time on things like that?" He replied, "I accept the judge's words as the truth." The general thought that he meant him, whereas he was really referring to Hashem. The general then said, "Rabbi, I see you have faith in me . . ." [turning to his men he said,] "I really was wondering, how could he have been led astray by such things?" Thereupon he said [to Rabbi Eliezer,] "I pardon you. You are free to go!"

You see that Rabbi Eliezer pretended to the general that he was a heretic, although in his heart he was devoted to Hashem. Heresy is much more serious than idolatry, as has been outlined throughout the Talmud. Yet according to the writings of this "devout"

---

underlying idea is that even when the Jewish people (Yaakov) transgress Hashem's laws, they remain His children and will receive His blessing.

[5]The Rambam is writing this sarcastically.

individual, Rabbi Eliezer should be disqualified. In this current persecution, [our transgression is far less serious] we do not pretend that we are idol worshippers, we only declare that we believe their creed. They are well aware that we do not believe one word of it. We are saying so only to deceive the king, similar to what the prophet said, *"Yet they deceived him with their speech, lied to him with their words"* (Tehillim 78:36).

It is well known what happened to the Jewish people in the days of the evil Nebuchadnezzar. The entire population of Babylon, except Chanaiah, Mishael, and Azariah, bowed to the statue. Hashem testified about that generation, stating, *"No more shall Yaakov be shamed, no longer his face grow pale"* (Yeshayah 29:22). Even the great Torah scholars, if they were present at the time, perhaps bowed down [to the image] in Babylon. I have not come across anyone who called them wicked, gentiles, or disqualified to testify as witnesses. Neither has Hashem counted their action as the sin of idolatry, because they were forced to do it. The Sages confirm this, with reference to the time of Haman, saying, "They performed [the act of prostrating themselves] outwardly, I will also deal with them only outwardly" (*Megillah* 12a).

The author of this response is no doubt a God-fearing man; [he should take a lesson from the Almighty how to treat his people]. *"Shame on him who argues with his Maker, a potsherd with the potsherds of earth! Shall the clay say to the potter, 'What are you doing?'"* (Yeshayah 45:9).

It is known what happened to the Jewish people under the wicked rule of the Greeks. Harsh and evil decrees were issued. There even was a rule that no one was allowed to close the door of his house, so that he would not be alone and be able to fulfill a mitzvah. In spite of this the Sages did not consider them gentiles or evildoers, but completely righteous. They pleaded for them to Hashem and added in the special prayer of thanksgiving, *Al Hanissim*—"For the Miracles"—the phrase, "and the wicked in the hands of the **righteous**."[6]

---

[6]Namely that the Greeks who were wicked were delivered into the hands of the Jews who were righteous, although they had transgressed the mitzvos out of duress.

The Importance of Every Mitzvah

PURPOSE OF THIS LETTER

If not for the fact that in my introductory remarks I resolved not to quote all the things this man has written, I would show you in detail how this person made a fool of himself. He not only said things that are foolish, but even took a pen in hand and wrote them down. In response to a question, he cited material that is totally beside the point. He brings proof from the laws of *eidim zomemim* — "the refuted witnesses" (see Devarim 19:15–21), from one who curses his father or mother, the mitzvah of *tzitzis*, the prohibition of plowing with an ox and a donkey together, and the prohibition of crossbreeding one's livestock with other species, as if the questioner had asked him to compile *Azharos*[1] for him and list all the mitzvos.

Then he says that the Moslems have an idol in Mecca and in other places. Did the questioner ask whether or not he should go on a pilgrimage to Mecca? He also states that the Madman [Mohammed] killed 24,000 Jews, as if he was asked whether Mohammed has a share in the world-to-come.

There are many more such irrelevant statements. This man really should have heeded Shlomoh's counsel, *"Keep your mouth from being rash, and let not your throat be quick to bring forth speech before God"* (Koheles 5:1). Had he paid attention to this verse, he would have realized that whoever answered or analyzed a question regarding permitted and forbidden things was interpreting God's word. He would not have blundered the way he did.

[Although I take issue with his accusation against the Jewish people], Hashem knows and is a good witness that even if he had insulted people more than he did and had babbled more than he

---

[1]*Azharos* is a list of the 613 mitzvos.

did, it would not hurt me. I am not looking for any support. On the contrary, I think, *"Let us lie down in our shame, let our disgrace cover us; for we have sinned against the Lord our God, we and our fathers* (Yirmiyah 3:25). I would have held him in great esteem and I would have said that he acted for the sake of Heaven. For, thank God, I know my worth, and I would not have made a fool of him. *"We acknowledge our wickedness, O Hashem—the iniquity of our fathers"* (Yirmiyah 14:20). But it would not have been right for me to look away and to keep quiet, since he said that any forced convert who prays receives no reward for his prayer but has, on the contrary, committed a sin [by praying]. I know that whatever is published in a book—whether it is true or false—will surely influence a wide readership. This is why so many wrong ideas circulate among people. The only way that a false idea reaches you is by way of a written book. Therefore, I was afraid that this response that turns people away from Hashem will fall into the hands of an unlearned person. He will read that he will receive no reward for praying, and he will not pray. He will reason that, in the same way, he will not be rewarded for performing any of the mitzvos. Eventually, this idea will surely lead to the creation of a new sect.

REFUTATION OF THE RABBI'S RESPONSE

I will now explain where this bombastic babbler slipped up. We read in *Tanach* a detailed account of how Achav, the son of Omri, denied God and worshiped idols, as Hashem testifies, *"Indeed there never was anyone like Achav who sold himself to do evil in the eyes of Hashem"* (Melachim I 21:25). He fasted two and a half hours and had the decree against him annulled (*Taanis* 25b), as it says, *"Then the word of Hashem came to Eliyahu the Tishbite, 'Have you seen how Achav has humbled himself before Me? Because he has humbled himself before Me, I will not bring disaster in his lifetime; I will bring disaster upon his house in his son's time' "* (Melachim I 21:28–29).

Eglon, the king of Moab, oppressed Yisrael, yet he was richly rewarded by God because he paid homage to Him. He rose from his seat when Ehud said to him, *"I have a message for you from God"* (Shoftim 3:20). Hashem rewarded him and preordained that the throne of Shlomoh, which is Hashem's throne, as it says, *"And Shlomoh sat on Hashem's throne"* (Divrei Hayamim I 29:23), and the throne of King Mashiach would come from [Eglon's] descendants. [Our Sages teach us that] Ruth the Moabite, great grandmother of King David, was Eglon's daughter (*Sanhedrin* 105b). The Rabbis noted that Hashem did not withhold his reward.

The wicked Nebuchadnezzar, who killed countless Jews and burned the House that is the footstool of God, was rewarded with forty years of royal rule like Shlomoh, because he ran four paces in order to place the name of God before the name of *Chizkiyahu* (*Sanhedrin* 96a). Again, Hashem did not withhold his reward.

The wicked Eisav was detested by Hashem, as He testifies, *"And I have hated Eisav"* (Malachi 1:3). The Sages outline his crimes as follows,

> That day, he committed five sins: he murdered, worshiped idols, raped an engaged girl, denied resurrection, and rejected his birthright. He then [deceived his father] by wrapping himself in his *tallis,* entering his father Yitzchak's room and saying to him, "Father, does the law of tithing apply to salt?" Said Yitzchak [to himself], "How carefully my son observes the mitzvos!"

Even so, as the reward for the one mitzvah—that of honoring his father—which he fulfilled, Hashem granted him uninterrupted kingship until the coming of King Mashiach. Our Sages say, "David's descendant (Mashiach) will not come before Eisav receives his reward for the mitzvah of honoring one's father and mother." They derived this from the verse, *"After honor he sent me unto the nations"*[2] (Zechariah 2:12). Our Sages formulated this idea in the following terms, "The Holy One, Blessed is He, does not deprive any creature of the reward due to it" (*Pesachim* 118a). He always rewards everyone for the good deeds he performs and punishes everyone for his misdeed; as long as he continues to do it.

Now if these well-known heretics were richly rewarded by Hashem for the little good they did, how can Hashem not reward Jews who were forced to convert but who nevertheless perform the mitzvos secretly? Can it be that Hashem does not distinguish between one who performs a mitzvah and one who does not, or between one who serves Hashem and one who does not? This man

---

[2]Our Sages interpreted this verse as follows—after the reward given to Eisav for honoring his father will Yisrael be sent unto the nations.

says [the opposite], that when he prays he commits a sin, and he backs this up by quoting the verse, *"For my people has done a twofold wrong"* (Yirmiyah 2:13). Now we have explained his error. He defames his contemporaries, and speaks contrary to the words of the rabbis, as we mentioned. He is even maligning the Creator, stating that He punishes a person for performing mitzvos. He stated, in fact, that the prayer of any of you is considered a sin. Shlomoh had such a situation in mind when he said, *"And don't plead before the messenger that it was an error"* (Koheles 5:5).

When I realized that this matter was a disease for the eyes, I set myself to gather herbs and choice spices from the books of the ancient pharmacists with which to concoct a medicine and an eye ointment for this disease. With God's help, it will bring about a cure.[3]

---

[3]The Rambam, who was a famous physician, uses a pharmaceutical metaphor to introduce his exhaustive response to the question regarding forced conversion to Islam.

Discussion of Kiddush Hashem

It is useful to divide my remarks on this subject into five parts: 1. The obligation to mitzvos during times of compulsion. 2. Parameters of *Chillul Hashem* – desecration of Hashem's Name – and its punishment. 3. The status of one who gives his life *al Kiddush Hashem* – for the sanctification of Hashem's name – and of one who transgresses under duress. 4. How the present persecution differs from previous ones, and how one should act during this situation. 5. How a person should perceive himself during this persecution, may Hashem end it soon. Amen.

I: THE OBLIGATION TO MITZVOS DURING TIMES OF RELIGIOUS COMPULSION

The three prohibitions of idolatry, incest, and manslaughter have a particular stringency. Whenever a person is forced to violate any of these, he is at all times, everywhere, and under all circumstances commanded to give up his life rather than transgress. When I say, "at all times" I mean in a time of persecution or otherwise; when I say "everywhere" I mean in private or in public; when I say, "under all circumstances" I mean whether the oppressor intends to make him violate his religious beliefs or not. [In any of these situations], he must choose death.

If he is forced to transgress any other commandment, excluding the aforementioned three, he must evaluate the circumstances. If the oppressor does it for his own benefit, be it at a time of persecution or not, privately or publicly, he may violate the law and thereby save his life. This may be found in the Talmud (*Sanhedrin* 74b) "But Esther was [forced to sin] in public? Abaye said, 'Esther was passive.' Rava said, 'If it is for his own enjoyment it makes a difference.' " We have a standing rule that the Halachah is decided according to Rava.

To summarize, if the oppressor is doing it for his personal benefit one should transgress and avoid being killed, even if it is in public and during a time of persecution.

If the oppressor intends to make him [violate his beliefs] and commit a sin, he must evaluate [the times]. In a time of persecution he must give up his life and not transgress, whether in private or in public. If it is not a time of persecution, he should transgress and save his life, if it is in private, but he should choose death if it is in public.

This is the relevant text in the Talmud; "When Rav Dimi [Ravin] arrived, he said in the name of Rabbi Yochanan that even if it is not a time of persecution, he may transgress and not die, only in private; in public he may not violate even a minor mitzvah, even changing the way he ties his shoes." By "in public" is meant [in the presence of] ten Jewish males.

II: PARAMETERS OF *CHILLUL HASHEM* AND ITS PUNISHMENT

The parameters of *Chillul Hashem* — desecration of Hashem's Name — can be divided into two categories: one that applies to [the] general [populace] and one to specific [people].

That which applies to the general populace takes two forms. The first form: When a person commits a sin out of spite, not for the pleasure or enjoyment to be derived from that act, but because he treats it lightly and disdainfully, he is thereby desecrating Hashem's Name. Hashem says concerning one who swears falsely, which is an act that brings him no pleasure or enjoyment, *"Do not swear falsely by My Name; [if you do so] you will be desecrating your God's Name"* (Vayikra 19:12). If he does it in public he is openly desecrating Hashem's Name. I explained above that "in public" means in the presence of ten Jews.

The second form: When someone consciously fails to correct his behavior to the point that people begin to talk disparagingly about him. He may not have committed a sin, but he has nonetheless desecrated Hashem's Name. When he is [being perceived as] sinning by his fellow man, a person should be as careful as he is of sinning to his Creator, for Hashem said, *"You shall be innocent before Hashem and Yisrael"* (Bamidbar 32:22).

The Talmud (*Yoma* 86a) asks regarding this subject, ["What is meant by *Chillul Hashem?*"] Rav Nachman bar Yitzchak replied, "For example, if people say about someone, May God forgive so-and-so." Another example cited is, "When friends are embarrassed by his reputation."

The parameters of *Chillul Hashem* that apply to specific people also take two forms:

The first form: When a learned person does something that a person of his stature should not do, even though others may do so without compunction. Because he has a reputation of being a man of virtue, people expect more of him. [By his action] he has desecrated Hashem's Name. Rav gave the following definition of *Chillul Hashem*, "For example, when I buy meat and do not pay right away" (*Yoma* 86a). In other words, a person of his eminence should not buy anything unless he pays immediately, at the time of purchase, although the practice [of buying on credit] is quite acceptable with the general public. Rabbi Yochanan said the following on the subject, "For example, if I walk four ells without wearing my *tefillin* and without being engrossed in Torah thoughts [it is considered a *Chillul Hashem*]." He is referring to a man of his stature. Very often we find that the Talmud draws a distinction when the person is an important personality.

The second form: When a learned man behaves in a lowly and loathsome way in his dealings with people. He receives people angrily and with contempt. He is not genial with people and does not treat them with decency and respect. Such a person has desecrated Hashem's Name. The Sages phrased it this way, "When a person is learned but is not honest in his dealings with people and does not speak gently to people, what do people say about him? Woe is to so-and-so who studied Torah!"

If I were not concerned about being long-winded and going off on a tangent, I would explain to you how a person should behave toward others, what his actions and words should be like, and how he should receive people. Thus anyone who spoke to him or had dealings with him would speak about him only in glowing terms. I would explain the meaning of the phrases "being honest in one's dealings with people" and "speaking gently to people." But this would require a full-length book. So I will pick up where I left off.

Kiddush Hashem—Sanctification of Hashem's Name is the opposite of *Chillul Hashem*. When a person fulfills a mitzvah and is inspired by no other motive than his love of Hashem and the desire to serve Him, he has publicly sanctified Hashem's Name. So too, if good things are said about him, he has sanctified Hashem's Name. The Sages phrased it like this, "When a person has studied Torah and Mishnah, attended to Torah scholars and dealt gently with people, what do people say about him? 'See how pleasant is his conduct, how seemly are his deeds!' " Scripture says this about such a man, *"And He said to me, 'You are My servant, Yisrael in whom I glory' "* (Yeshayah 49:3). Regarding *Kiddush Hashem* a great person is also special. If a great man avoids distasteful situations he is sanctifying Hashem's Name. And so we read, *"Put crooked speech away from you"* (Mishlei 4:24).

Chillul Hashem is a grave sin. Both the deliberate sinner and the inadvertent sinner are punished. The Rabbis phrased it succinctly, "Both unintentional and intentional, are liable regarding desecration of the Name" (*Avos* 4:5). A man is granted a delay in punishment for all sins, but not for the desecration of Hashem's Name. The Rabbis stated, "For the desecration of Hashem's Name no credit is extended. What do we mean that no credit is extended? He is not treated as he is by the storekeeper who extends credit" (*Kiddushin* 40a). In other words, he will be required to pay for his transgression immediately. The Sages also teach that, "Whoever desecrates Hashem's Name in secret, is punished in public" (*Avos* 4:5).

This sin is more serious than any other. Neither Yom Kippur, nor suffering, nor repentance can atone for *Chillul Hashem*. This is what the Rabbis say about it, "He who is guilty of *Chillul Hashem* cannot have his sin erased by either repentance, Yom Kippur or through suffering; they all suspend punishment until death affords forgiveness, for so it says, *"Then the Lord of Hosts revealed Himself to my ears: 'This iniquity shall never be forgiven you until you die' "* (Yeshayah 22:14). This entire discourse refers to the person who willingly desecrates the Name of Hashem, as I shall explain.

Just as *Chillul Hashem* is a grave sin, so is *Kiddush Hashem*—the Sanctification of Hashem's Name—a great mitzvah for which you are richly rewarded. Every Jew is required to sanctify Hashem's Name. It is written in Sifra, *"I am Hashem your God, who brought you out of the land of Egypt to give you the land of Canaan, [and] to be a God for you"* (Vayikra 25:38), on condition that you sanctify My Name publicly. We also find in the Talmud (*Sanhedrin* 74b) it says, "Rabbi Ami was asked, Is a Noachide commanded to sanctify Hashem's Name?" With regard to a Jew this question was not raised; obviously it may be inferred that a Jew is indeed commanded to sanctify His Name, as it is stated, *"I must be sanctified among the Israelites"* (Vayikra 22:32).

III: THE STATUS OF ONE WHO GIVES HIS LIFE *AL KIDDUSH HASHEM* AND OF ONE WHO TRANSGRESSES UNDER DURESS

You must realize that wherever the Sages ruled that one must give up his life rather than transgress, and he does so, he has sanctified Hashem's name. If ten Jews witnessed his death he has sanctified the Name publicly. For example: *Chananiah, Mishael* and *Azariah,*[1] *Daniel,*[2] the Ten Martyrs killed by the Romans,[3] the seven sons of *Channah,*[4] and all the other Jews who gave their lives for the sanctification of the Name, may the Merciful one speedily avenge their blood. The following verse applies to them, *"Bring in My devotees, who made a covenant with Me over sacrifice"* (Tehillim 50:5). Our Rabbis related the following verse to them, *"I adjure you, O maidens of Jerusalem, by gazelles or by hinds of the fields"* (*Shir Hashirim* 2:7). They expounded, *"I adjure you O maidens of Jerusalem"*—the persecuted generations; *"by the gazelles"*—those who did for Me what I desired, and I did what they desired; *"by the hinds of the field"*—those who shed their blood for Me like the blood of gazelles and hinds. The following verse also applies to them: *"It is for Your sake that we are slain all day long"* (Tehillim 44:23).

A person to whom God granted the privilege to rise to the lofty level of dying *al Kiddush Hashem*—for the Sanctification of Hashem's

---

[1]See Daniel, chapter 3. Nebuchadnezzar ordered everyone to bow down before a huge statue, but Daniel's three friends refused to do so. They were thrown into a furnace but were miraculously saved.

[2]Daniel who disobeyed King Darius' order and prayed to Hashem was miraculously saved from the lion's den into which he was thrown.

[3]The story of the ten great Tanna'im who were brutally killed by the Romans is told in the *Eileh Ezkera,* recited on Yom Kippur during Mussaf.

[4]They were killed by Antiochus, in the times of Chanukah, for refusing to worship the Greek idol.

Name, although he may not have been a Torah scholar, merits to be in the world to come, even if he was sinful as *Yerovam ben Nevat* and his colleagues. The Rabbis say of this, " 'No one can approach the high rank of those martyred by the government!' Who are we referring to? We cannot say that this refers to Rabbi Akiva and his colleagues [who were martyrs of the Roman government], because surely they had other claims to eminence. It must be referring to the martyrs of Lydda."[5]

If one did not allow himself to be killed, but under duress transgressed and remained alive, he did not do the right thing. Under duress he desecrated Hashem's Name. However, he does not incur any of the seven penalties enumerated in the Torah, namely: the four death penalties of the human court [stoning, burning, beheading, and strangling]; premature death—*kareis*; divinely caused death; and lashes. There is not a single case in the entire Torah in which a person acting under duress is sentenced to any of these punishments, whether his transgression was minor or major. Only a willful sinner is punished, not one who was forced. As it says, *"However, if a person commits [an act of idolatry] high-handedly, whether he is a native born or a proselyte, he is blaspheming Hashem, and that person shall be cut off [spiritually] from among his people"* (Bamidbar 15:30). The Talmud is full of statements to the effect that a person acting under duress is not guilty. According to the Torah, *". . . this case[6] is no different from the case where a man rises up against his neighbor and murders him"* (Devarim 22:26). We often read in the Talmud, "According to the Torah, a person who acted under duress, is exempt from punishment." He is not characterized as a sinner or a wicked man, and he is not disqualified [by this] from serving as a witness. Only if he [willfully] committed a sin that disqualifies him from serving as a witness. [All that can be said is that] he did not fulfill the mitzvah of *Kiddush Hashem*, but under no circumstances can he be considered as having willfully desecrated Hashem's Name.

---

[5]Two brothers, Lulianus and Pappus, who took upon themselves the guilt for the death of the Emperor's daughter, in order to save the entire nation. See Taanis 18b.

[6]The Torah is relating the punishment for one who forcibly cohabits with a betrothed girl. The Torah specifically excludes the girl from punishment, although technically she was involved in adultery.

Whoever says or thinks that a person should be sentenced to death because he violated a law of which the Sages said that he should give up his life rather than transgress, is completely wrong. It simply is not so, as I will explain. What is meant is that it is a mitzvah to offer his life, but if he did not, he is not liable to the death penalty. And even if he was forced to worship idols he is not liable to *kareis* (be cut off spiritually). He certainly is not executed by order of the court. This principle is clearly stated in *Toras Kohanim:* "Hashem says [concerning a man who gives any of his children to Molech,[7]] *"I will direct My anger against that person"* (Vayikra 20:5). Our Sages comment, "but not if he was forced, acted unwittingly, or was misled." It is clear then that if he was forced or misled he is not liable. We are speaking about a prohibition, that had it been done intentionally has the stringency of *kareis*. Certainly, if he was forced to commit sins that when done intentionally are punishable by lashes, he is not at all liable. The prohibition of *Chillul Hashem* is a negative commandment, [that is not liable to *kareis*]. As it is stated, *"Do not desecrate My holy Name"* (Vayikra 22:32). [Surely one who transgresses under duress is not liable.]

It is a known fact that making a false oath is a desecration of Hashem's Name. As it says, *"Do not swear falsely by My Name; [if you do], you will be desecrating your God's Name. I am Hashem"* (Vayikra 19:12). Still, the Mishnah reads, "One is allowed to vow to murderers, robbers and tax-collectors that what he has is *terumah,[8]* [thereby saving his produce]. Beis Shammai states that one may only use the form of a *neder* (vow). Beis Hillel says that one may also use the formula of *shevuah* (oath)" (*Nedarim* 3:4).

These things are clearly spelled out. There is no need to bring any proofs to support them; how can anyone say that the law regarding a person who acted under duress and one who acted voluntarily is the same? Our Sages ruled in many cases, "Let him transgress and not give up his life." Now this man [who wrote this response] considers himself to be more worthy than the Rabbis and more scrupulous in the observance of the mitzvos. He openly declares his willingness to surrender his life in all cases and thinks that he is sanctifying Hashem's Name. However, if he would indeed act this way [and surrender his life in every instance] he would

---

[7]A form of idol worship.
[8]Produce permitted only to a Kohain.

be a sinful and rebellious individual. He would bear guilt for his soul, for Hashem said, *"Keep My decrees and laws, since by keeping them a person will live"* (Vayikra 18:5) — and not die (*Sanhedrin* 74a).

IV: HOW THIS PERSECUTION DIFFERS FROM PREVIOUS ONES AND HOW ONE SHOULD ACT DURING THE PRESENT SITUATION

You have to realize that in all the persecutions that occurred in the time of the Sages, they were ordered to violate mitzvos and to perform [sinful] acts, as we are told in the Talmud: They were forbidden to study Torah and to circumcise their sons. They were ordered to have intercourse with their wives when they were ritually unclean. But in the present persecution they are not required to do any forbidden action, only to say something. If a person wishes to fulfill the 613 commandments of the Torah in secret he can do so. He is not guilty of anything unless he happens to desecrate the Shabbos without being forced to do so. This oppressive regime does not force anyone to do any prohibited act, just to make an oral affirmation [of faith]. They know very well that we do not mean what we say, and that the person making the affirmation is only doing so to escape the king's wrath and to satisfy him with a recitation of meaningless incantations.

If anyone asks me whether he should offer his life or make this acknowledgement, I tell him to acknowledge and not choose death. However if one died a martyr's death rather than affirm the divine mission of "that man" [Mohammed], we can say that he acted righteously. He will receive an abundant reward from Hashem. His position will be in the loftiest levels, for he has given his life for the sanctity of Hashem. However, one should not stay in the country under the rule of that king. [Until he is able to leave], he should stay home, do his work secretly and go out only if it is absolutely essential.

There has never been a persecution as unusual as this, where people are only compelled to say something. Our Rabbis ruled that a person should choose death and not transgress. We cannot infer that they meant speech that does not involve action. One must submit to martyrdom only when he is forced to do something that he is forbidden to do.

A person who is caught in this persecution should conduct himself along the following lines: Let him set his sights on observing as many of the mitzvos as he can. If he transgressed often or desecrated the Shabbos, he should still not carry what he is not allowed to carry.[9] He should not say to himself, "The transgressions I have made are more grave than [the carrying on Shabbos] from which I am abstaining now." Let him be as careful about observing the mitzvos as he can.

A person must be aware of this fundamental Torah principle. Yerovam ben Nevat and others like him are punished for [the grievous sin of] making the calves as well as for disregarding the [comparatively minor] law of *eiruv tavshilin*[10] and similar laws. Don't say that to him applies the rule of "he who has committed two offenses must be held answerable for the more severe one only" (*Gittin* 52b). This principle applies only to punishments meted out by man in this world. Hashem metes out punishment for minor and serious sins, and He rewards people for everything they do. A person should be aware that he is held accountable for every transgression he committed. He is rewarded for every mitzvah he performed. Things are not the way people think.

The recommendation I followed myself, and the advice I want to give to all my friends and anyone that consults me, is to leave those places and to go to where we can practice our religion and fulfill the Torah without compulsion and fear. Let him leave his family and his possessions. The Law of Hashem that He has given us as a heritage is very great. Our commitment to it takes precedence to material values. All thinkers scorn material wealth, which is transitory, but the fear of Hashem endures.

Let us say, there were two Jewish cities, one superior to the other in its deeds and conduct, more meticulous with mitzvos and more dedicated to their observance. A God-fearing person is required to leave the city where the actions are not quite proper and

---

[9]On Shabbos it is forbidden to carry an object from a private domain into a public domain, or vice versa, or to carry an object four ells in a public domain.

[10]*Eiruv tavshilin*, the law of "combination of dishes." When a *Yom Tov* falls on Friday, it is forbidden to cook or bake for Shabbos unless an *eiruv tavshilin* is performed.

move to the better city. Our Sages admonished us in this regard, stating, "You should not live in a city where there are fewer than ten righteous residents." They find support for this in the verse, [where Abraham pleads with Hashem to spare the city of Sodom, saying,] *"Suppose there are ten [righteous people] found there?"* And He answered, *"I will not destroy for the sake of the ten"* (Bereishis 18:32). This is what one should do when both cities are Jewish. Certainly, if a Jew lives in a place inhabited by gentiles, he must leave it and go to a more favorable place. He must make every effort to do so, although he may place himself in jeopardy. He must escape that bad place where he cannot practice his religion properly, and set out until he arrives at a decent place.

The prophets have postulated that he who lives among heretics is considered one of them. They derived it from [the words of King David who said, when he was banished from Eretz Yisrael], *"For they have driven me out today, so that I cannot have a share in Hashem's possession, rather I am told, 'Go and worship other gods'"* (Shmuel I 26:19). You see that [David] equates his dwelling among gentiles with the worship of other gods. In the same vein, David says, *"O Lord, You know I hate those who hate You and loathe Your adversaries"* (Tehillim 139:21), and also, *"I am a companion to all who fear You, to those who keep Your precepts"* (Tehillim 119:63). Similarly, we see that our father Abraham despised his family and his home town. He ran for his life to escape from the creed of the heretics.

He should make an effort to leave the nonbelievers' environment when they do not force him to follow in their ways. But when they coerce him to transgress even one of the mitzvos, he is forbidden to remain in that place. He must leave and abandon everything he owns, travel day and night, until he finds a spot where he can practice his religion. There is a big, wide world out there!

The excuse of the person who claims that he has to take care of his family and his household really does not hold water. *"A brother cannot redeem a man or pay his ransom to God"* (Tehillim 49:8). In my opinion, it is not right to make this claim to avoid the obligation. He should emigrate to a decent place, and under no circumstances continue to stay in the land of persecution. Whoever remains there is a transgressor and desecrates Hashem's Name, and is almost an intentional sinner.

There are those who delude themselves into believing that they should remain where they are until King Mashiach comes to the lands of the Maghreb. Then they will go to Jerusalem. I do not know how they will disentangle themselves from the present persecution. They are transgressors, and they cause others to sin. The prophet Yirmiyah had people like them in mind when he said, *"They offer healing offhand for the wounds of My people, saying, 'all is well, all is well' "* (Yirmiyah 6:14). There is no dependable set time for the coming of Mashiach. One does not know if he is coming soon or in the distant future. The obligation of keeping the mitzvos is not dependent on the coming of Mashiach. We are required to engross ourselves in Torah and mitzvos. We must strive to achieve perfection in both of them. Then, if Hashem grants us, our children or grandchildren the privilege to witness the coming of Mashiach, so much the better. If he does not come we have not lost anything. On the contrary, we have gained by doing what we had to do.

A person may be in a place where he sees Torah study coming to an end, the Jewish population declining and gradually disappearing, and he himself unable to practice his religion. He says, "I am going to stay here until Mashiach comes. Then I will be extricated from this predicament." Such a person is guilty of wickedness, destructive callousness, and of wiping out the Jewish faith and ideology. That is my opinion, and Hashem knows the truth.

V: HOW A PERSON SHOULD PERCEIVE HIMSELF DURING THIS PERSECUTION

A person may be unable to fulfill the aforementioned advice [to leave the land of persecution], either because of his fondness for his [native] country or because of his fear of the dangers of a sea voyage. He stays where he is. He, then, must regard himself as desecrating Hashem's Name, not quite deliberately, but almost so. He must consider himself as being scolded by God and punished for his bad deeds. At the same time, he should realize that if he performs a mitzvah, the Holy One, Blessed is He, will give him a two-fold reward. He did the mitzvah for the sake of Heaven, and not to impress others or to be regarded as an observant Jew. In addition, a person's reward for performing a mitzvah knowing that if caught, he will lose his life and all his possessions, is much greater than that of a person who fulfills a mitzvah without fear. The Torah, referring to a time like the present, [when observance of mitzvos is done for the sake of heaven and despite the fact that one's life is in danger], says: *"If only you seek Him with all your heart and soul"* (Devarim 4:29). Nevertheless, you should not take your mind off your plans to leave the provinces that Hashem is angry with, and do your utmost [to carry them out].

It is not right to shun and despise people who desecrate the Shabbos. Rather, you should reach out to them and encourage them to fulfill the mitzvos. The Rabbis ruled that a sinner who willfully transgressed should be welcomed to the synagogue and not humiliated. They based their pronouncement on Shlomoh's advice: *"A thief should not be despised for stealing to appease his hunger"* (Mishlei 6:30). This means, do not despise sinners in Yisrael when they come secretly to "steal" mitzvos.

Ever since we were banished from our land, persecutions have been our fate, as it says, *"From our youth it (the persecution) raised us as a father and from our mother's womb it has directed us"* (Iyov 31:18). It also says in many places in the Talmud, "a persecution is likely to pass" (*Kesuvos* 3b). May Hashem put an end to this one.

"In those days and at that time—declares Hashem—the iniquity of Yisrael shall be sought, and there shall be none; the sins of Yehudah, and none shall be found; for I will pardon those I allow to survive (Yirmiyah 50:12). Let the prophecy be fulfilled speedily in our days. May it be His will. Amen.

•3•

Commentary on The Mishnah

Translator's Introduction

The Rambam's early life was marred by persecution, flight, and restless wanderings. It was during these turbulent times that the Rambam, at the age of 23, wrote the Commentary on the Mishnah.

His introduction to this work—translated in this volume—is in itself a document of great importance, since it contains a comprehensive formulation of the process by which the Oral Law was transmitted, from Moshe until Rabbi Yehudah HaNasi, the compiler of the Mishnah.

The significance of this discourse lies in the fact that the Rambam conveys the proper outlook needed for the study of the Mishnah. He emphasizes that Halachah is not determined by prophetic pronouncements, but by analysis of the law by the Rabbis according to a set of prescribed rules.

This leads into a detailed discussion of prophecy, and the ways of distinguishing between a true and a false prophet.

The Rambam goes on to classify the Oral Law, clearly defining *Halachos leMoshe miSinai* (Laws received by Moses in Sinai), enactments (*takkanos*), and preventive measures (*gezeiros.*)

He then proceeds to give an outline of the Mishnah itself, describing the Six Orders (*Sedarim*) and the topics discussed in the various tractates (*mesechtos.*) He goes into greater detail with tractate *Avos* (Ethics of the Fathers), focusing on the role of a judge.

We are given an explanation of the origin of halachic disagreements and how these controversies led to the writing of the Talmud where these debates are recorded.

There follows a detailed overview of the nature of Aggadic *derashos* on which the Rambam explains that these seemingly bizarre tales must be seen as allegories concealing profound concepts that cannot be spelled out in simple language. This leads into a very enlightening philosophical discussion about the purpose of the creation of man, and the ideals man should pursue.

The Rambam then lists all the Orders and Tractates of the Talmud and concludes by describing his purpose in writing the commentary on the Mishnah.

The Introduction to the Mishnah is a work of sheer genius, for it offers in capsule form, a perspective on the contents of the entire Mishnah and the Talmud. More importantly, it fills us with awe and reverence for the towering Sages, the bearers of the torch, who handed the Oral Law to us in its pristine purity, link after link, in an unbroken chain.

The Rambam wrote his work in Arabic, in order to make it accessible to the widest spectrum of the Jews of his time whose native tongue this language was. It was translated into Hebrew by Rabbi Yehudah ben Shlomoh Charizi and can be found in the Vilna edition of *meseches Berachos,* in the commentary section, page 105.

In translating the Introduction I have attempted to make the difficult text accessible to a wide range of readers by presenting it in an informal, colloquial English, following the Rambam's example, who wrote in Arabic in order to reach the largest possible readership.

I kept the translation as literal as possible. Where the literal translation made it difficult to comprehend, I modified it slightly as the Rambam himself instructed to the translators of his works. Additions to the text and the translation of words that are necessary to understand the text, are placed in brackets. The translation of other words can be found in the glossary.

It is my hope that this volume will whet the readers' appetite for studying the Mishnah, *lilmod ulelameid, lishmor velaasos* — to learn, to teach, and to do.

The Written and the Oral Torah

Every *mitzvah* the Holy One, Blessed is He, gave to Moshe Rabbeinu, was given to him together with its explanation. Hashem would tell Moshe a verse of the Torah, and then He would give to him its explanation, its underlying principles and all the cases to which the verse applies.

Moshe, in person, taught each verse of the Torah to the assembly of the *B'nei Yisrael* in the presence of Aharon and the Elders.[1]

Afterwards, the people reviewed with one another what they had heard from Moshe, and wrote down the verse on scrolls. Supervisors would visit the people to teach and review the verse until everyone knew it accurately and was well versed in it. They

---

[1]The Talmud relates that Moshe taught the Torah to *B'nei Yisrael* in the following manner:

Moshe would enter his tent, and Aharon would be the first to follow. Moshe would tell Aharon the verse once and teach him its explanation. Aharon would then position himself on Moshe's right side, after which Aharon's sons, Elazar and Isamar, entered. Moshe would repeat to them what he had told Aharon, whereupon one son would take a seat on Moshe's right, and the other on Aharon's left. Next, the seventy elders would enter, and Moshe would repeat to them the instruction he had taught to Aharon and his sons.

Then the people at large, all those seeking Hashem, would come, and Moshe would present the verse to them, so that they would hear it entirely from his own lips.

As a result, Aharon heard each verse from Moshe's lips four times, his sons, three times, the elders, twice, and the rest of the people heard it once.

Moshe would then withdraw, and Aharon would explain to the assembled crowd the verse that he had heard from Moshe four times. Elazar and Isamar would then restate the verse to the people, after which the elders taught the same verse to the entire assemblage once more.

Consequently, *B'nei Yisrael* heard the verse four times: once from Moshe, once from Aharon, a third time from his sons, and a fourth time from the elders (*Eiruvin* 54b).

then taught the people the explanation of the God-given mitzvah in all its many details. Thus, the wording of the mitzvah would be recorded in writing, while its oral tradition would be learned by heart.

This fact [that the written verse was given with its oral explanation] is discussed by our Rabbis in a *Baraisa* (*Sifra, Vayikra* 25:1):

It is written, *"Hashem spoke to Moshe on Mount Sinai . . ."* (*Vayikra* 25:1). [This verse introduces a detailed discussion of the laws of *sh'mittah*—the Sabbatical year.] To what purpose does the verse mention Mount Sinai in connection with *sh'mittah?* After all, we know full well that *all* the laws of the Torah were given on Sinai—Mount Sinai is mentioned here to tell you: Just as the details and particulars of the laws of *sh'mittah* are written openly in the Torah and were obviously given at Sinai, so too the details of the other mitzvos [although not mentioned in the written Torah], were also given at Sinai.

For example, the Holy One, Blessed is He, told Moshe the verse, *"You must live in sukkos for seven days"* (*Vayikra* 23:42). Afterwards Hashem let Moshe know that this mitzvah needs to be fulfilled by all males but not by females (*Sukkah* 2:8), that the sick and travelers are not required to live in a *sukkah* (*Sukkah* 26a), that the roof of the *sukkah* must be made of something that grows from the ground (thus excluding wool, silk, and the like), and may not be made of utensils, even those made from plant material, such as quilts, pillows, and clothing (*Sukkah* 1:4). Hashem also let Moshe know that one must eat, drink, and sleep in the *sukkah* during all the seven days of *Sukkos,* and that the interior area of a *sukkah* may not be less than seven handbreadth square, and that it may not be less than ten handbreadth in height (*Sukkah* 16b). In this way, the mitzvah of *sukkah* was given to Moshe together with its detailed explanations.

And so it was with all the 613 mitzvos; Moshe received the mitzvos along with their explanations; the mitzvos he received in writing and their explanations, orally.

On the first of *Shevat,* in the fortieth year of the wandering of *B'nei Yisrael* in the desert, shortly before Moshe Rabbeinu's death, Moshe gathered the *B'nei Yisrael* and told them, "The time of my death is approaching. Whoever has heard a *Halachah* but forgot it, come and ask me, and I will explain it to you. Whoever is in doubt about something, tell me about it, and I will clarify it for you," as it says in the Torah, *"In the fortieth year on the first of the eleventh month; Moshe began to explain this Torah, saying"* (Devarim 1:5).

From the first of Sh'vat until the seventh of *Adar* [the day of Moshe's death], the *B'nei Yisrael* received clarification of the halachos directly from Moshe and studied the explanations. Shortly before his death, Moshe began to write the Torah on scrolls—thirteen parchment Torah scrolls—all containing the full Torah text from the *beis* of *bereishis* [the first letter in the Torah] to the last *lamed* of *le'einei kol Yisrael* [the last letter of the Torah].

He gave one scroll to each of the twelve tribes of Yisrael, instructing them to live according to its laws and to follow its decrees. The thirteenth scroll he gave to the *Levi'im*, telling them, *"Take this Torah scroll and place it beside the ark of the covenant of Hashem your God, leaving it there as a witness"* (Devarim 31:26).

After that, he climbed Mount Nevo on the seventh of Adar at noon, as has been calculated by traditional sources (*Megillah* 13b).

To us it seems as though Moshe had died, because he is no longer with us and we miss him; but in reality, he lives on, at a loftier level of existence, a higher plane to which he was elevated. The Sages had this in mind when they said, "Moshe Rabbeinu did not die, but rose on high and now serves Hashem in heaven" (*Sotah* 13a). However, a thorough discussion of this subject would take up too much space, and this is not the place for it.

After Moshe died, *Yehoshua* and the Sages of his time studied and researched the explanations they received from Moshe. No question or dispute arose regarding any matter that Yehoshua or any of the elders had explicitly heard from Moshe himself. However, related cases, for which Moshe had not given specific instruction, were solved by applying the Thirteen Rules by means of which the Torah is expounded—rules that were given on Sinai.

Some of the laws derived this way were undisputed and were unanimously agreed upon. Other laws gave rise to controversy. Depending on the precedent to which he compared the case at hand, one Sage would make a statement based on his logical reasoning insisting that he was right, while another Sage would just as vehemently insist that his rationale was right. When such disputes occurred among authorities they would follow the majority opinion, as it is stated, *"[A case] must be decided on the basis of the majority"* (Shemos 23:2).

The Power of Prophecy

Prophecy is of no use as a way of explaining the Torah, or as a means of influencing the Thirteen Rules by which subdivisions of mitzvos can be derived. In fact, what Yehoshua and Pinechas [disciples of Moshe] did with regard to analysis and explanation of the law is the same as what Ravina and Rav Ashi [who presided over the compilation of the Talmud, when the prophets no longer lived] were to do in their day.

Nevertheless, I assure you by my life that the extraordinary influence a prophet has on the mitzvos is one of the fundamental principles on which the Jewish faith rests and is based.

Although I recognize that this is the proper place to explain this fundamental principle [the role of the prophet], in greater detail, it is impossible to do so without first: (1) sorting out the various claims that can be made to possessing the power of prophecy, and (2) describing the method by which the truth of a prophecy can be verified, since this, too, represents a fundamental principle. The vast multitudes of mankind have already erred with regard to this subject, including a small number of their philosophers. They imagine that a person's power of prophecy is not proven unless he performs a miraculous sign, like one of the signs of Moshe Rabbeinu, changing the laws of nature as Eliyahu did when he revived the widow's son (Melachim I 17:22), or as Elisha did when he performed his famous miracles (Melachim II 2:2–9). This is not true. Eliyahu, Elisha, and the other prophets did not perform miracles in order to prove the truth of their prophecy. Their reputation as genuine prophets had already been established before that time. They performed those miracles only because the situation demanded it. Since they were so close to Hashem, He fulfilled their wishes, as He promised to the righteous, *"You will decree and it will be fulfilled"* (Iyov 22:28).

The procedure by which a prophecy can be authenticated I will discuss shortly.

PEOPLE CLAIMING TO POSSESS THE
POWER OF PROPHECY

Those who claim to have the power of prophecy can be divided into two groups: (1) Those who prophesy in the name of a foreign deity, and (2) those who prophesy in the name of Hashem.

Those who prophesy in the name of a foreign deity can be classified further into two categories: (1) The case of a prophet who arises and declares, "A certain star cast a spell over me and told me to worship it in a certain way, or call upon it in a certain way, so that it would save me," or the case where a prophet summons *others* to worship Baal or any image, declaring, "An image made itself known to me and told me to command **you** to worship it in a certain manner," as the prophets of Baal and Ashera used to do, and (2) a prophet who says, "The word of Hashem came to me, telling me to worship a given idol, or to influence a certain heavenly constellation for a given purpose." He then tells the people to perform one of the rituals that the Torah classifies as idol worship. This man is also considered as prophesying in the name of a foreign deity, even though he professes to speak in the name of Hashem. For the term "speaking in the name of a foreign deity" includes both a person who claims that the deity itself commanded him to worship it, or one who says that it was God who told him to worship any idol.

When a person claiming to be a prophet makes either of these statements, and there are witnesses who will testify to this, then according to Torah law, he must be put to death by strangling, as it says, *"That prophet or dreamer must be put to death"* (Devarim 13:6). We should not even attempt to verify his claim to prophecy, and we should not ask him to perform a sign. Even if he *did* perform amazing signs and wonders as proof of his prophetic powers, he still must be strangled. We should pay no attention to his signs, because the reason these miracles came about is, *"that Hashem is testing you . . ."* (Devarim 13:4). Besides, our intellect, which gives the lie to his testimony, is more reliable than our eye that sees his miracles. Great thinkers have offered undeniable proof that nothing should be revered and worshipped except the One, the Cause of all existence. He is One, with a Unity that is absolutely unique.

Those who prophesy in the name of Hashem can also be subdivided into two categories: The false prophet and the true prophet.

THE FALSE PROPHET

This prophet prophesies in the name of the Almighty, he summons the people to believe in Him, and commands them to worship Him. However he also says that the Holy One, Blessed is He, added a mitzvah or did away with one of the mitzvos of the Torah. He is considered a false prophet and should be put to death by strangling. It makes no difference whether he adds to or detracts from the written Torah verse or adds to or detracts from the traditional oral interpretation.

An example of detracting from a verse would be if he said, "Hashem told me that *orlah* [the prohibition of eating the fruit of newly planted trees for the first three years] applies for only *two years*, and afterwards you are allowed to eat the fruit." An example of adding to a Torah verse would be if he said, "Hashem told me that you are forbidden to eat *orlah* for *four years*," as opposed to what Hashem actually said, *"For three years the fruit shall be a forbidden growth, and it may not be eaten"* (Vayikra 19:23). Any similar statement brands him a false prophet.

If he makes the slightest change even in the Oral Law, he is considered a false prophet, even if the plain meaning of the verse seems to support his statement.

For example, it says in the Torah, *"If two men get into a fight with each other, and the wife of one comes up to defend her husband, grabbing his attacker by his private parts, you shall cut off her hand . . ."* (Devarim 25:11,12).

The Oral tradition explains that the statement *"cut off her hand"* should not be taken literally but rather to mean that she should pay a fine for the humiliation she caused her victim. Now if a prophet would say "Hashem told me that the phrase, *'you shall cut off her hand'* is to be understood in its literal sense," he is a false prophet and must be put to death by strangling, because he attributed to Hashem a statement He never made.

In this case, too, we should not pay attention to any sign or miracle this person might perform. The prophet Moshe, who awed the whole world with his miracles and convinced us of his legitimacy so that we believed in him, as it is written, *"they will believe in you forever"* (Shemos 19:9), already told us in the name of Hashem that no Law would ever come from the Creator other than that given to Moshe. This idea is derived from the verse *"It [The Torah] is not in heaven . . . It is in your mouth and in your heart, so that you can keep it"* (Devarim 30:12,14). The phrase *"in your mouth"* refers to the clearly stated Oral Law transmitted by Moshe, whereas the phrase *"in your heart"* refers to the implied laws that were derived through analytical research, which is a function of the heart.

We are expressly warned not to add to or detract from the laws of the Torah as it says, *"Be careful to observe everything that I am prescribing to you. Do not add to it and do not subtract from it"* (Devarim 13:1). The Sages therefore said, "A prophet is not allowed to introduce anything new, from now [the time of Moshe] on" (*Megillah* 2b).

Since we have established that such a claim of prophecy is, in fact, a false statement about Hashem, and that he attributes to Hashem sayings He never uttered, he is liable to the death penalty, as it is written, *"But any prophet who presumes to speak in My name when I have not commanded him to do so . . . then that prophet shall die"* (Devarim 19:20).

THE TRUE PROPHET

The second kind of prophet who speaks in the name of Hashem is one who calls on the people to worship Hashem, commands them to observe his mitzvos, and urges them to keep the Torah without additions or subtractions, as Malachi, the last of the prophets, did when he said, "Be mindful of the Torah of My servant Moshe" (Malachi 3:22). He promises a rich reward to those who fulfill the commandments of the Torah and warns those who violate it of the dire consequences, as did Yeshayah, Yirmiyah, Yechezkel, and all the other prophets. In addition, he may tell people to do certain things and forbid them to do other things, regarding matters that are not specifically mentioned in the Torah. For example, he might order the people to attack a certain city or nation, as Shmuel did when he commanded Shaul to attack Amalek (Shmuel I, 15); or he might prevent them from killing others, as Elisha did when he prohibited Yehoram from striking down the army of Aram, which had entered Shomron (Melachim II 6:22). The prophet might do as Yeshayah did when he halted the bringing of water to make cement to repair the cracks in the wall (Yeshayah 22:9), or he might act like

Yirmiyah, who prevented the Jews from going to *Eretz Yisrael* [before the end of the seventy years of exile] (Yirmiyah 29:4–10). Many other examples can be cited.

When a prophet claims to have the power of prophecy without basing it on any foreign source, and without adding to or detracting away from the Torah, but speaks of other matters, like those we have mentioned, then we need to check him out, to verify his testimony. If his testimony proves to be true, then any command he gives should be obeyed, from the smallest to the weightiest matter. Whoever violates one of such a prophet's commands is liable to the death penalty at the hands of the Heavenly Court, as Hashem said about a person who violates the command of a prophet, *"I will punish that person"* (Devarim 18:19).

But if this person's claim of being a prophet proves to be untrue, he must be put to death by strangling.

ESTABLISHING THE TRUTH OF A PROPHET'S CLAIM

The truth of a person's claim to being a prophet is established in the following manner:

> 1. He makes a valid claim to prophecy as was discussed above.
> 2. He has the characteristics befitting a prophet; he is a scholar, a pious, self-disciplined, intelligent person, and a man of noble character, in keeping with the saying that *"Prophecy rests only on one who is wise, strong and rich"* (Shabbos 92a). (The many qualities of this kind cannot all be listed here. Discussing them and deriving them from their Biblical sources would require a book in itself. Perhaps Hashem will help me to compose what should be written on this subject.)
> 3. We say to him, "Predict the future for us, and tell us some of the things Hashem has taught you." He must do so. If his predictions all come true, then we know that his entire prophecy was genuine. But if his prediction does not come true in its entirety, even if it is missing only a minor detail, then we know that he is a false prophet.

This test is described in the Torah, *"You may ask yourselves, 'How can we know that a declaration was not spoken by Hashem?' If the prophet predicts something in Hashem's name, and the prediction does not material-*

ize or come true, then the message was not spoken by Hashem. That prophet has spoken deceitfully, and you must not fear him" (Devarim 18:21,22).

However, even if one or two of his predictions do come true, we do not yet have proof that his prophecy was genuine. Rather, the matter is left undecided until everything he has declared in the name of Hashem is repeatedly confirmed, over and over again. This is borne out by the story of Shmuel, where we are told that only after it became known that all of Shmuel's predictions had come true, *"All Yisrael, from Dan to Beersheva, knew that Shmuel was trustworthy as a prophet of Hashem"* (Shmuel I 3:20).

The people would not hesitate to ask a prophet for help even regarding personal problems. If it had not been for this practice, Shaul, at the beginning of his career, would have never gone to Shmuel to ask him for help in finding the donkeys he lost (Shmuel I 9:3–10). Without a doubt, this was the accepted custom, for Hashem gave us prophets instead of astrologers, fortunetellers, and diviners, so that we would ask them for advice of a general nature and about specific problems. They would give us dependable answers, unlike the fortunetellers whose predictions may or may not come true, as it says, *"The nations that you are driving out listen to astrologers and diviners, but what Hashem has given you is totally different. Hashem your God will raise up for you a prophet from among your own people, like myself; him you heed"* (Devarim 18:15,16).

Because of this power [that the prophet could foresee events], a prophet was called a *ro'eh*, a seer, as it is written, *"for the prophet of today was formerly called a ro'eh [seer]"* (Shmuel I 9:9).

DIFFERENCE BETWEEN PROPHECY AND THE OCCULT

One should not think, "Since a prophet proves he is genuine by the fact that his predictions come true, then all fortunetellers, astrologers, and mind readers can claim to be prophets, because we see with our own eyes that they predict the future every day!"

I want to emphasize that this is an important issue that needs to be clarified so that people clearly understand the sharp difference that exists between the message of a prophet who speaks in the name of Hashem and the words of a fortuneteller.

I want to put it this way: Fortunetellers, astrologers, and all others in this category do indeed predict future events, but their predictions are only partially true, while the remainder inevitably turns out to be false. We see this happen all the time, and even the fortunetellers themselves do not deny this. The only way that one fortuneteller is better than the next is that he told fewer lies than his colleague did. But that all of a fortuneteller's predictions should come true is simply impossible.

These crystal gazers do not even pretend or boast that their predictions will come true in all details. One fortuneteller might say, "This year there will be a drought; there will be no rainfall at all this year," when, in fact, a small amount of rain will fall. Or another might say, "Tomorrow it will rain," while it actually will rain on the day after. And even such a near-miss will happen only to an eminent expert in the art of the occult, one of the authorities who are quoted in books. Yeshayah spoke about these diviners when he challenged Babylonia, *"You are helpless despite all your art. Let them stand up and help you now, the astrologers, the star-gazers, who predict parts of the months' events, whatever will come upon you"* (Yeshayah 47:13). Our Rabbis commented that Yeshayah stated, "who predict *parts* of the events," and that he did not state, "who predict those events in their entirety."

The testimonies and predictions of the prophets, however, are altogether different. All their prophesies come true word for word and letter for letter, and not even the slightest detail of anything they say in the name of Hashem remains unfulfilled. Therefore, if any portion of a prophecy does not come true, we know that the man who proclaimed it is an impostor, *"for nothing that Hashem has spoken will remain unfulfilled"* (Melachim II, 10:10).

This is what Yirmiyah had in mind when he said that the visions of people who claim to have prophetic power must be proven to be correct in every detail. He would discredit the false prophets and demolish their claims to prophecy, saying, *"Let the prophet who has a dream tell the dream; and let him who has received My word report My word faithfully! How can straw be compared to grain?"* says Hashem (Yirmiyah 23:28). The Sages explain this to mean that prophecy is crystal clear without any elements of falsehood blended in, just as grain kernels are separate from straw. The dreams of the fortunetellers are mostly false, like straw that contains a few kernels of wheat. "Just as it is impossible to have grain without straw, so too it is impossible [for an ordinary person] to have a dream without senseless matters" (*Berachos* 55a).

THREATENING PREDICTIONS

There still remains one important point on which we should comment, namely, if a prophet foretells catastrophic events such as famine, war, earthquakes, a disastrous hail storm, or similar calamities, as a punishment to the people. Heaven may have mercy, and the punishment will not arrive. In fact everything will remain peaceful and quiet. This does not mean that the prophet lied. It would be incorrect to say that he is a false prophet and deserving the death penalty, because although a punishment was decreed, Hashem abrogated the decree. It may very well be that the people repented of their despicable behavior, or that Hashem mercifully postponed their punishment and will show His anger at another time, as He did with Achav when He said through Eliyahu, *"I will not bring the disaster in his lifetime; I will bring the disaster upon his house in his son's time"* (Melachim I 21:29), or He may have had pity on them because of good deeds they did earlier. The statement, *"The prediction does not materialize or come true"* (Devarim 18:21) [which is the sign of a false prophet] does not apply to this prophet.

GOOD TIDINGS

However, if the prophet forecasts tidings of good things to occur at a set time, and he says, "This will be a year of quiet and tranquility," yet a war breaks out, or if he predicts, "This will be a year of rain and blessing," but famine and drought occur, then we know that he is a false prophet, and his fraudulent claim to prophecy is exposed. This is expressed in the verse, *"The prophet has spoken deceitfully, and you must not fear him"* (Devarim 18:21), meaning, "do not let him frighten you or terrify you into refraining from killing him, [by reminding you of] his piety, righteousness and wisdom. He is guilty of brazenly making such a momentous declaration and speaking rebelliously against Hashem. For when Hashem sends good tidings through a prophet, it is impossible to say that He will not fulfill His promise, for He will certainly confirm the promise the prophet made to the people. Our Sages put it this way, "Any good tidings Hashem announces, even if it is subject to certain conditions, He does not go back on" (*Berachos* 7a).

Now there is the puzzling fact that *Yaakov* [as he returned to Eretz Yisrael and Esav was preparing to attack him] feared for his life, as it says, *"Yaakov was very frightened and distressed"* (Bereishis 32:8), even though Hashem had assured him of good fortune, saying, *"I am with you. I will protect you wherever you go"* (Bereishis 28:15). The Sages explain that Yaakov was afraid that he had committed a sin that would cause his death (*Berachos* 4a).

This incident teaches us that although Hashem promises good fortune to someone, his sins may stand in the way and these promises may not be realized. But we must realize that this will only happen in matters that are between Hashem and the prophet alone, but when Hashem tells a prophet to bring good tidings to other people in a definite and unconditional message, then for this good not to come about is absurd and unthinkable. Otherwise, we have no way of establishing the genuineness of anyone's prophetic message; yet Hashem gave us in His Torah the fundamental principle that the proof of a prophet's genuineness is in the fact that his predictions come true.

It was this fundamental principle that Yirmiyah referred to in his dispute with Chananiah ben Azur. Yirmiyah was prophesying disaster and death, declaring that Nebuchadnezzar would be victorious and succeed in destroying the Beis Hamikdash. Chananiah ben Azur was predicting good tidings, that the vessels of the Beis Hamikdash, which had been carted off to Babylonia, would be returned to Yerushalayim. During the ensuing debate Yirmiyah said that if his own prediction would not come true, and Nebuchadnezzar would not be victorious and the vessels would be returned to the Beis Hamikdash, as Chananiah said would happen, this would not disprove his own (Yirmiyah's) prophecy, for it is possible that Hashem had mercy on the people. But if Chananiah's predictions would not come true, and the vessels would **not** be returned to the Beis Hamikdash, this will be clear proof that Chananiah's prophecy was false. Chananiah's prophetic mission would only be established when all his predictions of good fortune came true.

"But listen to this word which I address to you and to all the people. The prophets who lived before you and me from ancient times prophesied war, disaster and pestilence against many lands and great kingdoms. If a prophet prophesies good fortune, when the word of the prophet comes true it will be known that Hashem really sent him" (Yirmiyah 28:7-9). What Yirmiyah means to say is that we cannot tell by the bad tidings of

prophets whether they are true or false prophets. But we *do* know with certainty that they are true prophets if they foretell good fortune and their promises come true.

THE PROPHET'S POWERS AND RESTRICTIONS

When a prophet's predictions have come true according to the guidelines we have established, and that prophet becomes famous like Shmuel, Eliyahu, and others, that prophet has the power to modify the Torah in a way that no one else may do. If he would order the cancellation of any of the positive commandments of the Torah, or he would permit something that is forbidden by a negative commandment, as a temporary emergency measure, then as long as it is not a command to worship idols, it is our duty to obey him and to carry out his command. Whoever violates his orders will be put to death by Hashem. The Sages of the Talmud stated this clearly:

"Regarding any matter, if a prophet tells you to violate the words of the Torah, you should obey him; except for idol worship" (*Sanhedrin* 90a).

However, this is only true provided that it is not a permanent ruling. He may not say that Hashem has decreed that this mitzvah be nullified forever. He may only order a suspension of a mitzvah for a temporary need. That prophet himself, when asked about his order to violate one of the mitzvos that Hashem gave us through Moshe, will answer that the suspension of this mitzvah is not permanent, but only a temporary measure for the present moment. This is similar to the power that the *Beis Din* [Rabbinical High Court] has to issue an emergency order to nullify temporarily certain mitzvos. Eliyahu made use of this principle when he sacrificed on Mount Carmel (Melachim I, 18:20–40), while the Beis Hamikdash was standing. Doing such a thing without the command of a prophet is punishable by *kares* [premature death]. The Torah cautions against this, stating, *"Be careful not to offer your burnt offerings in any place that you may see fit"* (Devarim 12:13). And we are told that a person who offers a sacrifice outside of Yerushalayim is subject to *kares* in the verse, *"Bloodguilt shall be counted for that man; he has spilled blood; that man shall be cut off from among his people"* (Vayikra 17:4).

If anyone had asked Eliyahu at the time he was offering the sacrifice on Mount Carmel, "Are we allowed to do such a thing from now on?" he would have answered that it was not permitted, and anyone offering sacrifices outside the Beis Hamikdash was liable to *kares*, but that the present ceremony was a one-time emergency action designed to expose the falsehood of the prophets of Baal and to smash their pagan belief.

In the same way, the prophet Elisha, when ordering an attack on Moab, decreed the cutting of every fruit-bearing tree, *"You shall cut down every good tree"* (Melachim II 3:19), although Hashem prohibited this in the Torah, stating, *"You must not destroy its trees, wielding an ax against any food producing tree"* (Devarim 20:19). Now, if people had asked Elisha whether this prohibition had been lifted, and it was permitted from now on to cut down fruit-bearing trees when laying siege to a city, he would have replied that it was not permitted, and that the present decree was a one-time emergency measure.

Let me give you an illustration that will explain to you this principle as it applies to all the mitzvos.

Suppose a prophet whose credentials are impeccable told us on Shabbos that all B'nei Yisrael—men and women alike—should light a fire, make weapons with it, put on battle attire and attack a certain place on this Shabbos day, and that we should plunder the enemies' possessions and take their women captive. As Torah observers we would have the duty to get up immediately, and do as he told us, with eagerness and extraordinary love, without qualms or reservations. And we must believe that with whatever we were doing, whether it was making a fire, performing forbidden labors, killing the enemy, or fighting a war, we were performing a mitzvah, notwithstanding that it was Shabbos. We should expect to be richly rewarded for it by Hashem because by fulfilling a command of a prophet we are observing a positive commandment, *"Hashem your God will raise up for you a prophet from among your own people, **and it is to him that you must listen**"* (Devarim 18:15). The Oral Law expounded on this verse, "In all matters, if a prophet tells you to violate the words of the Torah, you should listen to him—except for idol worship" (*Sanhedrin* 90a). For example, if he told you, "Worship this image only today," or "Burn incense for this star only for this hour," he must be killed, and no one should listen to him.

Conversely, take the case of a person who considers himself a righteous and God-fearing man. He is old, well advanced in years, and he says to himself, "I have reached old age, and never in my life have I transgressed any of the mitzvos. How can I go and commit on this Shabbos a transgression for which the penalty is stoning? How can I go out to fight in the war? After all, I cannot contribute anything to the outcome. Let them find others to take my place; there are many others who can do it!"

This man is a rebel, he is breaking Hashem's law, and for violating the prophet's command he incurs death by God's hand. He who commanded us to keep the Shabbos commanded us to obey the words and decrees of the prophet, as it is written, *"If any person shall not listen to the word that he declares in My name, I will punish that person"* (Devarim 18:19).

All the same, if, while doing the work on Shabbos that the prophet has commanded, a person tied a double knot [which is one of the thirty-nine labors that are forbidden on Shabbos] that was not needed for that work, then he is liable for stoning.

If this same prophet who commanded us as he did and we obeyed him, would tell us that the Shabbos boundary is one *amah* less or one *amah* more than two thousand *amas* [thereby changing one of the laws of Shabbos], claiming that he received this knowledge by way of prophecy rather than through Scriptural analysis and logical argument, then we know that he is a false prophet and must be executed by strangling.

This illustration gives you the means of understanding what a prophet may command you and of grasping all that is written in the Torah on the subject of a prophet who contradicts any part of the mitzvos. This fundamental principle is the key to understanding the entire subject matter, and it is only in this respect [temporary emergency measure] that a prophet is different from other people, regarding mitzvos. But as far as deriving mitzvos through analysis, logical reasoning, and deductive thinking is concerned, he is on the same level as the other sages who do not possess prophetic powers. If a prophet advances a logical argument in support of a halachic ruling and someone who is not a prophet likewise advances a different rational argument, but the prophet declares, "Hashem told me that my reasoning is correct," you should not pay attention to him. And even if one thousand prophets of the caliber of Eliyahu and Elisha would support one line of reasoning and one thousand and one sages would support an opposing logic, we would follow the majority, and the Halachah would be decided according to the view of the 1,001 sages, and *not* according to the one thousand honorable prophets.

The Sages of the Talmud said it like this, "By God! Even if Yehoshua bin Nun personally would tell this to me I would not listen to him or pay attention to him" (*Chullin* 124a).

They also said, "If Eliyahu would come and say, '*Chalitzah* should be performed with a shoe,' listen to him, but if he would say, 'with a sandal,' then do not listen to him" (*Yevamos* 102a).

What they mean to say is that under no circumstances may anything be added to or taken away from the mitzvos on the basis of prophecy. Similarly, if a prophet declared that Hashem told him that the practical application of a given mitzvah is such-and-such, and that the rationale offered by one Sage rather than that of another is correct, then this prophet must be put to death because he is a false prophet, as we have established as a fundamental rule: No Torah was given after the first prophet Moshe, and nothing may be added or taken away from it, as it says, *"It is not in heaven"* [*requiring prophetic insight*] (Devarim 30:12). Hashem did not permit us to learn the Torah laws from the prophets, but only from the Sages, men who derive the law from logical inferences and opinions. Hashem does not say, *"If you are unable to reach a decision . . . you must approach the prophet who exists at the time"* but rather, *"You must approach the Kohanim-Levi'im [and other members of] the supreme court that exists at the time"* (Devarim 17:9). The Sages have discussed this subject extensively, and this is a true presentation of their views.

The Transmission of the Oral Torah

When Yehoshua bin Nun was nearing his death, he taught the elders the oral explanation that he had received from Moshe. He also transmitted to them the new applications of the laws that were agreed upon by all the Sages and those laws that were not agreed upon by all the Sages but were decided by a majority vote of the elders.

This, that the elders received the oral tradition from Yehoshua is referred to in the verse, *"Yisrael served Hashem during the lifetime of Yehoshua and the lifetime of the elders who lived on after Yehoshua, and who had experienced all that Hashem had done for Yisrael"* (Yehoshua 24:31). In the following generation these elders taught the prophets all that they had received from Yehoshua. Each prophet in turn taught the next. During all this time there was constant analysis of the law and new laws were derived according to the established rules.

The Sages of each generation regarded the teachings of the earlier Sages as authoritative. They would study them and extract new ideas from them, but they would never disagree with them. This process of transmission continued until the era of the Men of the Great Assembly [a legislative body consisting of 120 Sages], including in its ranks [the prophets] Chaggai, Zechariah, Malachi, Daniel, Chananiah, Mishael, Azariah, Ezra HaSofer, Nechemiah ben Chachalyah, Mordechai, and Zerubavel ben She'altiel. The remainder of the 120 Sages were comprised of the [elite Torah scholars referred to in the Scriptures (Melachim II 24:16) as the] "craftsmen and locksmiths" [in reference to their profound scholarship]. Like their predecessors, they too, researched the Oral Tradition, enacted precautionary decrees to prevent violations of the law, and issued ordinances.

The last of this illustrious group was one of the earliest Sages mentioned in the Mishnah, Shimon Hatzaddik, who was the *Kohein Gadol* of that generation.

RABBI YEHUDAH HANASI [REBBI]

In the course of time, Rabbeinu Hakadosh arrived on the scene, a personality who was outstanding in his generation and unique in his time; a man of such perfect piety and sterling character, that his contemporaries called him Rabbeinu Hakadosh—Our Holy Teacher. His name was Rabbi Yehudah [HaNasi—the Prince. He was affectionately called Rebbi-our teacher—because he was regarded by all as their teacher]. He was supreme in wisdom and grandeur, to the extent that the Talmud says of him, "From Moshe until Rebbi, we do not find Torah scholarship and majesty combined in one person" (*Gittin* 59a). He exemplified piety and humility, and shunned all pleasures of life, as it says, "Since Rebbi died, humility and fear of sin have vanished" (*Sotah* 49a). He expressed himself clearly and surpassed everyone in his command of the holy tongue, to the point that the Sages learned the meaning of Biblical words about which they were in doubt from the way his servants and maids used these words. This is mentioned in a well-known passage in the Talmud (*Rosh Hashanah* 26b). He was immensely wealthy and wielded great power, so that people said about him, "Rebbi's butler is wealthier than Shabor, the king of Persia" (*Bava Metzia* 85a). He relieved the plight of needy scholars and students and spread Torah knowledge among the Jewish people. He collected the oral tradition, including the words of the Sages and their conflicting views that were handed down since the days of Moshe Rabbeinu until his own time.

He himself was a link in the chain of transmission of the Oral Torah, since he received it from his father, Rabbi Shimon III, and Shimon III received it from his father Rabban Gamliel II, who received it from Rabban Shimon II, who received it from Hillel; he from Shemayah and Avtalyon; they from Yehudah ben Tabbai and Shimon ben Shetach; they from Yehoshua ben Perachyah and Nitai of Arbela; they from Yosei ben Yo'ezer and Yosei ben Yochanan; they from Antignos Ish Socho; he from Shimon Hatzaddik, who received it from Ezra and the Men of the Great Assembly. Ezra received the Oral Torah from Baruch ben Neriah his teacher, Baruch from Yirmiyah, and in the same way, Yirmiyah definitely received it from the prophets that went before him, reaching back from prophet to prophet to the elders who received the Oral Torah from Yehoshua bin Nun who, in turn, received it from Moshe.

Categories of the Oral Torah

After collecting all the opinions and the statements of the previous Sages, Rabbi Yehudah HaNasi began to compile the Mishnah. He incorporated into the Mishnah the explanation of all the mitzvos of the Torah. Some of these are explanations that were received directly from Moshe, as well as expositions and laws that had not been learned from tradition, but had been added by the use of the Thirteen Principles by which the Torah is expounded. Of these, there were some that were agreed upon by all, and others about which differences of opinion had arisen between two authorities. Rabbi Yehudah HaNasi would record these disputes, writing, "This Rabbi says this, but that Rabbi says that." Even if the majority opinion was opposed by only one rabbi, Rabbi Yehudah HaNasi would record the single dissenting opinion and the majority view. He did this for very important reasons, which are mentioned in the Mishnah in *Eiduyos* (1:6). I will refer to them later [page 111], but first I must discuss a very basic principle:

HALACHAH LEMOSHE MISINAI

[The Talmud refers to certain laws as *Halachah leMoshe miSinai*— accepted tradition received directly from Moshe at Sinai, and as such, not open to debate]. You may wonder, if all the explanations of the laws of the Torah were received from Moshe, as we are taught, "the general principles, the specifics and the details of each law of the Torah were told on Mount Sinai" (*Toras Kohanim, Vayikra* 25:1) [as outlined above], then in what way are the laws that are known as *Halachah leMoshe miSinai* different than all other laws?

Let me explain this elementary issue very clearly:

[In regard to the fact that tradition handed down from Moshe is accepted as reliable and not open for debate, there is no distinction between *Halachah leMoshe miSinai* and other explanations handed down from Moshe.] Therefore, there never existed an argument about the basic interpretation of the verses of the Torah. There never has arisen a dispute among authorities of any time or era— from Moshe until Rav Ashi [who finalized the Talmud]—in which one sage would say that the phrase *"an eye for an eye"* (Devarim 19:21) should be taken literally, and another sage would say that the Torah is referring to monetary compensation.

Likewise, there never arose a dispute over the meaning of the verse, *"On the first day you shall take the fruit of a hadar tree,"* (Vayikra 23:40), whereby one sage said that this fruit was an *esrog,* and another said that it referred to a quince, a pomegranate, or some other fruit.

Nor have we come across an argument about the fact that *anaf eitz avos,* "branches of an *avos* tree" (Vayikra 23:40) refers to myrtle branches, or a disagreement about the fact that *"you must cut off her hand"* (Devarim 25:12) is not to be taken literally but means monetary compensation.

Similarly, no one ever disputed the fact that the death sentence in the verse, *"If a kohein's daughter defiles herself by acting promiscuously . . . she must be burned with fire"* (Vayikra 21:9) is carried out only if she was a married woman. In line with this, no one—from Moshe until today—has ever denied that the punishment of stoning for a girl who was found not to have been a virgin (Devarim 22:20) applied only if she was a married woman, and witnesses testified that after her betrothal she committed adultery in their presence and that they had warned her beforehand. There is no disagreement about these and similar commandments, because the explanations of all these laws were received from Moshe. It is with regard to such mitzvos that the Sages said, "The general outline and the specifics of the entire Torah were told on Sinai."

However, although these explanations were received from Moshe and cannot be disputed, we can trace these explanations to the Torah text by means of the rules of Torah interpretation, through reasoning, comparisons, proofs, and allusions.

When you find the Sages in the Talmud disagreeing with one another, bringing proofs for any of these explanations or others like it, they are not arguing over the validity of the explanation, but rather how this explanation is derived from the text itself. For example, when they discuss the meaning of the term "fruit of a *hadar* tree," some Rabbis bring Scriptural proof from the juxtaposition in the text of the words "fruit" and "tree" to indicate that it must be the fruit of a tree whose bark tastes the same as its fruit [which is true of the esrog]. Another Sage finds a hint for the esrog in the word *hadar*, explaining that the word *hadar* can be interpreted to mean—*that dwells*; it is a fruit that dwells in the tree from year to year, which can only be an esrog. A third Sage, noting a kinship between *hadar* and the Greek *hydor*, meaning water, says that it is a fruit that grows on much water—an esrog. The Rabbis did not bring these proofs because they were not sure of what the Torah meant by "fruit of *hadar*" until these hints were found. Of course, ever since the days of Yehoshua, Jews took a *lulav* and an *esrog* in hand, year after year; there was no quarrel about that. The Rabbis merely searched for a hint in the Torah for this accepted tradition. The same is true for the proofs the Rabbis brought for the *hadas* [myrtle branch], and their proofs for the law requiring monetary restitution for inflicting bodily injury (*Bava Kamma* 83), as well as their proof for the law concerning the death penalty for a *kohein's* daughter who had committed adultery (*Sanhedrin* 50b).

All proofs like these are meant to serve as Scriptural allusions to well-known and long-established traditions. This is the meaning of the statement, "The general outlines and the specifics were told on Sinai." In other words, those matters that can be drawn out from the text through the rule of *k'lal up'rat*, "a general statement limited by a specification" or through any of the other Rules of Interpretation, were handed down to us by Moshe, who received them on Sinai.

Although we received all these laws from Moshe, we do not call them *Halachah leMoshe miSinai*—Laws Given to Moshe on Sinai. You cannot say that the tradition that *peri eitz hadar* means an *esrog*, or the law that if someone wounds his fellow Jew, he must pay monetary compensation are *Halachah leMoshe miSinai*, because although all these explanations came to us from Moshe, there are indications for them in the text or they have been derived by logical analysis, as we have mentioned. Only those laws for which no hint or allusion can be found in Scripture and cannot be derived from the text by means of one of the methods of interpretation are termed *Halachah leMoshe miSinai*.

This is the reason why when it was said that "Legal measurements are *Halachah leMoshe miSinai*," the question was raised, "How can you say that legal measurements are *Halachah leMoshe miSinai* when legal measurements are alluded to in the verse, *'It is a land of wheat, barley, grapes, figs and pomegranates, a land of oil olives and honey dates?'* " (Devarim 8:8). The answer was: Legal measurements are indeed *Halachah leMoshe miSinai*, and they cannot logically be derived from the verse; there is not even a suggestion for them anywhere in the Torah. The association of legal measurements with this verse is only a way to jog the memory and make it easier to remember them; it has nothing to do with the actual meaning of the verse. This is what the Sages meant whenever they said, "It is merely an *asmachta*," a mnemonic device.

Now I will list most—and possibly all—of the laws that are termed *Halachah leMoshe miSinai*. You will then realize that what I said was correct, that not one of these laws has been derived from the Torah by means of logical reasoning, and that none of them can be related to a Scriptural verse, except as a way of jogging the memory. We do not find that the Rabbis analyzed these laws or brought proofs for them. The Rabbis learned them from Moshe, exactly as Hashem had instructed him.

THE LIST OF *HALACHOS LEMOSHE MISINAI*

1. The measurement of one-half log of oil needed to be mixed with the loaves that are presented along with a thanksgiving offering (Vayikra 7:12).

2. The measurement of one-fourth log of oil needed for the loaves offered by a *nazir* when the term of his nazirite vow is complete.

3. The law that there are 11 days between two *niddah* periods.

4. The law that a wall is considered as being extended vertically under certain conditions.

5. The law that an empty space of less than three handbreadth wide separating a solid surface is considered as solid surface.

6. The law that a ceiling may be considered as a part of the wall from which it extends.

7. Minimum quantities, sizes, and measurements.

8. Definition of what constitutes a separation between one's body and the water of a *mikveh*.

9. Minimum dimensions of a partition.

10. The parchment required for the *tefillin*.

11. The parchment required for a *mezuzah* scroll.

12. The parchment required for a Torah scroll.

13. The form of the letter *shin* on the head *tefillin*.

14. The formation of the knot on the straps of the head and arm *tefillin*.

15. The requirement of black straps for *tefillin*.

16. The requirement for *tefillin* to be shaped like a cube.

17. The requirement of a sleeve on the bases of the *tefillin* boxes through which the leather straps are pulled.

18. The requirement that the parchments are tied in a roll with threads made from the hair of kosher animals, before being placed in the *tefillin* boxes.

19. The requirement that the compartments of the *tefillin* be sewn together with threads made from parts of kosher animals.

20. The composition of the ink that must be used in writing a Torah scroll.

21. The requirement that there be ruled guidelines etched above the lettering in a Torah Scroll.

22. The rule that a girl under the age of 3 years and 1 day retains her status of virginity despite cohabitation.

23. The rule that the number of *pei'ah* gifts from a field on which more than one kind of grain is growing depends on whether the different grains are stored together or separately [*Pei'ah* 2:5].

24. The law that even a seed so fine that a small amount will suffice to plant an entire field, has the same rule as other seeds— insofar as the rule that they are considered insignificant in a mixture when there is less than one twenty-fourth [*Kilayim* 2:2].

25. Although in a standard field the restriction of plowing begins prior to the actual *sh'mittah* [sabbatical] year, if the field contains at least ten saplings the entire field may be plowed up to the beginning of the *sh'mittah year* [*Shevi'is* 1:6].

26. If a ring of figs is partly *tamei* [ritually unclean], one may give the full percentage of *terumah* due from both the *tamei* and *tahor* parts, from the *tahor* part alone [*Terumos* 2:1].

27. On Shabbos, the teacher may find the place by lamplight from which the students are to begin reading [*Shabbos* 1:3].

28. A woman must bring a sin offering if she carries an object in her apron on Shabbos, even if she placed the object in the front of her apron, and it inadvertently moved to her back [*Shabbos* 10:4].

29. The right of a wine seller to mix strong wine into his soft wine without being guilty of deception (since he is improving the product) [*Bava Metzia* 4:11].

30. The law that Jews living in Ammon and Moab must give *ma'aseir ani* [the tithe for the needy] in the seventh year.

Whenever we will come across one of these laws in our Commentary on the Mishnah, we will elaborate on it, with God's help.

FIVE CATEGORIES OF THE ORAL LAW

The Oral Law can now be divided into five categories:

1. Explanations that were received directly from Moshe, that are hinted at in the verse, and that can be drawn from text by means of logical reasoning. Such laws may not be disputed, and when someone says, "This is what I received," there can be no further debate.

2. The laws that are known as *Halachah leMoshe miSinai*, and that cannot be proven as we explained. These laws may not be disputed either.

3. Laws that were derived by reasoning, about which there may arise differences of opinion, as we mentioned earlier. In such cases, the law is decided on the basis of the majority vote. Such disputes come about when different rational approaches are used. Therefore the Rabbis say, "If it is a stated Halachah then we must accept it, but if it is open for discussion let us debate it" (*Yevamos* 8:3).

Disputes arose only regarding matters about which no clear-cut *Halachah* was received. Throughout the entire Talmud you find the Sages looking for the underlying reasons for the disputes among the earlier authorities. They will ask, "What is the point at issue?" or "What reason does this Rabbi give?" or "What is the practical difference between them?" In most instances the Sages answer these questions, giving the reason for the dispute. They might say, for example, "This Rabbi holds this for such a reason, and that Rabbi holds that because of another reason."

Do not think for a moment that the Sages received the disputed laws from Moshe, or that the conflicts arose because some Sages made errors or were forgetful, or that one Sage heard the law correctly and his opponent heard it incorrectly, or forgot it, or heard it only partially. And do not try to defend your [mistaken] theory by quoting the saying, "Ever since a growing number of students of Hillel and Shammai did not study under their teachers sufficiently, disputes increased in Yisrael, and the Torah came to be understood two different ways" (*Sanhedrin* 88b). To say such a thing is disgraceful. Only an ignorant and unlearned person would say this, a person who does not understand the fundamentals of Judaism and who slurs the people from whom we received the commandments. Such statements amount to empty talk; they are without rhyme or reason. What brings people to believe such false ideas is that they did not study the words of the Sages in the Talmud sufficiently. Although they correctly concluded that explanations came from Moshe, they failed to draw a distinction between those basic explanations that were explicitly given by Moshe and those details and offshoots the Sages themselves derived through their own analysis.

Now, when it comes to the controversy between Beis Shammai and Beis Hillel over whether "you should clear the table first and then you rinse your hands," or, "you should rinse your hands first and then clear the table" (*Berachos* 51b), don't let it enter your mind that either one of these statements was relayed to us directly by Moshe. The underlying reason for Beis Shammai and Beis Hillel's dispute is mentioned in the Talmud: one of them forbids us to employ an ignorant servant and the other does not.[1] [Their argument is obviously not what was handed down from Moshe, rather based on logical arguments.] All similar controversies should be understood the same way.

Let us explain the statement, "Ever since a growing number of students of Hillel and Shammai did not study sufficiently, disputes increased in Yisrael." If you have two men with the same intelligence, thinking power, and knowledge of the basic facts from which to draw conclusions, they will have very few, if any, disagreements. Shammai and Hillel, who disagreed on only a few laws, are an example of this. They thought along the same lines when it came to deriving new laws, and they both interpreted the

---

[1]We are concerned that water might drip from the hands and spoil pieces of bread that are lying on the table. Beis Hillel forbids the use of an ignorant servant who does not know to remove the larger pieces of bread. Therefore, Beis Hillel states that it is not necessary to clear the table before rinsing the hands. Beis Shammai permits the use of an ignorant servant, so they require that the table be cleared before rinsing your hands.

basic facts the same way. But when the students became less interested in learning and their reasoning became blurred in comparison to their teachers Hillel and Shammai, then often disputes surfaced between them based upon their analysis of the many laws. Each one made assumptions according to his own reasoning power and according to his understanding of the basic principles.

Still, we should not find fault in them because of this. For we cannot ask of two Sages that they conduct their debate on the intellectual level of Yehoshua and Pinchas. Neither do we harbor any doubt about the things that they disagreed on, even though they are not as great as Shammai and Hillel were, or as Sages who were even greater. For Hashem did not command us to serve Him in such a way [demanding that we obey only those Sages who are as great as the early sages], but He did command us to obey the Sages of our own generation, as it says, *"You must approach the judge that exists at that time"* (Devarim 17:9).

This was the way conflicts arose; not because scholars erred regarding the tradition handed down from Moshe, and that one was right and the other wrong. If you think about it, it will become crystal clear to you, and you will realize what a precious and great ground rule about the mitzvos this is.

[In the following category the Rambam discusses those parts of the Oral Law that are not explanations of the Written Law.]

4. Preventive measures that the prophets and sages established in each generation, in order to "make a hedge" for the Torah. Hashem ordered them to issue such preventive measures, which fall under the heading of *"Safeguard My charges"* (Vayikra 18:30), which the Oral Law explains to mean, "Make precautions to protect My charges" (*Yevamos* 21a). The Sages called these preventive measures *gezeiros*.

Disputes sometimes arose about these *gezeiros*. One Sage might prohibit something as a precaution and another disagreed with him. You find this very often in the Talmud where it will say: "This Rabbi prohibited such-and-such because of this-and-that, and that Rabbi did not." This is another one of the various causes of disputes. For example, the Torah forbids only the mixing of dairy products with meat of an animal. The Sages prohibited mixing poultry with dairy products in order to prevent an unintentional violation of the Torah prohibition through the confusion of poultry with meat. There was one Sage, Rabbi Yosei Hagelili, who did not impose this decree, and who permitted eating poultry with milk, and the people of his city ate the two together, as related in the Talmud (*Chullin* 116a).

Once a *gezeirah* is adopted by the Sages, no one is allowed to oppose it in any way, shape, or form. And once a *gezeirah* becomes widely accepted among all the Jewish people, it can never be revoked. Not even a prophet was allowed to nullify a *gezeirah*. In this connection we read in the Talmud that "Eliyahu would have been unable to annul any of the eighteen *gezeiros* that were instituted by Beis Shammai and Beis Hillel," and the reason given was, "that their prohibitions were widely accepted throughout Yisrael" (*Avodah Zarah* 36a).

5. Laws that were enacted by the Rabbis in order to preserve harmony among the people, which neither add to nor take away from any mitzvah and practices which would be useful in promoting Torah observance. These enactments are called *takkanos* and *minhagim* [customs], and you are forbidden to disregard either of them. *Shlomoh* had this to say about anyone ignoring them, *"He who breaches a fence will be bitten by a snake"* (Koheles 10:8).

The Talmud and the Mishnah mention a great many of these *takkanos*, some of them dealing with ritual matters and others with monetary issues. Some were enacted by prophets like Moshe, Yehoshua, and Ezra, as it says, "Moshe established for the Jews the practice of inquiring and holding lectures on the subject matter of the day: the laws of Pesach on Pesach etc." (*Megillah* 4a), and Moshe composed the first *berachah* of *Birchas Hamazon* in gratitude for the manna with which Hashem sustained Yisrael in the desert (*Berachos* 48b). There are many *takkanos* that were enacted by Yehoshua and Ezra.

Some *takkanos* are associated with individual Sages, as it says, "Hillel made the *takkanah* of *pruzbul*" (*Shevi'is* 10:3); Rabban Gamliel the Elder decreed . . . ; Rabbi Yochanan ben Zakkai decreed . . . (*Rosh Hashanah* 4:1). There are many examples of this in the Talmud.

Other *takkanos* are linked to the full assembly of the Sages of the Mishnah. Such *takkanos* are introduced with the phrase, "In Usha they enacted . . . ," or "The Sages enacted . . . ," or "This is an enactment of the Sages . . . ," or similar statements.

To sum it up, the laws that are recorded in the Mishnah can be divided into these five categories:

1. Explanations that were received from Moshe, but that are also hinted at in the Torah, or that can be derived from the verse.

2. *Halachah leMoshe miSinai.*

3. Laws that were extracted by comparing and analyzing the text; about these laws there have been disputes.

4. *Gezeiros,* preventive measures.

5. *Takkanos.*

Dissenting Opinions

Rabbi Yehudah HaNasi, the compiler of the Mishnah, found it necessary to include the opinions of both sides to a dispute. Had he only written the final decisions, leaving out the opinions that were rejected, this could raise serious problems. It could happen that one who had received a contradictory *Halachah* from a Sage who held an opposing view might cause us to wonder, "How could this man, who obviously is a trustworthy person, receive a tradition that a certain food is forbidden, when the Mishnah says that it is permitted; or vice versa, that something is permitted when the Mishnah says it is forbidden?"

Now that the opposing view is also written in the Mishnah, such misunderstandings will not happen. For if someone should say, "I have heard that such-and-such is forbidden," we will be able to tell him, "You are quite right; what you have heard is indeed the opinion of one Rabbi, but the majority disagreed with him," or "Another Rabbi disagreed with him, and the *Halachah* was decided according to the other Rabbi, either because his reasoning was more logical, or because we found another opinion supporting him" (*Eiduyos* 1:6).

Rabbi Yehudah HaNasi also felt it was necessary to record the opinion of an individual even when the opposing view was the majority view. This was because the final law may eventually be decided according to the individual. The fact that he did so teaches us that if an individual's argument is clear and straightforward, we should listen to it, even if a large number of people oppose it.

He also recorded the original opinion of a Sage who later changed his mind. For example, "Beis Shammai say one thing, and Beis Hillel say something else, but Beis Hillel changed their mind and agreed with Beis Shammai" (*Eiduyos* 1:2). He did this to show how much they loved the truth, and in order to promote righteousness and integrity. These men were respected, pious, noble, and very learned, yet when one realized that his opponent's reasoning

111

was better than his own, and his opponent's analysis was correct, he admitted it. Certainly, we, too, should admit when we are wrong and should not be stubborn.

This is what the Torah means when it says, *"Pursue perfect honesty"* (Devarim 16:20), and the Sages comment on this, "Acknowledge the truth" (*Avos* 5:9), meaning, "Although you could defend yourself through convincing arguments; if you know that your opponent's claims are right, but that he is intimidated or that you have greater verbal skill and can convince him that you are correct, withdraw your opinion and accept his."

The Structure of the Mishnah

THE SIX ORDERS OF THE MISHNAH

When Rabbi Yehudah HaNasi edited and compiled the Mishnah he divided his work into six parts; he called each part a *Seder* [order].

The first Seder is called *Seder Zera'im* [Seeds], which deals with *mitzvos* that apply to agriculture, like *kilayim* (mingled seeds), *sh'mittah* (the sabbatical year), *orlah* (fruit of a tree in the first three years after planting), *terumos* (contributions of produce given to *kohanim*), and *ma'aseros* (tithe given to the *levi'im*), and other obligatory contributions.

The second is *Seder Mo'eid* [Festivals], which deals with mitzvos relating to the Festivals, the specific obligations of each individual Yom Tov and the things that are forbidden and permitted on each Yom Tov, and all other laws pertaining to the Festivals.

The third is *Seder Nashim* [Women], which is concerned with the laws of marriage, and the different precepts that involve men and women, for example, *yibbum* (levirate marriage), *chalitzah* (the ceremony of removing the obligation of *yibbum*), *kesuvah* (the writing of a marriage contract), *kiddushin* (the betrothal ceremony), *gittin* (writ of divorce), and all other laws that belong in this category.

The fourth is *Seder Nezikin* [Damages], which discusses civil laws, the settling of disputes concerning ownerships, business transactions, partnerships in real estate, and similar issues.

The fifth is *Seder Kodashim* [Sacred Objects], which deals with the sacrifices that are offered in the *Beis Hamikdash*.

The sixth is *Seder Teharos* [Ritual Purity], which discusses the laws of ritual purity of objects used for holy purposes, and what renders them ritually impure.

Rabbi Yehudah HaNasi began the Mishnah with *Seder Zera'im* because it deals with agriculture—the source of sustenance of all life. Man, who was created to serve Hashem, needs food to stay alive. Therefore, Rabbi Yehudah HaNasi opened the Mishnah with the laws dealing with agriculture.

Next in line he placed *Seder Mo'eid*, in keeping with the sequence in which these subjects are arranged in the Torah. First we read about agriculture, *"You may plant your land for six years and gather its crops. But during the seventh year, you must leave it alone and withdraw from it"* (Shemos 23:10–11). This is followed by the laws concerning Shabbos and Yom Tov, *"You may do whatever you must during the six weekdays, but you must stop on the seventh day . . . Celebrate for me three festivals in the year"* (Shemos 23:12, 14).

He then arranged *Seder Nashim* (Women) ahead of *Seder Nezikin* (Damages), in line with the order of the verses: *"If a man sells his daughter as a maidservant . . ."* (Shemos 21:7), which is followed by *"When two men fight and harm a pregnant woman . . ."* (Shemos 21:22), and *"If an ox gores a man"* (Shemos 21:28).

You will notice that the subjects that are discussed in the four orders: *Seder Zera'im, Mo'eid, Nashim,* and *Nezikin,* are all included in the Book of Shemos.

After discussing the laws of the Book of Shemos, he goes on outlining the contents of the Book of Vayikra. Therefore, *Nezikin* is followed by *Kodashim. Kodashim,* the laws of offerings, precedes *Taharos,* the laws of ritual purity. This, too, is consistent with the order of the verses. For the Torah lists the laws of sacrifices ahead of the laws of ritual purity and impurity; the laws of sacrifices are in the beginning of Vayikra, whereas the laws of purity start only in *parashas Shemini* (Vayikra, chapter 11).

THE ORDER AND LIST OF THE *MASECHTOS*

When Rabbi Yehudah HaNasi compiled these six sections, he subdivided each section of general topics into separate parts. Each of these parts he called a *masechta*. These *masechtos* he then split up into chapters, each dealing with a single concept. He called each chapter a *perek*.

He then divided each *perek* into small paragraphs that are simple to understand and easy to memorize and teach to others. He called each paragraph a *Halachah* [or *Mishnah*].

I. *Seder Zera'im* — Agricultural Produce

1. Maseches Berachos — *Blessings*

He began with *maseches Berachos* for a very logical reason. A good doctor who wants to keep a person's health intact will begin by prescribing a balanced diet. With this in mind, Rabbi Yehudah HaNasi began with *Berachos*, because you may not eat anything unless you first say a *berachah*. By assigning first place to *maseches Berachos*, he wanted to make a meaningful improvement in the food by introducing a spiritual component into it.

However, in order to keep a unified theme, he included the laws of all *Berachos*, those you say over food as well as those you say before performing a mitzvah.

There is only one Biblical mitzvah you have to do each and every day and that is the mitzvah of *Kerias Shema*.[1] Now, it would not be right to discuss the *berachos* of *Kerias Shema* unless you first reviewed the laws of *Kerias Shema* itself. That is why he began *maseches Berachos* with the words, "*Mei'eimasai korin es Shema* — From what time in the evening may you recite the *Shema*?" and spoke about all other aspects of the *Shema*. He then went on to discuss the laws of the other *Berachos* and finally those you say over food.

He then returned to the topic of agriculture.

2. Pei'ah — *Edge of the Field*[2] (Vayikra 19:9)

Maseches Pei'ah is the first *Masechta* to follow *Berachos* because it is the only gift of produce a farmer must make while the standing grain is still rooted in the earth.

3. Demai — *Questionable Produce*[3]

After *Pei'ah* comes *Demai* because the poor may use *demai* just as they use *pei'ah*, as it says, "We let the poor eat *demai*" (*Demai* 3:1).

---

[1] *Kerias Shema* — the obligation to recite the "*Shema Yisrael*" in the morning and evening.

[2] A farmer must leave a portion at the edge of his field for the poor.

[3] Since some unlearned people did not set aside the required tithes of their produce, all produce bought from such people was called *demai* [questionable] and had to be tithed before eating it. This rule did not apply to the poor.

4. Kilayim—*Mixture of Seeds*

After *Demai* comes *Kilayim*, in line with the order of the verses in *parashas Kedoshim*, where it first says, *"Do not completely harvest the ends of your fields"* (Vayikra 19:9), and afterwards, *"Do not plant your field with different species of seeds"* (Vayikra 19:19).

5. Shevi'is—*Sabbatical Year*

After *Kilayim* comes *Shevi'is*. By rights, Rabbi Yehudah HaNasi should have placed *Maseches Orlah* after *Kilayim* because that is the order in which they appear in the Torah. But he realized that *orlah* is not a mitzvah that every farmer must observe (as long as he does not plant a tree, the prohibition of *orlah* does not apply to him), and *shevi'is* is a mitzvah everyone must observe. Furthermore, the Torah devotes an entire *sidrah* to *shemittah* (the sabbatical year), which is the subject of *maseches Shevi'is*. Therefore, he placed *Shevi'is* before *Orlah*.

6. Terumah—*Offering of Produce to the Kohein*[4]

After *Shevi'is* comes *Terumah*, because the *terumah* offering is the first gift that is offered from the grain.

7. Ma'aseros—*Tithes*

After *Terumah* comes *Ma'aseros*, which deals with *ma'aseir rishon* [the first tithe]—the annual offering given to the *levi'im* (Bamidbar 18:21, 24), because it is set aside after the *terumah*.

8. Ma'aseir Sheini—*Second Tithe*[5]

After *ma'aseir rishon* [first tithe], he discusses *ma'aseir sheini* [second tithe], which is given after *ma'aseir rishon*.

9. Challah—*Dough Offering*[6]

This is followed by *maseches Challah*, because after a person has given all the above-mentioned offerings [*terumah, ma'aseir rishon,* and *ma'aseir sheini*]—he grinds the grain into flour and kneads the

---

[4]The first offering to be set aside of the grain produce is the *terumah*, which must be given to the *kohen* (Devarim 18:4 and Bamidbar 18:8).

[5]In the first, second, fourth, and fifth year of a six-year cycle, a second tithe, called *ma'aseir sheini* had to be set aside. This produce had to be eaten in Yerushalayim, or its equivalent in money had to be spent on food and eaten in Yerushalayim (Devarim 14:28, 29).

[6]The dough offering given to the *kohanim*, (Bamidbar 15:17–21).

flour into dough. At that point, *challah* must be separated from the dough.

10. Orlah — *Prohibited Fruit*[7]
After he finishes discussing the laws of the offerings that are given from the grain, he begins to speak about fruits. And so he arranged the *maseches Orlah* after *Challah.*

11. Bikkurim — *First-Fruit*[8]
Bikkurim follows *Orlah* in accordance with their sequence in the Torah: The laws of *orlah* are discussed in Vayikra 19:23, and the laws of *bikkurim* are described in Devarim 26:1–11.

Thus, *Seder Zera'im* consists of a total of eleven *masechtos.*

II. *Seder Mo'eid* — Festivals

1. Shabbos
He began with *maseches Shabbos* because it outranks the Festivals in its holiness, and because it occurs regularly every week. Furthermore, the chapter in the Torah outlining the Festivals begins with Shabbos (Vayikra 23:3).

2. Eiruvin — *Combining Domains*[9]
After *maseches Shabbos* he placed *maseches Eiruvin,* since the subject matter has to do with Shabbos.

3. Pesachim — Pesach
The next *masechta* is *Pesachim* [dealing with the laws of *Pesach*], which is the first mitzvah given through Moshe (Shemos 12). It is also the mitzvah that follows after Shabbos in the Torah chapter of the Festivals (Vayikra 23).

---

[7]The fruit of a tree may not be eaten for the first three years; such fruit is called *orlah* (Vayikra 19:23).

[8]The first fruits (*bikkurim*) of the seven species mentioned in Devarim 8:8 must be brought to the Beis Hamikdash and presented to the *kohanim* in a festive ceremony that is described in Devarim 26:1–11.

[9]On Shabbos you are forbidden to carry from a private domain into a public domain and vice versa. Private homes in a common courtyard may be combined by means of an *eiruv,* enabling the residents to carry from one house to another.

4. Shekalim—*Shekels*[10]

Then comes *Shekalim,* in line with the order in which it appears in the Torah in *Parshas Ki Sisa* (Shemos 20:12).

5. Yoma—*Yom Kippur*

Shekalim is followed by *Yoma* [in keeping with the order in the Torah], where the topic of Yom Kippur is elaborated on in *Parshas Acharei Mos.*

6. Sukkah—*Sukkos*

Rabbi Yehudah HaNasi wanted to end his discussion of the *Shalosh Regalim* [the Three Pilgrimage Festivals]. Since he had already discussed the laws of *Pesach,* there remained *Shavuos* and *Sukkos* to be dealt with. However, there are no obligations that are unique to Shavuos. All the things he had to say about *Shavuos* applied to *all* Festivals. Therefore, after *maseches Yoma* he would have placed *Beitzah,* which deals with the general laws of Yom Tov. But because there are so many special mitzvos connected with *Sukkos,* he set *Sukkah* before *Beitzah.*

7. Beitzah—*Laws of Yom Tov*

8. Rosh Hashanah

At this point, the only Yom Tov listed in the Torah still to be discussed was Rosh Hashanah, and so, after *Beitzah,* he took up *Rosh Hashanah.*

9. Ta'anis—*Fasts*

After he finished speaking about the Festivals listed in the Torah, he turned to the fasts instituted by the prophets, which are mentioned in the Prophets. Therefore, after Rosh Hashanah he placed *maseches Ta'anis.*

10. Megillah—*Laws of Purim*

Next came *maseches Megillah,* because the reading of the *Megillah* was instituted by prophets who lived after those that instituted the fast days.

---

[10]The obligation upon each person to donate a half *shekel* [coin] to the Beis Hamikdash each year, which was used to buy communal sacrifices.

11. Mo'eid Katan—*Intermediate Days*

After *Megillah* comes *Mo'eid Katan*, which deals with the laws of *Chol Hamo'eid* [the intermediate days of *Pesach* and *Sukkos*], because *Megillah* and *Mo'eid Katan* have one common feature: both on Purim and *Chol Hamo'eid* it is forbidden to fast or eulogize.

12. Chagigah—*Festival Offering*

After he completed the subject of the *Yamim Tovim* and the things you must do on them and everything related to them, he closed the discussion with *maseches Chagigah*, which deals with a special obligation related to the *Shalosh Regalim* [the Three Pilgrim Festivals], namely, to come to the Beis Hamikdash with an offering (Devarim 16:16). He left this topic over for the end, because it does not apply to everyone—only to the men—as it says, *"Three times each year, every male among you must appear before Hashem"* (Shemos 23:17).

Thus, *Seder Mo'eid* consists of a total of twelve *masechtos*.

III. *Seder Nashim*—Women

1. Yevamos—*Levirate Marriages*[11]He then subdivided *Seder Nashim*, beginning with *maseches Yevamos*. It would have been more sensible to start with *maseches Kesuvos*, since it deals with marriage contracts. However, Rabbi Yehudah HaNasi was prompted by the following consideration: Marriage is a voluntary act, and the Beis Din has no power to force a man into marriage. However, the Beis Din does have the power to tell a man, "Either perform *yibbum* and marry your late brother's wife or perform the *chalitzah* ceremony." Thinking that it is right and proper to place laws that are enforceable ahead of laws that are not, he began with *maseches Yevamos*.

2. Kesuvos—*Marriage Contracts*

He then placed *Kesuvos* next in order.

3. Nedarim—*Vows*

After *Kesuvos* comes *Nedarim*. The chapter in the Torah dealing with vows and the Talmudic debates about it concentrate on vows made

---

[11]Levirate marriages or *yibbum*, the law described in Devarim 25:5-10 where it is stated that a man must marry his deceased brother's wife if he is childless. If he does not wish to take his sister-in-law as a wife, the *chalitzah* ceremony is performed, whereupon she is free to marry another man.

by women, as it says, *"These are the rules that Hashem commanded Moshe regarding the relationship between a man and his wife, and between a father and his daughter"* (*Bamidbar* 30:17). Also when a woman is legally married, her husband has the right to annul her vows. That is why *maseches Nedarim* was placed after *Kesuvos*.

4. Nazir—*Nazirite*[12]
After *Nedarim* he placed *Nazir*, because a nazir also takes a vow, and when a woman takes a nazirite vow, her husband can nullify her vow. Therefore, after *Nedarim* comes *Nazir*.

5. Gittin—*Divorce Law*
After completing the discussion of the laws of marriage and the related subject of annulling vows, he began the topic of divorce, placing *Gittin*, after *Nazir*.

6. Sotah—*The Suspected Adulteress*
After *Gittin* he recorded *Sotah*, because it is related to the subject of divorce. If a wife commits adultery, the husband and the wife are forced to divorce, as I will explain in my commentary on the Mishnah.

7. Kiddushin—*Sanctification of the Marriage*
After *Sotah* comes *Kiddushin*. You may wonder why *Kiddushin* [the betrothal ceremony] was left for the last, and why it was not placed ahead of *Kesuvos* [which deals with the rights and obligations between husband and wife after their marriage]. The answer is that Rabbi Yehudah HaNasi did not arrange *Kiddushin* before *Kesuvos* so as not to create a separation between *Yevamos* and *Kesuvos*, both of which deal with marital relations and should therefore be linked together.

The question remains: Why didn't he at least arrange *Kiddushin* before *Gittin*, and follow the natural sequence of marriage before divorce?

The reason that he set *Gittin* before *Kiddushin* is that he wanted to follow the pattern of the Torah where divorce is mentioned before marriage: *". . . he shall write her a bill of divorce and place it in her*

---

[12]A person who takes a nazirite vow must abstain from wine or any grape beverage, may not cut his hair, and may not have any contact with the dead.

hand . . . *When she thus leaves his household, she may go and marry another man"* (Devarim 24:1–2). From the words "and marry another man" we derive a basic law of *Kiddushin,* as the Talmud explains, "we compare marriage law to divorce law" (*Kiddushin* 5a).

Seder Nashim consists of a total of seven *masechtos.*

IV. *Seder Nezikin* — Damages

1. Masechta Nezikin

He divided the first *masechta* into three parts:

a. Bava Kamma — *[First Gate]*

The first part is *Bava Kamma,* which deals with damages caused to property that are classified under the headings of Ox, Pit, Fire, and personal injury. Since the primary duty of the court is to remove the sources of damages, Rabbi Yehudah HaNasi began with *Bava Kamma.*

b. Bava Metzia — *[Middle Gate]*

After *Bava Kamma* comes *Bava Metzia,* which is concerned with conflicting claims of ownership, law concerning things held in safekeeping, wages, laws concerning borrowing and renting, and everything related to these topics.

He followed the order of the Torah verses; after the laws of damages (Ox, Pit, Fire) (Shemos 21:22–33, 22:4–5) and *"when two men fight"* (Shemos 21:22), the Torah discusses the laws of the "Four Custodians"[13] (Shemos 22:6–14).

c. Bava Basra — *[Last Gate]*

Then comes *Bava Basra,* which deals with laws concerning the division of property held in partnership, adjacent dwellings under co-ownership, cancellations of sales contracts when merchandise is found to be defective, buying and selling, guarantees, and hereditary succession.

He made this section the last of the "Three Gates" because its subject matter is based entirely on the Oral Torah and logical reasoning, and is not explicitly mentioned in the Torah.

---

[13]The Torah distinguishes four categories of custodians, (a) the unpaid custodian, (b) the paid custodian, (c) the borrower, (d) the renter.

2. Sanhedrin — *Judicial Body*
Now that we are familiar with the civil laws, Rabbi Yehudah HaNasi deals with the judges who administer these laws. Thus, he arranged *Sanhedrin* after *Bava Basra*.

3. Makkos — *Flogging*
In some editions of the Talmud, *maseches Makkos* [which deals with the punishment of flogging to be administered by the Beis Din], is joined with *maseches Sanhedrin* and is counted as one *masechta* with the explanation that since *Sanhedrin* ends with "The following offenders are to be put to death by strangling," Rabbi Yehudah HaNasi attached to it "The following offenders are to be punished by flogging" [the first words of *maseches Makkos*]. This simply is not so. *Makkos* is a *masechta* all by itself. It was placed next to *Sanhedrin* because no one, except the judge, has the right to give a flogging, as it says, ". . . *the judge shall make him lean over and have him flogged*" (Devarim 25:2).

4. Shavuos — *Oaths*
Makkos is followed by *Shavuos* because of the similarity of the laws between those at the end of *Makkos* and those at the beginning of *Shavuos*. The Talmud in *Shavuos* comments on this. Another reason for juxtaposing these two *masechtos* is that, similar to flogging, only a judge can compel someone to take an oath.

5. Eiduyos — *Testimonies*
When he completed his discussion of the civil laws, the judges, and their powers, such as administering flogging and oaths, Rebbi went on to speak about *Eiduyos*, which consists largely of a collection of *halachos* about whose reliability we have the testimony of trustworthy men. We may depend on their testimony. The testimony of witnesses in court is the basis of the judicial system, and these men testified before the Beis Din as to the authenticity of these *halachos*. Therefore, it belongs near the laws of Beis Din. Rabbi Yehudah HaNasi arranged *Eiduyos* [though it is more closely related to *Sanhedrin*], after *Shavuos*, whose subject matter is oaths, because people take oaths all the time, whereas *Eiduyos* consists of testimonies that were given to the judges at certain special occasions, and that were then accepted by them.

6. Avodah Zarah—*Idolatry*

Rabbi Yehudah HaNasi then began to discuss the subject of idolatry, because in order to be qualified, a judge must be thoroughly familiar with the rituals and cults of idol worshipers. When he knows these ceremonies, he will be able to apply the law that states that a person who worships the planet Saturn by performing the rites that apply to the planet Venus, or who prays to Jupiter with the prayers of Mars, does not deserve to be put to death, as the Oral Law clearly declares.

He left this *masechta* for the last, because idol worship happens only in extremely rare cases.

7. Avos—*Ethics of the Fathers*

When he finished discussing the requirements of a judge, he began *maseches Avos*, Ethics of the Fathers. He wrote this *masechta* for two reasons.

First, it clearly states that accepted oral tradition is absolutely true and that it was transmitted from generation to generation in an unbroken chain, reaching back to Moshe. You will come to honor the Sage of your generation and treat him with utmost respect, because he is the bearer of the Tradition. It has been transmitted through the ages down to him in his generation, just as the earlier Sages received it in their generation. As we are taught, "If we were to investigate the Beis Din of Rabban Gamliel, then we would have to put on trial each Beis Din which ever stood, from the days of Moshe until the present" (*Rosh Hashanah* 2:9). "Shimshon was as authoritative in his generation as Shmuel was in his" (*Rosh Hashanah* 25b). There is an important lesson in this for all of us. We should not say, "Why should we accept the decision of this Judge or abide by the ordinance enacted by that Judge?" This attitude is wrong, because the decision was not rendered by the judge alone, but also by Hashem who said, *"Judgment belongs to God"* (Devarim 1:17). It is all one and the same system of justice that was transmitted over the ages, from generation to generation.

The second reason for including *maseches Avos* in *Seder Nezikin* is that Rabbi Yehudah HaNasi recorded the ethical sayings of the outstanding Sages to teach us good character traits. No one needs good character traits more than a judge. If an ignorant person is not a paragon of virtue, he does no harm to the community; he only hurts himself. But if a judge is not an ethical and humble man, he will not only hurt himself, but also bring harm to the community. Therefore, he begins *maseches Avos* by admonishing the judges, "Be deliberate in judgment" (*Avos* 1:1).

A judge must take to heart all the words of advice that are found in *maseches Avos*, such as to be deliberate in judgment, and not to rush into rendering a verdict, for there may be important aspects that have been withheld by the witnesses; rendering the case a *din merumeh* [suspect to legal trickery or conspiracy] (*Sanhedrin* 32b). On the other hand, he should not draw out the court proceedings unnecessarily, if he knows that there are no suspicious aspects; this would be called *inui hadin* [delaying justice]. He must do his best to interrogate the witnesses thoroughly, and to be careful with his words, and not unwittingly give the witnesses guidance through his line of questioning. Neither should he counsel the litigants on how to plead their case. This is called *orechei hadayanim* [a judge acting as a lawyer]. He should not disgrace himself by associating with ignorant people, for he will lose his dignity. He should not seclude himself, so that people cannot reach him when they need him. He should not pursue leisure and pleasures for in his passion for enjoyment he will lose sight of the truth. He should not want to rank himself higher than his colleagues in the seating order, and he should not make a strong bid for the post of judgeship, for he might be suspected of harboring ulterior motives. He should always try to work out a settlement. If he never in his life rendered a verdict but always reached a settlement, how wonderful that would be. But if a settlement cannot be reached, then he should render a legal decision. He should not be abrupt, but should allow the opposing litigant ample time to plead his case, even if he talks too much and speaks nonsense. If this is impossible, since he cannot see any justification at all in his claim, he should render his decision immediately. We see how our Sages often took immediate decisive action when there was a need for it. The Talmud said about such cases, "Let the law pierce the mountain." (*Sanhedrin* 6b).

To sum it up, a judge must be like a capable doctor. If he can cure a patient by putting him on a diet, he will not prescribe medicine. When he sees that the patient does not respond to the change in the diet, he will prescribe natural medicines, like potions, brews, and sweet-smelling herbs. Only if he sees that none of these medications have an effect will he prescribe strong bad-tasting medicines like laxatives. Similarly, a judge should begin by trying to reach a settlement. If he cannot, he should pronounce judgment in a quiet way, gently appeasing the losing party. If he cannot appease him because the man is stubborn and insists on winning the case no matter what, then he must become more firm, as it says, *"See every proud man and humble him, and crush the wicked where they stand"* (Iyov 40:12).

A judge should not chase after the pleasures of the world, wealth and social status, as it says about judges, *"men . . . who hate improper gain"* (Shemos 18:21) and *"A king, by justice sustains the land"* (Mishlei 29:4) — "If a judge is like a king who needs nothing, then he sustains the land; but if he behaves like a *kohen* who comes to the threshing floors to collect his *terumah*, then he destroys the land" (*Kesuvos* 105b).

Now that we have seen that a judge needs all these admonitions, how perfectly appropriate is it for *maseches Avos* to be placed after *Sanhedrin*. Once *Avos* contained all this valuable advice to judges, similar wise counsel was added, designed to promote abstention from the empty pleasures of the world, respect for the Sages, integrity, and the fear of Heaven.

8. Horayos — *Erroneous Rulings*

When Rabbi Yehudah HaNasi completed the ethical admonitions to the judges, he began to discuss what should be done in case judges render an erroneous decision, for it is impossible for anyone made of flesh and blood not to make mistakes. Therefore, *Horayos* [which deals with erroneous rulings] follows *Avos*, and with it *Seder Nezikin* is ended.

Thus, *Seder Nezikin* comprises eight *masechtos*.

V. *Seder Kodashim* — Sacred Objects

1. Zevachim — *Animal Offerings*

He began *Kodashim* with the animal offerings that form *maseches Zevachim*.

2. Menachos — *Meal Offerings*

After *Zevachim* comes *Menachos* [offerings made of flour] in keeping with the order of these subjects in the Torah (Vayikra 1–2).

3. Chullin—*Nonsacred Meat*

Having completed the entire subject of sacrificial offerings, he turned to the laws of slaughtering for nonsacrificial purposes, following the order of the verses. After Hashem said, *"There will be a site that Hashem will choose as the place dedicated to His name. It is there that you will have to bring all that I am prescribing to you"* (Devarim 12:11), He said, *"In all your settlements, you may slaughter animals to satisfy your wants, so that you will be able to eat the meat that Hashem gives you as His blessing"* (Devarim 12:15). Thus, after *Menachos* comes *Chullin*.

4. Bechoros—*The First-Born*

After *Chullin* comes *Bechoros*, again following the order in which these subjects are mentioned in the Torah. Speaking of nonsacred meat, the Torah says, *"In all your settlements, you may slaughter animals to satisfy your wants"* (Devarim 12:15). After that it says, *"However, in your settlements, you may not eat the tithes of your grain, wine and oil, the* **first-born of your cattle and flocks,** *any general pledges you make, your specific pledges, or your hand-delivered elevated gifts"* (Devarim 12:17).

5. Arachin—*Valuations*

After discussing the laws regarding things set aside for sacred purposes, he deals with the laws concerning the valuations of objects pledged for sacred purposes. The monetary value of these objects also become sacred. Thus, after *Bechoros*, he arranged *maseches Arachin*.

6. Temurah—*Exchanges*[14]

Temurah follows *Arachin* following the order of the Torah verses.

7. Kereisos[15]

Having completed the discussion of these various offerings, he continues with *maseches Kereisos*, which deals with all transgres-

---

[14]The Torah states, "One may neither exchange [the animal that was donated] nor offer a substitute for it, whether it be a better animal for a worse one, or a worse animal for a better one. If he replaces one animal with another, both [the original animal] and its replacement shall be consecrated" (Vayikra 27:10).

[15]Divine punishment by premature death.

sions that are punishable by *kares* and related topics. The reason he placed this *masechta* in *Seder Kodashim* [which has to do with offerings] is because every transgression that is punishable by *kares* if done intentionally requires a sin-offering if it was done inadvertently.

8. Me'ilah—*Misuse of Sacred Objects*[16]

After *Kereisos* he proceeded with *Me'ilah*, because the transgressions for which a person must bring a *me'ilah*—guilt offering—are less serious than the transgressions for which a sin-offering must be brought.

9. Tamid—*Daily Offering*

After *Me'ilah* comes *maseches Tamid*. He left this *masechta* for the end, because it contains no learned discussions or expositions on things that are forbidden and permitted. Rather, it tells the story of how the daily offering was brought, in order that we will be able to bring it in the future.

10. Midos—*Measurements*

After *Tamid* follows *Midos*, which relates a series of facts. It describes the shape and structure of the Beis Hamikdash as well as its measurements. This is useful, for when the Beis Hamikdash will be rebuilt, speedily in our days, we will have to be very careful to build it according to this layout, design, and size, since its dimensions were revealed through *ruach hakodesh* [a divine gift of superior understanding, akin to prophecy], as David said to his son Shlomoh, *"All this that Hashem made me understand by His hand on me, I give you in writing—the plan of [the Beis Hamikdash] all the works"* (Divrei Hayamim I 28:19).

11. Kinim—*Birds*

After completing the discussion of animal sacrifices, and the design of the Beis Hamikdash where these sacrifices were offered, he turned to *maseches Kinim*. The only topic discussed in this *masechta* is what should be done if different kinds of bird offerings were mixed up. This subject was left for last because such a mix-up does

---

[16]Which speaks about the offering that has to be brought by a person who used an article that was set aside for sacred purposes, for his own benefit (Vayikra 5:15–16).

not necessarily happen. Besides, the discussion is very short, as will be explained.

With this *masechta*, *Seder Kodashim* is ended. Thus, *Seder Kodashim* contains eleven *masechtos*.

VI. *Seder Teharos*—Ritual Purity

1. Keilim—*Vessels*

He began *Seder Taharos*, with *maseches Keilim*, which concerns the main sources of *tum'ah* [ritual uncleanness], and lists all things that are and are not receptive to *tum'ah*.

2. Ohalos—*Tents*

After *Keilim* comes *Ohalos*, which discusses the *tum'ah* of a dead human being. He assigns first place to this masechta, because the *tum'ah* of a dead body is the most potent source of *tum'ah*.

3. Nega'im—*Plagues*

Following *Ohalos* is *Nega'im*, which deals with the *tum'ah* caused by the disease of *tzora'as* [plague of leprosy], because a person suffering from *tzora'as* spreads *tum'ah* to everything within the tent or room he occupies. In this respect, it has some similarity to the spreading of *tum'ah* by a corpse.

4. Parah—*Red Cow*

After ending the discussion of the *tum'ah* produced by a dead body and of similar *tum'ah*, he goes on to speak about *Taharah*, ritual purity, which is attained through the red cow. Therefore, he arranged *maseches Parah* after *Nega'im*.

5. Teharos—*Ritual Purity*

When he finished the discussion of the more potent sources of *tum'ah* and the process by which ritual purity is attained, he turned to the weaker forms of *tum'ah*, which may be ended at sunset by immersing in a *mikveh*. Thus, he placed *maseches Teharos* after *Parah*. Euphemistically, he named it *Teharos*, substituting that name for the actual subject matter, which deals with the weaker forms of *tum'ah*. Another reason for the name *Teharos* is that in order to know the various stages of *tum'ah*, you must be familiar with the concept of *Taharah*.

Don't think for a moment that giving the name *Teharos* to a *masechta* and giving the same name to the entire *Seder Teharos* was an error on the part of the author. Among philosophers this is not considered an error. They often use the same term for a specific part as for the general concept.

6. Mikva'os—*Ritual Immersion Pools*
After completing the discussion of the more potent and the weaker forms of *tum'ah* and the ways by which ritual cleansing may be attained, he dealt with the specific laws of ritual cleansing. Thus, he arranged *maseches Mikva'os* after *Teharos*.

7. Niddah—*Menstrual Period*
He discussed *Niddah* [dealing with the laws relating to a woman who has a menstrual flow] after all these other forms of *tum'ah*, because it is not a universal *tum'ah*, as it applies only to women. Thus, he placed *Niddah* after *Mikva'os*.

8. Mach'shirin—*Requirements*
Niddah is followed by *Mach'shirin* [which outlines the ways food must be prepared to enable it to become contaminated by *tum'ah*, see Vayikra 11:34].
After *Mach'shirin* comes *Zavim*.

9. Zavim—*Venereal Discharge*[17]
Zavim really should have been placed immediately after *Niddah*, but he put *Mach'shirin* ahead of *Zavim*, to conform with the order in which these topics appear in the Torah. The subject of *Mach'shirin* appears in *parashas Shemini* (Vayikra 11:34), and the laws of *Zavim* are found in *parashas Metzora* (Vayikra chapter 15).

10. T'vul Yom—*Immersed on that Day*[18]
After *Zavim* comes *T'vul Yom*, following the order of the verses, as it says, *"This is the law concerning the man who is unclean because of a discharge or seminal emission"* (Vayikra 15:32).

---

[17]The laws of *tum'ah* that arise as a result of venereal discharge.

[18]Detailing the laws of one who has immersed in the *mikveh* and must wait until sunset to become ritually clean (Vayikra 22:6–7).

11. Yadayim—*Hands*

The previous forms of *tum'ah* involved the entire body, in other words, if a person came in contact with these forms of *tum'ah*, his entire body becomes *tamei*. Therefore, Rabbi Yehudah HaNasi now takes up the forms of *tum'ah* that affect only one part of the body, placing *Yadayim* (Hands) after *T'vul Yom*.

12. Uktzim—*Stems*[19]

He left this *masechta* for the last because its laws are derived through reasoning and they are not explicitly mentioned in the Torah. With this *masechta* he closed his work.

Thus, *Seder Teharos* contains a total of twelve *masechtos*.

The total number of *masechtos* in the entire Mishnah adds up to sixty-one. The total number of chapters of all *masechtos* amounts to 523.

---

[19]The laws concerning the stems of foods in regard to *tum'ah*.

Expounding the Mishnah

In compiling the Mishnah, Rabbi Yehudah HaNasi was content to trace the transmission of the Oral Law only as far back as Shimon HaTzaddik. He wrote the Mishnah in a lucid and concise style. To his brilliant mind everything was very clear, but a person of lesser intelligence had difficulty grasping the concepts, since the early Sages wrote on their own level of comprehension. Because of this, Rabbi Chiya, one of Rabbi Yehudah's students, wrote a book patterned after his master's work in which he explained the things that might be puzzling. This is the *Tosefta* [Supplement]. Its purpose is to explain the Mishnah and to provide insights that could not be discovered without a great deal of diligent study. He presented these insights in order to teach us how to derive and develop concepts from the Mishnah.

Rabbi Hoshiah wrote similar works, and so did Rav, who wrote the braisos—[literally, "outside texts"—teaching not found in the Mishnah], the *Sifra* [a commentary on *Vayikra*], and *Sifrei* [a commentary on *Bamidbar* and *Devarim*]. There were many other Sages who wrote similar works, as it says in the Talmud, "When a Rabbi came, he brought a *baraisa* with him." However, none of these *baraisos* matched the Mishnah in the smooth flow of language, clarity, and brevity. The Mishnah became the accepted text, and all the other works ranked second to it. The Mishnah was preferred and admired by everyone. [In comparison to other texts], its praise could be summed up in the verse, *"Maidens see her and acclaim her; queens and concubines, and praise her"* (*Shir Hashirim* 6:9).

All those who came after the time of the Mishnah, devoted their energies to nothing but the study of the Mishnah. Generation after generation researched, analyzed and expounded the Mishnah, each scholar according to his wisdom and understanding. With the passing years, differences of opinion arose about the interpretation of some laws. Whenever scholars studied together, invariably they probed and delved into the Mishnah, discovered

131

new insights and increased their knowledge in general. This process of research and analysis continued up to the time of Ravina and Rav Ashi, the last of the Talmudic Sages.

THE *GEMARA*

Rav Ashi (353–427 C.E.) set himself the task of compiling the *Gemara* [Talmud]. He followed the example of Rabbeinu Hakadosh [Rabbi Yehudah HaNasi], who had collected all the statements of those who came after Moshe. He too gathered all the sayings of the Sages who followed Rabbeinu Hakadosh, including all the explanations of the commentators and the fine legal points they made. He compiled them, digested them with his God-given intellect, and composed the *Gemara.* He had four goals in mind:

The First, to explain the Mishnah by (1) showing the various interpretations of its text, (2) showing the reasoning of the contending sages, and (3) revealing which line of reasoning holds true. This was his main purpose.

The Second, to set down the final *Halachah* according to one of the sages, whether concerning the text or the meaning of the Mishnah, or about new laws that were derived from the Mishnah.

The Third, to put on record new applications of the law that the Sages of each generation derived from the Mishnah, including the principles and proofs on which the teachers of the Mishnah based their statements, and arranged them in their present form. And to record the preventive measures (*gezeiros*) and enactments that were instituted from Rabbi Yehudah HaNasi's days until his day.

The Fourth, to write down the *Aggadic derashos* [homilies], that fit the theme of the chapter where they are found.

AGGADIC DERASHOS

The *Aggadic derashos* are not to be taken lightly. On the contrary, one should view them seriously, because they are full of great wisdom, amazing secrets and precious treasures. If you look at these *derashos* from an intellectual perspective, you will discover in them the supreme, essential good. These *derashos* contain ideas about God and the essential good that the mystics keep hidden and do not want to reveal. They also contain all the ideas that the philosophers dealt with. Yet, on the surface they seem to be utter nonsense.

The Sages had very good reasons for disguising these lofty ideas. In the first place, they wanted to sharpen their students' wits and broaden their minds. Also, they wanted to pull the wool over the eyes of the fools, who would not be able to grasp their real meaning. If the fools would be shown the splendor of these truths, in their ignorance they would ridicule them. The Talmud says about these fools, "Do not reveal the secret to them" (*Kiddushin* 71a), since they do not have enough intelligence to grasp the mystical truth.

Even to one another the Sages did not want to reveal the mysteries of Kabbalistic wisdom. The Talmud speaks about this:

> One of the Sages got together with some people who were well-versed in the knowledge of *Ma'aseh Bereishis* [the Kabbalistic study of Creation]. He himself was an expert on *Ma'aseh Merkavah* [the mystical description of the Divine Chariot in *Yechezkel, chapter 1*]. He said to them, "You teach me *Ma'aseh Bereishis* and I will teach you *Ma'aseh Merkavah*." They agreed. However, after they taught him *Ma'aseh Bereishis*, he refused to teach them *Ma'aseh Merkavah*. (*Chagigah* 13a)

Now, this man certainly did not do this because he was not generous with his scholarship, nor because he wanted to pride himself that he knew more than they did. Heaven forbid! Even fools do not stoop that low, let alone such a respected and pious man. He did this because he thought that he was qualified to understand what they knew, but that they were not capable of grasping what he knew. He found a verse to support his view, *"Honey and milk are under your tongue"* (*Shir Hashirim* 4:11), meaning, those sweet sciences for which the soul craves like the palate craves honey and milk, must be kept hidden, should not be talked about, and should not even be mentioned or hinted at. That is why it says, *"under* your tongue"—these topics should not be studied and meditated on in public. These secrets are alluded to in the text of the Talmud; and when Hashem will see fit to lift the veil of ignorance from a person's heart, then, if he makes a strong effort and familiarizes himself with the secrets of Kabbalah, he will understand as much as his intelligence can absorb. Having made a sincere effort, there is nothing left for him to do, other than to leave the matter in the hand of the

Creator. He should pray to Him and beg Him that He may enlighten him and reveal to him the mysteries that are hidden in the Holy Books. David did this when he said, *"Open my eyes, that I may perceive the wonders of Your teaching"* (Tehillim 119:18).

When Hashem opens a man's eyes and reveals to him some of these mystical secrets, he must hide them from others, as we have said. And if he does hint at it ever so slightly, he should do so only to someone who has a brilliant mind and who is known for his integrity, as has been illustrated in many stories in the Talmud. A scholar should reveal his Kabbalistic knowledge only to someone who is more learned than he is, or at least his equal. If he revealed it to a fool, the fool may not disparage him, but he certainly will not appreciate it. *Shlomoh* said about this, *"Do not speak to a fool, for he will disdain your sensible words"* (Mishlei 23:9).

A third reason the Sages wrote their *derashos* in the form of symbolism was to teach the masses through allegories and parables. Women, young boys, and children will enjoy the stories, and when their intellect has ripened, they will understand the lofty ideas that are at the heart of these stories. Shlomoh hinted at this when he said, *"For understanding proverb and parable, the words of the wise and their allusions"* (Mishlei 1:6).

If you come across a parable and you cannot grasp its simple meaning, you should be pained by this fact. Don't blame the *derash*, blame your weak mind that is far removed from understanding the basic truth. For it is a fact that some people are smarter than others, which is due to differences in their physical makeup. Just as one man may be stronger than another, so is one man's brainpower greater than someone else's. Secondly, even one who is naturally very smart will fail to comprehend many things if he is ignorant of knowledge. The understanding of a man who developed his intellect to understand an intricate matter is definitely greater than that of one who has not developed his intellect. The one who has worked to develop himself has what is called "actual brainpower," while the one who has not worked, has "potential brainpower." Because of that, some people clearly see the truth of certain things, while others find these things to be far-fetched and even impossible. It depends on their intelligence and on how they have developed.

Let me give you an illustration. Think of a man who is a physician, well versed in arithmetic, a scholar of music, a physicist, and an all-around bright fellow, but who knows nothing about geometry and astronomy. Suppose we were to ask his opinion of a man who claimed that the sun, which we see as a small disk, is really a large sphere, that this sphere is 166-3/8 times as large as the earth, that the earth's sphere has a circumference of 24,000 miles, and that by this method the circumference of the sun can be calculated. No doubt, our bright scientist will be unable to accept such a theory. To him it will sound outlandish and utterly baffling. He will argue immediately that these claims make no sense at all, for how can a man who takes up only a few inches of space on earth know the size of the sun as if it were a piece of real estate? He will exclaim, "How is this possible? Look, the sun in heaven is very far away. We cannot even clearly see the outline of the sun; all we can see is its glow. So how can anyone go up there to survey it and measure it, down to a fraction of 3/8th? This is nothing but absolute nonsense." He will have no doubt at all that these claims are baseless and absurd.

But if he would study geometry and learn the basic theorems of the proportions of spheres and other geometrical shapes, and he would then study the authoritative text on this subject, namely *Almagesti* [written by Ptolemy], the famous work on the calculations of the heavenly orbits, then he would clearly understand this claim, and he would realize that it is undeniably true and can be proven. He would accept the dimensions of the sun, just as he is convinced that the sun exists. He would adjust his mind to believing firmly all the things that he considered incredible earlier. A scenario like this could very well happen. We did not ask a man who is ignorant about science the question, but one who is intelligent, good-natured, and wise. The person we asked was familiar with mathematics, a science with its thought process similar to theology. Certainly, if a man who has no common sense and knows nothing about science, a man whose brainpower has not developed, were asked about Divine ideas that are hidden in the allegories of the *derashos*, he surely would find them hopelessly unbelievable and would not understand one word of them.

Therefore, we should make allowances for these *derashos*, and analyze them carefully. Let us not be quick to dismiss even one word in them; and when something strikes us as bizarre, let us study the various intellectual sciences, until we understand the concepts that are involved. Even the Sages, although they were eager to study diligently, had brilliant minds, studied in the company of great scholars, and kept away from worldly things, still would consider themselves inferior in comparison to earlier sages. They said about themselves, "The wisdom of the early Sages was as wide as the entrance to the hall of the Beis Hamikdash, and that of the later sages is not even as wide as the eye of a needle" (*Eiruvin* 53a). This certainly applies to us—we have no wisdom at all, as Hashem told us, *"The wisdom of the wise men shall fail, and the prudence of the prudent shall vanish"* (Yeshayah 29:14). The prophet Yeshayah in this chapter identifies four negative qualities in us: (1) weak intelligence, (2) a strong appetite for pleasure, (3) laziness in the search for wisdom, and (4) greediness. With these four bad character traits, how can we *not* feel inferior when we compare ourselves to the early sages?

Because the later sages were aware of the fact that all the words of the earlier sages were clear, pure, and perfect, they warned us not to ridicule them. They said, "Whoever makes fun of the words of the sages, is sentenced to boiling excrements" (*Gittin* 57a). And there is no greater boiling excrement than the foolishness that makes one belittle the words of the sages. Only a dull-witted, pleasure-seeking sensualist will dismiss their words.

Because they saw the truth of the early rabbis' words, they devoted their entire lives to studying the Torah and commanded us to immerse ourselves in it at night and part of the day. They considered the study of Torah the height of wisdom, and so it is.

MODEL OF A DERASHAH

The Sages said, "The Holy One Blessed is He has nothing in this world except for the four cubits of *Halachah*" (*Berachos* 8a). Now, pay close attention to this statement. For if you take it at face value, you will find that it appears untrue—as if the four cubits of *Halachah* were the only worthwhile pursuit, and all other sciences were worthless. And furthermore, if this were so, from the days of *Shem* and *Eiver* and onwards until the giving of the Torah, can we say that Hashem had nothing to concern Himself with in this world?

However, if you think about this statement, you will find that it contains a marvelous and profound idea. I will explain it to you, so that it may serve as a model for any other *derashos* you may come across. So, please pay close attention.

THE PURPOSE OF EXISTENCE

The ancient philosophers, after delving deeply into the problem of existence, came to the conclusion that every existing thing needs to have a purpose for which it came into being. Things do not exist without a purpose. Once they established this general rule, they began to sort out all existing things in order to find out the purpose of each object. They discovered that the purpose of every manmade object is known and needs no investigation, for a craftsman will not make an object unless he has a certain purpose in mind. For example, a carpenter would not have made a saw unless he first wondered how to cut a piece of wood, imagined the shape of a saw, and began to make it in order to cut wood with it. So we know that the purpose of a saw is to cut wood, the purpose of an ax is to chop, the purpose of a needle is to sew, and so it is with all man-made objects.

But when it comes to things that were created by the Divine wisdom through nature, such as trees, herbs, minerals, different rock formations, and various kinds of animals, the purpose of some of these are readily apparent, others are not apparent without careful observation and study, while the purpose of others cannot possibly be known unless it is revealed through prophecy or through the power of knowledge of the future.

It is beyond man's ability to explore the reason why some ants have wings and others do not, or why some worms have many legs and others have few, and what the purpose of a particular species of worm or ant is.

However, in regards to larger things whose functions are more obvious, it is possible for wise men to argue the purpose of their creation. The wiser a man is, and the greater his hunger and motivation for learning, the more perfect will be his knowledge.

When Hashem granted Shlomoh the wisdom He had promised him, he understood whatever mortal man could possibly comprehend of the secrets of the creation of all species. He spoke about the purpose of the creation of trees, herbs, and animals, as it says, *"He spoke about trees, from the cedar in the Lebanon to the moss that grows out of the wall; and he spoke about the beasts, birds, creeping things and fishes"* (Melachim I 5:3). This was proof that he had the Divine Spirit. Then it says, *"Men of all peoples came to hear Shlomoh's wisdom"* (Melachim I 5:14).

MAN IS THE PURPOSE

You should understand that all things that exist beneath the orbit of the moon were created only for the sake of man. Some of the animals are meant to be eaten, like sheep and cattle and other species. Some are here to serve purposes other than nourishment, like a donkey, which is meant to carry heavy burdens, or horses, which are meant to help man reach distant places in a short time. The benefit of some species we do not know; they do have benefits, though, but we are not aware of what these benefits are. In the same way, some trees, plants, and herbs can be eaten; others are used as medicines.

Now, if you find animals or plants that you think cannot be eaten and seem to have no purpose, you should blame it on your lack of knowledge. It is impossible for any herb, fruit, or animal—from the elephant to the worm—not to be beneficial for man. Proof of this is that in each generation, extremely beneficial herbs and fruits are discovered that were unknown to earlier generations. The human mind cannot grasp the advantages of each plant, but their benefits will become known through scientific experiments in time to come.

Now you may ask, "For what purpose were deadly poisons created, such as the herb called *beish* or blood herb, which kills people and which has no benefit at all?"

Even these specimens have benefits. For although one dies when eating them, they are not lethal when they are used as an ointment on the body. You should realize that if the venoms of rattlesnakes and viper have great medicinal value, surely things that are less harmful must also carry great benefits.

MAN'S PURPOSE IS TO THINK

Now that we have stated that the purpose of all things is to benefit man, we must also probe the question as to why and for what purpose was man created. After a long investigation, the philosophers concluded that man has a great many functions, in contrast to all species of animals and trees, which have only one or two functions. For example, a palm tree has only one function: to produce dates. The same goes for all other trees. Similarly, some animals will be able to spin, like the spider; others will be able to build, like the swallow, which builds intricate nests during the summer. Lions can pounce and attack. But man does many different things. They analyzed each of his functions, in order to discover the purpose for which man was created, and they found that his main purpose is to perform one function only. It is for the sake of this one function that he was created, and all his other functions only serve to keep him alive so that he can fulfill his main function. This function is: To form abstract ideas and to know the essential truths. Logic tells you that it is wrong and incorrect to think that the purpose of man's life is to eat, drink, and to pursue physical pleasures, or to build a stronghold, because all these activities are passing, short-lived events; they do not improve his inner worth, and besides, all other creatures do the same things. On the other hand, wisdom does add to his inner being and lifts him from disgrace to esteem. Originally he was only a potential man, but wisdom made him an actual man. Before developing his knowledge, a man is no better than a beast, for the only thing that makes him different than other living creatures is his ability to think logically and form abstract ideas. Now, the loftiest idea a man can think of is the Unity of Hashem and all theological concepts that flow from this. All other fields of study are only exercises by which to train your mind until it reaches knowledge of Hashem. A full discussion of this subject would take up too much space.

As you attain understanding of these lofty thoughts, you must learn to stay away from most sensual pleasures. It is a fundamental rule that your soul suffers when you indulge your body, and your soul is restored when you restrain your body. A person who chases after bodily pleasures and lets his intellect be dominated by his feelings becomes like an animal that can only think of eating, drinking, and mating; such a person loses his God-given power to think abstract thoughts. He will turn into a vulgar creature, roaming around in a sea of emptiness.

We have made it clear that the purpose of the world and all that is in it is the wise and good man, the person who understands that wisdom and deeds are what make him a man. By "wisdom" I mean the ability to see the truth as it really is, and to understand whatever man can understand. By "deeds" I mean refining and curbing your innate tendencies, not to be swept along by sensual desires, but enjoying only those things that will benefit your physical, mental, and spiritual health. A man who lives according to these notions is the ideal and accomplished man.

We have heard this not only from the prophets, but even the scholars of the various nations, men who have never seen a prophet or heard his wisdom—even they knew that a man is not perfect unless he represents "wisdom and deeds." It will be enough if I just quote the words of the famous philosopher [Aristotle] who said, "God demands of us that we are wise and upright men." If a man is supposedly wise and righteous but runs after worldly delights, that man is not really a wise man. Wisdom demands that a person should enjoy luxuries only if they are good for his health. (In our commentary on *maseches Avos*, we will give this theme the full attention it deserves).

Along similar lines, we find that the prophet reprimands a person who boasts that he is wise, yet rebels against the mitzvos, and seeks hedonistic pleasures, *"How can you say, 'We are wise, and we possess Hashem's Torah?'* . . . *See, they reject the word of Hashem, so their wisdom amounts to nothing"* (Yirmiyah 8:8-9).

On the other hand, if a man serves Hashem, abstains from enjoyment—except for that which he needs for his health—lives a life of moderation, has the best character traits—but does not possess wisdom, he is not perfect either. But he certainly is better than the first person we discussed; only, his deeds don't have proper direction, and are not performed truthfully. The Sages said about such a person, "A boor cannot be fearful of sin, an unlearned person cannot be scrupulously pious" (*Avos* 2:6). Anyone who says about an ignorant man that he is pious, denies simple logic and contradicts the sages, who made a clear-cut statement about this. Indeed, the Torah always mentions first the command, *"you should study [the mitzvos],"* and only afterwards says, *"You should keep them"* (Devarim 5:1). Learning is mentioned before doing, because knowledge helps you to do things the right way, but by doing you do not increase your knowledge. The Sages put it this way, "Learning leads to doing" (*Kiddushin* 40b).

PURPOSE OF THE UNLEARNED

There is still one problem: You may ask, "You have just told me that Divine wisdom does not create anything useless, everything has a purpose. You also said that man is the preeminent creature, and was created for the purpose of conceiving thoughts and ideas. Now, if that is the case, why did Hashem call into being all those people who cannot form a creative thought? We see that most people are dense and empty-headed, seeking only worldly pleasures, while there are only very few outstanding wise men who reject material values. In fact, you may find no more than one wise man in several generations.

Those ignorant people were created for two reasons: The first reason is to attend to the needs of that one wise man. If all human beings were thinkers and philosophers, the world economy would be destroyed and the human race would perish within a short time. Man is basically a helpless creature who needs many services. The wise man would have to learn how to plow, harvest, thresh, grind and bake, and to make the necessary tools for all this work in order to prepare his food. He would have to learn how to spin and weave in order to make clothing. Then he would have to learn how to build a place to live, and fashion the tools for all these jobs. Even if he lived as long as Mesushelach he would not have enough time to learn all the trades that are essential for him to survive. When would he find time to study and acquire wisdom? Therefore, the rest of mankind was created to provide all the services of a smooth-running society so that the scholar's needs are met, the nation's economy will function well, and scholarship will flourish. How apt is the saying, "If it were not for the foolish the world would lay in ruin." The fool referred to here is the folly of an ordinary man. He has a weak constitution, yet he travels from one end of the world to other, crossing oceans during the winter, traveling through dry desert land in the scorching heat of summer, risking his life by exposing himself to wild animals and snakes, in order to earn a few dollars. And when he accumulates some money for which he jeopardized his life, he will pay it out to laborers to build a foundation deep in the earth, made of cement and stones, in order to erect on it a stronghold that will stand for many years, although he knows full well that there are not enough years left in his life to outlast a building made of reeds. Can there be a greater foolishness and idiocy than this? By the same token, all worldly pleasures are madness and insanity; still they are needed to keep the world going. This is why the Sages called an ignorant person an *am ha'aretz* [a "person of the land"], meaning that he was created just to keep the land going.

Someone may argue, "Do we not find at times a fool, who enjoys life and does not work hard, while others serve him and take care of his business? It might very well be that a wise man is taking care of his business!"

Things are not the way they look on the surface. The pleasure of that imbecile also serves a purpose; it is preparing something good for someone whom the Creator wants to give it to in the future. Because he relaxes and enjoys his money, the imbecile will order his employees to build him a beautiful palace or plant an impressive vineyard, like kings or princes do. It is quite possible that this palace is really being built for a pious man who, one day many years later, will come and find shelter from the scorching sun in the shade of one of its walls. The palace will actually have saved him from death. This thought is expressed in the verse, *"Should he pile up silver like dust, lay up clothing like dirt—he may lay it up, but the righteous will wear it, and the innocent will share his silver"* (Iyov 27:17). Or one day a cup of wine from that vineyard will be used to make a medicine called *tri'aka*, which will save the life of a perfectly righteous man who was bitten by a snake. This is Hashem's way and this is His wisdom with which he directs nature, *"for You planned ideas of long ago, fulfilled in steadfast faithfulness"* (Yeshayah 25:1).

This concept was taught by the Sages, "When Ben Zoma would stand on the Temple Mount and see Israel coming to celebrate, he would say, 'Blessed is He Who created all these to care for me" (*Berachos* 58b), for he was the greatest Sage in his generation.

The second reason for the existence of people who have no wisdom is that there are only very few wise men. Hashem in His wisdom wanted it that way. You cannot ask why this is so, any more than you can ask why there are nine heavenly spheres, seven planets, and four basic elements, because all these matters and others like them were willed by Hashem when He created the universe. The Sages explained this, "Rabbi Shimon ben Yochai said about his contemporaries, [although they were towering personalities], 'I have seen scholars who have reached eminence, and there are only a few; . . . if there are two, they are myself and my son' " (*Sukkah* 45b).

Since there are only very few Sages, the masses were created to provide companionship for the Sages.

You might think that this is an unimportant benefit; on the contrary, it is essential and even more important than the first. For

Hashem Himself settled evil people in *Eretz Yisrael* to provide a preexisting society for the Children of Israel, and in order to keep the pious ones from being alone, as it says, *"I will not drive them out in a single year, lest the land becomes depopulated . . ."* (Shemos 23:29).

The Sages commented on this idea, in explaining the verse, *"fear God and keep his commandments—because this is all man"* (Koheles 12:13). Literally translated it means, "this" [fearing God and keeping his commandments] is the purpose of all man. The Sages interpret it as follows: "because of this" [the perfect man], all man was created.

To sum it up, it has become clear that the goal of Creation was to bring into being the perfect man who possesses both "wisdom" and "good deeds," as we explained.

When you will study and think about what the words of the Sages teach us about these two concepts (wisdom and deeds), then you will see that they were correct when they said, "The Holy One, Blessed is He has nothing in this world except the four cubits of *Halachah*."[1]

We have strayed a little from our topic, but I brought up these matters because they strengthen the faith, and stimulate a desire for wisdom, and, in my opinion, they are quite important.

Now, let us get back to our subject.

---

[1] The Rambam's original question was "How can we say that Hashem has nothing in the world besides the four cubits of *Halachah* when in fact there exists many sciences in the world other than *Halachah*? We also find many generations where there wasn't Torah study." His answer appears to be that once we have established that although there are many sciences and unlearned generations, their ultimate purpose is to serve the perfect man. It is correct to say the purpose of the entire world is the perfect man. Since man will not attain perfection without learning *Halachah* we can properly say that *Hashem has nothing in the world except the four cubits of Halachah.*

Following the Completion of the Talmud

When Rav Ashi completed the compilation of the Talmud as we have it today, the magnificence and the extraordinary usefulness of this work attested to the fact *"that the spirit of God was in him"* (Daniel 4:5).

Of the sixty-one *masechtos* of the Mishnah, only thirty-five are expounded on in Rav Ashi's work: We find no *Gemara* on *Seder Zera'im*, except for *maseches Berachos*.

There is no *Gemara* on *Shekalim*, in *Seder Mo'eid*.

There is no *Gemara* on *Eiduyos* and *Avos*, in *Seder Nezikin*.

There is no *Gemara* on *Midos* and *Kinim*, in *Seder Kodashim*.

There is no *Gemara* on any *masechta* in *Seder Tehoros*, except for *Niddah*.

Rav Ashi passed away in Babylonia after he completed the Talmud. [This Talmud is referred to as the Babylonian Talmud.] The Sages of *Eretz Yisrael* did what Rav Ashi had done and composed the Jerusalem Talmud. It was compiled by Rabbi Yochanan.

We find all the *masechtos* of five *sedarim* expounded on in the Jerusalem Talmud. However, no *masechta* of *Seder Tehoros* is expounded in the Talmud, neither in the Babylonian nor in the Jerusalem Talmud, except for *Niddah*, as we mentioned. But if you work hard and study diligently at it you can understand this *Seder*, with the help of the *Tosefta* and the *Baraisos*. One can assemble all the relevant laws scattered throughout the Talmud and by a process of analysis deduce the underlying principles and themes of these *halachos*, as you will see me do when I explain that *Seder*, with God's help.

When all the Sages had passed away, the last of whom were Ravina and Rav Ashi, the Talmud was completed and its text firmly established. All sages who came afterwards strived with all their might to understand the recorded text only; no one was permitted either to add to the text or subtract from it.

The *Geonim* wrote many commentaries, but none of them, as far as we know, had the opportunity of completing a commentary on the entire Talmud. Some of them did not live long enough; others were busy settling legal disputes. However, they did compose complete halachic codes, some in Arabic, others in Hebrew, such as *Halachos Gedolos* [Great Laws], *Halachos Ketanos* [Brief Laws], *Halachos Pesukos* [Legal Decisions], *Halachos Rav Acha MiShavcha* [Decisions of Rav Acha of Shavcha], and others. Then there were the *halachos* written by the illustrious Rabbi Yitzchak Alfasi. This work is equivalent to all previous works because it includes all the decisions and laws we need in our time of the Exile. In his work, the *Rif* [an acronym for Rabbi Yitzchak Alfasi] clears up all errors in the books of earlier authorities. His work I have found flawless, except for fewer than ten *halachos*.

However, each of the existing commentaries of the *Geonim* has its own merits, according to the author's intelligence. A discerning person who studies the Talmud in depth can judge each gaon's intellectual power by his words and commentaries.

Now that it is our turn, we have done our utmost to research the works of the earlier authorities, and to toil to the utmost of our capabilities, hoping to find favor in the eyes of our Creator. I have collected anything I could lay my hands on from the commentaries of my father, and others, which they received from Rabbi Yosef HaLevi ibn Migash. Rabbi Yosef ibn Migash, a student of the Rif, succeeded him as rabbi of Alusina (Lucene) Spain. The passion this man had for studying the Talmud astonishes anyone who studies his works. The depth of his intellect is such that one could almost say of him, *"There was no king like him before"* (Melachim II 23:25) in his method and approach to research. I also assembled whatever I found of his personal notes on the halachos, and whatever I was able to learn from the various commentaries and what I have learned from the various branches of science. I then wrote a commentary on the three *Sedarim: Mo'ed, Nashim,* and *Nezikin,* except for four *masechtos.* I am planning now to write on them, too, but I have not yet found the time to do so. I also wrote a commentary on *Chullin* because there is an urgent need for it.

And that is what I have been working on.

Discussion about the Commentary on the Mishnah

I then decided to write a sorely needed commentary on the Mishnah following the pattern that I will discuss at the end of this chapter.

I was prompted to write this work by the following consideration:

I saw that the *Gemara* tells us things about the Mishnah that you could never deduce through logical analysis. For example, the *Gemara* will say, "This Mishnah is speaking about a specific circumstance," or, "There are certain words missing in this Mishnah, and it should be amended to read . . . ," or "This Mishnah is according to so-and-so whose opinion is such . . ." In addition, the *Gemara* adds words to the Mishnah or deletes words from it, and reveals the underlying reason of the Mishnah. By writing this commentary on the Mishnah I hoped to be helpful in four ways:

1. To give a clear interpretation of the Mishnah and explanation of its words. For if you would ask any of the great Sages for an explanation of a law in a Mishnah, he could not tell you a thing unless he knew the *Gemara* on that Mishnah by heart. Or he would tell you, "Let me look up what the *Gemara* has to say about this." Now, no one can know the entire *Gemara* by heart, and certainly not when the discussion of that particular law takes up four or five pages in the *Gemara*. There are so many intricacies, claims, rebuttals, questions, and answers that only an expert in analytical thought can extract a clear-cut decision from the *Gemara's* discussion of the Mishnah. Even such a person will find it difficult when it comes to decisions that are based on knowledge of two or three *masechtos.*

2. The second benefit of my commentary is that it will state the final decision. I will clearly tell you according to whose opinion each law was decided.

3. The third advantage is that it will serve as an introduction for any beginner to in-depth Talmudic analysis. He will

gather from it an approach of how to reduce a statement to its elements and assess its meaning. With the help of this system, the entire Talmud will become like an open book to him.

4. The fourth advantage is that it will help anyone who has mastered the Talmud to memorize it, so that whatever he has read will be permanently imprinted in his mind, and he will have the Mishnah and the *Gemara* at his fingertips.

As I imagined such a project, I took courage to carry out my plan. My primary goal is to clarify the Mishnah according to the *Gemara's* explanation, selecting only valid interpretations, staying away from explanations that the Talmud rejects. I will tell the underlying reasons that led to differences of opinion between the opposing parties, and I will state according to whom the law was decided as it is explained in the *Gemara*. I will make sure to be brief, in order not to confuse the reader. Our commentary is not meant to teach someone who is obstinate like stone, but to enlighten those who want to understand.

I decided to arrange my work along the lines of all commentators, that is, I will first copy the words of the Mishnah until the end of the law. Then I will discuss the explanation of that law in the way I described. I will then deal with the next law in the same way, and so, until the end of the Mishnah. Laws that are well known and whose meaning need no explanation, I will simply write down, and it will not be necessary to comment on it.

Let me point out that wherever the opinions of Beis Shammai and Beis Hillel are in conflict, the *Halachah* is decided according to Beis Hillel, with certain exceptions. Only in those cases will I make an exception and state that the *Halachah* follows Beis Shammai.

In the same way, the law is always decided according to an anonymous Mishnah in which there is no dispute, except in a few isolated cases. Again, only in those rare cases will I tell you that this anonymous Mishnah is rejected and is not the *Halachah*.

It is not necessary to deal at great length with other halachic disputes; I will immediately tell you according to which authority the law is decided. And even in a case where it is one individual's opinion against a majority, I will state that the *Halachah* is decided according to the majority.

May the Almighty show me the way to the truth, and steer me away from untruth.

Written with the help of God Who is uplifted and exalted.

Appendix

I have decided to include in this introduction ten sections relating to the Mishnah. However, they certainly are not quite as important as our primary subject. Still, anyone wishing to know the Mishnah thoroughly would do well to study these sections.

The first section deals with those Sages who are mentioned in the Mishnah, and in whose names the law is quoted.

The second section deals with those Sages who are mentioned in the Mishnah because they played a part in an incident, or because of a moral lesson that can be learned from them, or because of a homiletical explanation they gave to a verse.

The third section offers information about the hereditary status of the Sages in the Mishnah.

The fourth section tells you the chronological order of the Sages and which of the Sages of the Mishnah were contemporaries.

The fifth section identifies the Sages and their disciples.

The sixth section identifies the Sages whose names are vague and undefined.

The seventh section discusses the various titles the author of the Mishnah assigned to the Sages.

The eighth section discusses the various nicknames given to the Sages relating to country, occupation, people, or family.

The ninth section discusses the Sages who were involved in most of the disputes in the Mishnah.

The tenth section discusses the number of times a Sage is mentioned in the Mishnah.

SECTION ONE

Sages whose laws are quoted in the Mishnah. As we have said earlier, the author of the Mishnah began his list of the men involved in transmitting the Oral Law with Shimon HaTzaddik and his colleagues. The total number of Sages of the Mishnah whose names are associated with the laws, questions, enactments, and preventive measures adds up to ninety-one. They are:

1. Rabbi Eliezer ben Hyrkanos
2. Rabbi Eliezer ben Yaakov
3. Rabbi Eliezer son of Rabbi Yosei Hagelili
4. Rabbi Yehoshua ben Perachyah
5. Rabbi Yehoshua ben Chananiah
6. Rabbi Yehoshua ben Korchah
7. Rabbi Yehoshua ben Beseira
8. Rabbi Yehoshua ben Hyrkanos
9. Rabbi Eliezer ben Azariah
10. Rabbi Elazar ben Yehudah of Bartusa
11. Rabbi Elazar ben Rabbi Tzadok
12. Rabbi Elazar ben Shamua
13. Rabbi Elazar Chasma
14. Rabbi Elazar ben Parta
15. Rabbi Elazar ben Rabbi Shimon
16. Rabbi Elazar ben Pavi
17. Rabbi Yehudah ben Rabbi Ila'i
18. Rabbi Yehudah ben Beseira
19. Rabbi Yehudah ben Bava
20. Rabbi Yehudah ben Abba
21. Rabbi Yehudah ben Tabbai
22. Rabban Shimon ben Gamliel
23. Rabbi Shimon ben Yochai
24. Rabbi Shimon Hashezuri
25. Rabbi Shimon ben Nannas
26. Rabbi Shimon ben HaSegan
27. Shimon ben Shetach
28. Shimon HaTeimani
29. Rabbi Shimon ben Azzai
30. Rabbi Shimon ben Zoma
31. Rabbi Shimon ben Elazar
32. Rabbi Shimon ben Yehudah
33. Rabbi Shimon ben Beseira
34. Shimon achi Azariah
35. Rabbi Chanania Segan HaKohanim
36. Rabbi Chanina ben Antigonus
37. Rabbi Chaninah ben Chachina'i
38. Rabbi Chananiah ben Gamliel
39. Rabbi Nechunia ben Elchanan Ish K'far HaBavli

40. Rabbi Yishmael
41. Rabbi Nechemiah
42. Rabbi Nechemiah Ish K'far HaBavli
43. Rabbi Yochanan ben Nuri
44. Yochanan Kohein Gadol
45. Rabban Yochanan ben Zakkai
46. Rabbi Yochanan ben Beroka
47. Yochanan ben Gudgoda
48. Rabbi Yochanan HaSandler
49. Rabbi Yochanan ben Yashua, son of Rabbi Akiva's father-in-law
50. Rabbi Yosi
51. Rabbi Yosi ben Meshullam
52. Rabbi Yosi ben HaChoteif Efrasi
53. Rabbi Yosi HaGelili
54. Yosef ben Yo'ezer
55. Yosef ben Yochanan
56. Rabbi Yosi ben Rabbi Yehudah
57. Rabbi Yosi HaKohen
58. Yosi ben Choni
59. Rabban Gamliel
60. Rabbi Gamliel HaZaken
61. Dusta'i Ish K'far D'mai
62. Rabbi Dusta'i ben Rabbi Yannai
63. Abba Shaul
64. Rabbi Tarfon
65. Rabbi Meir
66. Rabbi Akiva
67. Rabbi Chutzpis
68. Rabbi Nassan
69. Nachum HaLavlar
70. Rabbi Miyasha
71. Rabbi Tzadok
72. Nachum HaMadi
73. Rabbi Dosa ben Hyrkanos
74. Rabbi Ila'i
75. Rabbi Kuvri
76. Rabbi Pappaias
77. Rabbi Masya ben Cheresh
78. Nitai HaArbeli
79. Shemayah
80. Avtalyon
81. Hillel

82. Shammai
83. Rabbi Zechariah ben HaKatzav
84. Admon
85. Chanan ben Avshalom
86. Rabbi Yadua HaBavli
87. Akavya ben Mehalalel
88. Rabbi Yakim Ish Chadid
89. Menachem ben Signa'i
90. Rabbi Yaakov

We have not listed these names in chronological order.

[This list contains only ninety names instead of ninety-one. The Rambam meant to say that including Rabbi Yehudah HaNasi, the compiler of the Mishnah, the number of Sages would total ninety-one.]

SECTION TWO

Sages mentioned in the Mishnah because they played a part in an incident, because of a moral lesson that can be learned from them, or because of a homiletic explanation they gave to a verse. Many Sages in the Mishnah are not associated with a law, but they are mentioned because of an incident that happened during their time, or because they taught moral lessons like those in *maseches Avos*. The number of Sages mentioned in the Mishnah for these or similar reasons amounts to thirty-seven:

1. Rabbi Yehoshua ben Levi
2. Rabbi Elazar Hakapar
3. Rabbi Elazar ben Arach
4. Rabbi Elazar Hamodai
5. Yehudah ben Teima
6. Rabbi Shimon ben Nesanel
7. Rabbi Shimon ben Akashya
8. Rabbi Shimon ben Chalafta
9. Chanina ben Dosa
10. Chanina ben Chizkiya ben Garon
11. Rabbi Chanania ben Teradyon
12. Rabbi Nechunia ben Hakanah
13. Rabbi Yishmael ben Pavi
14. Yochanan ben Hachoroni

15. Rabbi Yosi ben Rabbi Yehudah Ish K'far HaBavli
16. Rabbi Yosi ben Durmaskis
17. Rabban Gamliel, son of Rabbi Yehudah HaNasi
18. Rabbi Shimon Ish Hamitzpah
19. Choni Hame'ageil
20. Rabbi Hyrkanos
21. Rabbi Yannai
22. Rabbi Nehora'i
23. Antignos Ish Socho
24. Rabbi Chalafta Ish K'far Chanania
25. Rabbi Levitas Ish Yavneh
26. Rabbi Yonasan
27. Shmuel HaKatan
28. Ben Bag Bag
29. Ben Hei Hei
30. Eliho'eini ben Hakaf
31. Chanamel HaMitzri
32. Rabbi Shimon ben Menasia
33. Abba Shaul ben Botnis
34. Zechariah ben Kevutal
35. Bava ben Buta
36. Rabbi Yishmael son of Rabbi Yochanan ben Beroka
37. Rabbi Yishmael ben Rabbi Yosi

Here, too, I have not listed the names in chronological order.

Consequently, the total number of Sages mentioned in the Mishnah is 128. However, there are two names we have omitted: Elisha *Acher* (the Other), whom we did not count among the virtuous Sages because of his dishonorable conduct, which is well known, and Menachem, mentioned as a colleague of Shammai who was not listed because we found no place for him in any of the classifications we have created.

SECTION THREE

The hereditary status of the Sages of the Mishnah.
The Sages who were of noble birth:

Rabban Gamliel III, son of
Rabbi Yehudah HaNasi, son of
Rabban Shimon III, son of

Rabban Gamliel II of Yavneh, son of
Rabban Shimon II, son of
Rabban Gamliel the Elder, son of
Rabban Shimon I, son of,

Hillel HaNasi: this is the Hillel of Babylonia who was the leader of the assembly of later Sages who upheld his decisions and who were known as Beis Hillel.

Hillel himself was a descendant of Shefatya, son of Avital, who was the son of David. Therefore, these seven Sages issuing from Hillel are all descendants of King David.

Four of the Sages mentioned in the Mishnah are converts or descendants of converts to Judaism:

1. Shemayah
2. Avtalyon
3. Rabbi Akiva
4. Rabbi Meir

Some of the Sages were *kohanim:*

1. Shimon HaTzaddik, to whom the entire Oral Law can be traced, in fulfillment of the prophecy concerning *kohanim,* *"They shall teach your laws to Jacob"* (*Devarim* 33:10)
2. Rabbi Elazar ben Azariah, the tenth generation after Ezra
3. His uncle, Shimon, known as Shimon achi Azariah
4. Rabbi Elazar ben Shamua
5. Rabbi Chanania Segan HaKohanim
6. His son, Rabbi Shimon, known as Rabbi Shimon ben HaSegan
7. Yishmael ben Pavi
8. Yochanan Kohen Gadol
9. Rabbi Yochanan ben Zakkai
10. Yosi ben Yoezer
11. Rabbi Yosi HaKohen
12. Rabbi Tarfon
13. Eliho'eini ben Hakaf
14. Chanamel HaMitzri

The rest of the Sages were non-*kohanim* and, as far as I know, were not of prominent ancestry.

SECTION FOUR

The chronological order of the Sages in the Mishnah and which of the Sages were contemporaries are:

Shimon HaTzaddik and Rabbi Dosa ben Hyrkanos were contemporaries. Rabbi Dosa ben Hyrkanos lived an extremely long life, living into the generation of Rabbi Akiva. These two are known as the First-Generation Group.

The Second Generation Group comprised

Antignos Ish Socho and
Rabbi Elazar ben Charsom

The Third Generation Group comprised

Yosi ben Yoezer Ish Tzereidah and
Yosi ben Yochanan Ish Yerushalayim

The Fourth Generation Group comprised

Yochanan ben Mattisyah
Yehoshuah ben Perachyah and
Nitai Ha'arbeili

The Fifth Generation Group comprised

Choni HaMe'ageil
Eliho'eini ben Hakaf
Yehudah ben Tabbai and
Shimon ben Shetach

The Sixth Generation Group comprised

Akavya ben Mehalalel
Shemaya
Avtalyon
Admon and Chanon
Rabbi Myasha

The Seventh Generation Group comprised

Shammai

Hillel
Menachem
Yehudah ben Beseirah
Rabbi Pappias
Rabbi Yochanan ben Bag
Chanania ben Chizkiah ben Garon
Nechuniah ben Hakanah
Bava ben Buta
Rabbi Yochanan ben Hachoroni
Rabban Gamliel the Elder and
Nachum HaLavlar

These seven groups spanned the era beginning with the Second Beis Hamikdash, until its destruction. None of them saw its destruction.

[The Eighth Generation] witnessed the destruction. They comprised:

Rabbi Eliezer ben Yaakov
Rabbi Tzadok
Rabbi Eliezer, his son
Rabbi Yochanan ben Zakkai and his students
Rabbi Yishmael ben Elisha, the Kohen Gadol
Abba Shaul
Rabbi Elazar HaModa'i
Rabbi Chanina Segan HaKohanim
Rabban Gamliel
Rabbi Shimon, his son
Rabbi Chanina ben Antignos
Rabbi Chanina ben Dosa
Rabbi Chanina ben Teradyon
Shmuel Hakatan
Rabbi Elazar ben Parta
Rabbi Elazar ben Dama
Chanania ben Chachina'i
Rabbi Yehudah ben Abba

[The Ninth Generation, which was] the second generation after the Destruction, comprised:

Rabbi Tarfon
Rabbi Akiva
Rabbi Elazar ben Azariah

Rabbi Yishmael
Rabbi Yehoshua ben Korcha
Chanania Ish Ono
Shimon ben Nannas
Yochanan ben Baroka
Rabbi Yishmael, his son
Rabbi Yochanan ben Gudgoda
Rabbi Elazar Chasma
Rabbi Yehudah ben Teima

[The Tenth Generation Group, which was] the third generation of Tanna'im after the Destruction, comprised:

Rabbi Meir
Rabbi Yehudah ben Ila'i
Rabbi Yosi
Rabbi Nassan
Rabbi Yochanan HaSandler
Rabbi Yosi HaGelili
Rabbi Elazar ben Shamua
Shimon ben Azai
Shimon ben Zoma
Rabbi Chutzpis HaMeturgeman

[The Eleventh Generation Group, which was] the fourth generation of Tanna'im after the Destruction, comprised:

Rabbi Yehudah HaNasi
Rabban Gamliel III
Rabbi Shimon IV
Rabbi Shimon ben Yochai
Rabbi Elazar, his son
Rabbi Shimon ben Elazar
Rabbi Yishmael ben Rabbi Yosi and
Rabbi Yonasan

This group represents the last generation of Sages mentioned in the Mishnah.

SECTION FIVE

The Sages and their disciples.

1. In our opening remarks we indicated that Rabbi Yehudah HaNasi, the compiler of the Mishnah, was a disciple of his father. In the same way, each of his predecessors was the student of his father, going back to Hillel and further back to Shimon HaTzaddik.

2. Rabban Yochanan ben Zakkai was also a disciple of Hillel; he had five disciples:

Rabbi Eliezer ben Hyrkanos
Rabbi Yehoshua ben Chananiah
Rabbi Yosi HaKohen
Rabbi Shimon ben Nesanel and
Rabbi Elazar ben Arach

This is the group that was assured of life in the World to Come for themselves and their disciples, as it says in the Talmud (*Chagigah* 14).

3. Rabbi Akiva was the disciple of Rabbi Eliezer ben Hyrkanos, his primary teacher. Rabbi Akiva also studied with Rabbi Tarfon for a short time, but as a colleague rather than a student. However, Rabbi Akiva would respect Rabbi Tarfon and address him as "Rabbi," while Rabbi Tarfon would address Rabbi Akiva simply as "Akiva." Rabbi Akiva's esteem of Rabbi Tarfon can be seen in the fact that Rabbi Akiva said, "Allow me to review before you something you have taught me." (*Sifra* 4)

4. Rabbi Meir and Rabbi Shimon ben Yochai were disciples of Rabbi Akiva, who was their primary teacher. Rabbi Meir also studied under Rabbi Yishmael and others (*Eiruvin 13a*).

5. Rabbi Yehudah ben Ila'i studied mainly under Rabbi Elazar ben Azariah.

6. Whenever it says in the Mishnah "This Rabbi said in the name of That Rabbi," it means that the former was a student of the latter, and that is why he received the statement from him.

7. Rabbi Yehudah HaNasi received part of his instruction studying under Rabbi Elazar ben Shamua (*Yevamos* 84a).

8. Sumchus was a disciple of Rabbi Meir. After Rabbi Meir's death, Sumchus planned to study under Rabbi Yehudah, but his plan did not materialize.

SECTION SIX

The following are Sages whose names are vague and undefined.

1. If the Mishnah mentions a Sage simply as "Rabbi Eliezer" without any further identification, it refers to Rabbi Eliezer ben Hyrkanos, a disciple of Rabban Yochanan ben Zakkai.

2. "Rabbi Yehoshua" without any further identification refers to Rabbi Yehoshua ben Chanania, a student of Rabban Yochanan ben Zakkai.

3. "Rabbi Yehudah" without further qualification refers in the Mishnah to Rabbi Yehudah ben Ila'i. It is he whom the Talmud has in mind when it says, "An incident happened with a certain *chasid*," for he was known by that title.

4. "Rabbi Elazar" without further identification, refers to Rabbi Elazar ben Shamua HaKohen, who lived in Rabban Gamliel's generation. It was his disciples who refused to allow Rabbi Yehudah HaNasi to give a lecture in their Beis Midrash (*Yevamos* 84a).

5. "Rabbi Shimon," simply stated, refers to Rabbi Shimon ben Yochai, a disciple of Rabbi Akiva, whose episode involving a Roman Caesar is well known. [After making an unflattering remark about the Roman government, Rabbi Shimon ben Yocha'i was condemned to death. He hid in a cave for twelve years, emerging only after the Caesar's death (*Shabbos* 33b).]

6. "Rabbi Elazar ben Rabbi Shimon" refers to Rabbi Shimon ben Yocha'i's son (*Shabbos* 33b).

7. "Ben Azzai, Ben Zoma, Ben Nannas" refers to Shimon ben Azzai, Shimon ben Zoma, and Shimon ben Nannas.

8. "Ben Beseira" refers to Rabbi Yehoshua ben Beseira.

9. "Ben Bag Bag" refers to Rabbi Yochanan ben Bag Bag.

10. "Yochanan Kohen Gadol" is the famous Yochanan ben Mattisyahu who is mentioned in our prayers when we give thanks for our victory over the Greek rulers [*Al HaNissim* on Chanukah].

11. Rabbi Meir and Rabbi Nassan once wanted to embarrass Rabban Shimon, the father of Rabbi Yehudah HaNasi (because of an incident that is too involved to be mentioned here). Thereupon, Rabban Gamliel denied them entry into his yeshivah (*Horayos* 13b). Therefore, when a *Halachah* was quoted in the name of Rabbi Meir, they would quote it as "others

say . . ." If it was quoted in Rabbi Nassan's name they would quote it as "some say . . ."

12. When Rabbi Yehudah HaNasi says in the Mishnah, "A certain disciple said before Rabbi Akiva, in the name of Rabbi Yishmael," that is *his* way of referring to Rabbi Meir (*Eiruvin* 13a).

13. "The learned ones said before the Sages . . ." refers to five scholars:

Rabbi Shimon ben Azzai
Rabbi Shimon ben Zoma
Rabbi Shimon ben Nannas
Chanan, and
Chananiah Ish Ono

14. Rabbi Meir is also called Rabbi Nehora'i. Both names have the same meaning (brilliant light). His original name was Rabbi Nechemiah.

15. When the Mishnah refers to *Chachamim,* "Sages," it sometimes is referring to one of the personalities we mentioned earlier, and sometimes it means the entire body of Sages; sometimes the *Gemara* explains who is meant by asking, "Who is meant by the term *'chachamim'* "? And the *Gemara* will answer, "Rabbi so-and-so." This will happen if that particular Sage's opinion was accepted by many. Therefore, he is referred to as *chachamim,* although it was the opinion of only one individual.

16. When the Mishnah mentions Beis Shammai and Beis Hillel [House of Shammai and House of Hillel], it refers to the group that followed Shammai's or Hillel's opinion, because a person's students are his household.

17. The title "Rebbi" refers to Rabbeinu HaKadosh, our holy teacher, Rabbi Yehudah HaNasi, the sixth in lineage after Hillel the Elder. He is the compiler of the Mishnah.

18. Wherever it says in the Mishnah, *"Be'emes ameru*—In truth they said . . . ,"* it signifies *Halachah leMoshe miSinai.*

19. An anonymous Mishnah contains one of the following:

a. A derived law that the full body of Sages unanimously agreed on or
b. That which the full body of the Sages received from the Sages that came before it, as a law handed down generation

after generation from Moshe. The last Sage in the line of transmission before Rabbi Yehudah HaNasi was Rabbi Meir, and
that is what is meant by the phrase, "An anonymous Mishnah
is by Rabbi Meir."

c. Some of the anonymous *mishnayos* may reflect Rabbi Meir's
individual view, with which others disagree or

d. It may be by someone other than Rabbi Meir, whom the
Gemara will identify.

When in my commentary, I will record the final *Halachah*, it
will become clear which of the above alternatives is the case in each
Mishnah.

SECTION SEVEN

This deals with the various titles the author of the Mishnah assigned to each of the Sages.

Rabbi Yehudah HaNasi classified the 128 Sages mentioned
in the Mishnah into three categories. Those whom he ranked
highest in eminence he simply called by their name. For example,
he refers to Hillel and Shammai, to Shemaya and Avtalyon by their
name and nothing else. He does this because of their towering
greatness, since it was impossible to find a suitable title to express
their magnificent stature, just as we give no accolades to the
prophets.

Those Sages who, in his judgment, were below that level he
gave the title "Rabban." For example, he speaks of *Rabban* Gamliel
and *Rabban* Yochanan ben Zakkai.

Those who, in his opinion, were below this latter level, he
gave the title "Rabbi," like *Rabbi* Meir and *Rabbi* Yehudah. He
also called men on this level by the title *"Abba"* (Father), like
Abba Shaul.

Sometimes he omits a title, without any particular reason,
such as when he refers to Shimon Achi Azariah and Elazar Ish
Bartosa.

Those personalities who are called simply by their names out
of honor, and who therefore have no titles before their names are:

Shimon HaTzaddik
Antignos Ish Socho

Yosi ben Yoezer
Yosi ben Yochanan
Yochanan Kohen Gadol
Yehoshua ben Perachyah
Nitai HaArbeili
Choni HaMe'ageil
Eliho'eini ben Hakaf
Chanamel HaMitzri
Yehudah ben Tabbai
Shimon ben Shetach
Sh'mayah
Avtalyon
Chanan
Admon
Akavya ben Mehalalel
Hillel
Shammai
Nachum HaLavlar
Chananiah ben Chizkiah ben Garon
Bava ben Buta

Anyone mentioned in the Mishnah by his name alone, besides those in the above list, does have a title, but it has been omitted by Rabbi Yehudah HaNasi for no particular reason.

SECTION EIGHT

The various nicknames relating to country of origin, occupation, people, and family.

The compiler of the Mishnah added various nicknames to the names of the transmitters of the Oral Law. Some of these have to do with their trade, such as Nachum HaLavlar, "the scribe," and Rabbi Shimon HaShezuri, "the spinner of threads."

Others he connected to their native lands, such as Ish Chadid [the man from Chadid], Ish Ono, and Ish Bartosa. The meaning of the nicknames Ish Tzereida [the personality of Tzereida], Ish Yerushalayim, and other common places is that he is the outstanding citizen of that place.

Others have their father's or brother's name added to their name, such as "This Rabbi ben [the son of] That Rabbi" or "This Rabbi achi [the brother of] That Rabbi." This happens very often.

And some were identified by their family status, such a "So-and-so the Kohen."

SECTION NINE

This deals with the Sages who were involved in most of the disputes in the Mishnah.

Those personalities who most often are involved in disputes in the Mishnah are:

Rabbi Meir
Rabbi Yehudah (ben Ila'i)
Rabbi Shimon (ben Yocha'i) and
Rabbi Yosi (ben Chalafta)

Controversies arise between any two in this group, and also among all four of them.

You will also find Rabbi Elazar disagreeing with any one of those four, but not as often as there are conflicts among these four.

The same is true for

Rabbi Akiva
Rabbi Eliezer and
Rabbi Yehoshua (ben Chanania)

You may find disputes between any two of them and among all three of them, but not as often as between the above-mentioned four.

You will find disagreements also among

Rabbi Akiva
Rabbi Yishmael
Rabbi Tarfon and
Rabbi Elazar ben Azariah

but fewer than among those mentioned above.

Fewer still are the disputes between Beis Shammai and Beis Hillel.

Fewer yet are the conflicts between Rabban Gamliel or Rabban Shimon ben Gamliel and Rebbi, and each one of the Sages mentioned above.

It is among these men that every dispute occurs in the majority of the Mishnah, with the exception of rare instances.

SECTION TEN

The number of times a Sage is mentioned in the Mishnah.

Some of the Sages who received the Oral Law have many laws quoted in their names, such as Rabbi Meir and Rabbi Yehudah. Others have only a few recorded in their names, for example, Rabbi Elazar ben Yaakov, as the Sages said, "The Mishnah of Rabbi Eliezer ben Yaakov is small but good" (*Eiruvin* 62b), meaning his legal opinions are few in number, but we accept his decisions.

The more often a person is involved in disputes, the more often his name will be quoted in the Mishnah.

Some of the Sages are mentioned only once in the Mishnah, and their names never occur again in connection with any legal matter.

There are thirty-seven such Sages:

    1. Nachum HaLavlar and
    2. Rabbi Miyasha are mentioned only in *maseches Pei'ah* (1:6), and their names never occur again elsewhere.
    3. Chananiah ben Chachina'i and
    4. Rabbi Yosef ben Hachotef Efrasi, in *Kilayim* (3:7 and 4:8) only.
    5. Rabbi Elazar Chisma and
    6. Rabbi Yosi ben Meshullam in *Terumos* (3:5; 4:8) only.
    7. Rabbi Chutzpis in *Shevi'is* (10:6) only.
    8. Rabbi Elazar ben Yehudah Ish Bartosa and
    9. Dusta'i Ish K'far Demai, in *Orlah* (1:4; 2:5) only.
    10. Nachum Hamadi in *Shabbos* (2:1) only.
    11. Rabbi Ila'i and
    12. Rabbi Dusta'i bar Rabbi Yannai, in *Eiruvin* (2:6; 5:4) only.
    13. Rabbi Shimon ben HaSegan, and
    14. ben Kovri, in *Shekalim* (1:4; 8:5) only.
    15. Yehudah ben Tabbai
    16. Shimon ben Shetach
    17. Yosi ben Yoezer
    18. Yosi ben Yochanan
    19. Nitai HaArbeli and

20. Yehoshua ben Perachyah in *Chagigah* (2:2) only.
21. Shimon HaTeimani and
22. Nechemiah Ish Beis D'li, in *Yevamos* (4:13; 16:7) only.
23. Rabbi Elazar, son of Rabbi Yosi HaGelili and
24. Rabbi Yehoshua ben Hyrkanos in *Sotah* (5:3–5) only.
25. Yadua HaBavli in *Bava Metzia* (7:9) only.
26. Rabbi Shimon ben Yehudah in *Shavuos* (1:5) only.
27. Rabbi Shimon ben Beseira
28. Rabbi Nechuniah ben Elnasan Ish K'far HaBavli,
29. Rabbi Yosi HaKohen
30. Rabbi Yakim Ish Chadid and
31. Menachem ben Segana'i are mentioned in *Eiduyos* (6:2; 7:5–8; 8:1–2) only.
32. Shimon achi Azariah and
33. Yosi ben Choni in *Zevachim* (1:2) only.
34. Rabbi Elazar ben Rabbi Shimon in *Temurah* (4:4) only
35. Rabbi Yaakov in *Nega'im* (4:10), only.
36. Rabbi Elazar ben Pavi in *Tehoros* (7:9), only.
37. Rabbi Yochanan ben Yashua, son of Rabbi Akiva's father-in-law, in *Yadayim* (3:5), only.

All the Sages in this list have only one single *Halachah* in the entire Mishnah quoted in their name, in the *masechta* we indicated.
This completes our Introduction to the Mishnah.

•4•

Shemonah Perakim
The Eight Chapters

An Introduction to the Ethics of the Fathers

Introduction

We explained in the *Introduction to the Commentary on the Mishnah* why Rabbi Yehudah HaNassi, the compiler of the Mishnah, placed *Avos* (The Tractate of the Fathers) in *Seder Nezikin*. We also mentioned the great benefit that can be derived from this small Tractate, and we promised a more lengthy discussion of the Tractate's important points.

Although the contents of this Tractate seem clear and apparently easy to understand and carry out, the matter is not so simple. What the Tractate speaks of can lead to perfection and happiness; yet, not all of its points can be understood without a detailed commentary. Because the subject is so important and so complex, I think it requires my discussing it at some length.

Our Rabbis have said, "Whoever wants to be pious should practice the ethical teachings of Tractate Avos" (*Bava Kama* 30a). The only thing that ranks higher than piety is prophecy, and piety is what paves the way to prophecy, as our Rabbis said, "Piety leads to *ruach hakodesh* (holy inspiration)."

From these words of the Rabbis, it is clear that fulfilling the teachings of this Tractate can bring one to the level of prophecy. Later, I will explain the truth of this statement because it is the basis of a number of ethical principles.

I think it advisable to preface my commentary on Tractate Avos with a few helpful chapters that will introduce the reader to the subject and provide a key to my commentary. Let me note, however, that the ideas or explanations I will be presenting in these pages are not my own. Rather I have derived them from the Rabbis cited in the Midrash and the Talmud, from the writings of other Jewish sages, from the words of ancient and current philosophers, and from the works of various authors, accepting the truth from anyone who has stated it.

Sometimes, I quote an author word for word without naming the writer. In these instances I am not presenting someone else's writings as my own, since I have just acknowledged that my writings are based on numerous sources. I do not interrupt my text to say, "so-and-so said," because that would add unnecessary wordiness. Also, the mention of the author might cause an unintelligent person to dismiss the statement itself as inaccurate and wrong.[1] Therefore, because my aim is to serve the reader and to explain the thoughts hidden in this Tractate, I prefer not to mention sources.

I will now begin the introductory chapters, which I call, *Shemonah Perakim, The Eight Chapters.*

---

[1]Rabbi Shem Tov ibn Falquiera, a student of the Rambam, explains in the introduction to his work, *Hama'alos,* that the Rambam had in mind unlearned people who would not understand his quoting non-Jewish philosophers.

Chapter One

The Human Soul and Its Powers

You must understand that the human soul is a single entity that has many different activities. Indeed, some of these activities have themselves been called souls, which has led people to think that man has many souls. Physicians, for example, believe in this multiplicity, and the most prominent among them[2] states in the introduction to his book that there are three souls: the physical, the vital, and the psychological.

The activities of the soul have also been called *powers* or *parts*, and the phrase *parts of the soul* is a common expression that is often used by philosophers. However, when philosophers speak of parts, they do not mean that the soul is actually divided into sections like the parts of bodies. They merely enumerate the soul's different activities as aspects of a whole that together constitute the soul.

You should know that the improvement of character traits results from healing the soul and its activities. The physician who attempts to cure the human body must be thoroughly familiar with the anatomy and physiology of the body. He must know what causes sickness and should be avoided, and he must know what will cure a patient and should be pursued. Similarly, a healer of the soul who wants to improve a person's character traits must understand the complete soul and its parts. He must know what makes it ill and what can restore it to health.

Therefore I begin by enumerating the powers and parts of the soul.

---

[2]Hippocrates (c. 460–377 B.C.E.), a Greek physician of antiquity who is regarded as the father of medical science.

THE FIVE POWERS OF THE SOUL

The soul has five powers: the nutritive or growth power; the power of feeling, the power of imagination, the power of desire, and the power of reasoning.

Remember that what we say applies only to the human soul; for the nutritive power by which man is fed is not the same as that of a donkey or a horse. Man is sustained by the nutritive power of the human soul; a donkey is fed by the nutritive power of its donkey soul, and an eagle thrives on the nutritive power of its eagle soul. Although we use the term *nutritive power* for all of these beings, the meaning is not quite the same. In the same way, we apply the term *feeling* indiscriminately to both man and beast, but we do not mean to imply that the feeling of one species is the same as that of another. Each species has its own specific soul that is distinct from every other. As a result, each soul produces activities that are uniquely its own. It is possible that an activity of one soul may seem similar to that of another, so that one may think that both are the same. But this is not so.

By way of analogy, let us imagine that three dark places are differently illuminated: one from the sun, the second from the moon, and the third from a lamp. There is light in each of these places, but there is sunlight in only one. The second has moonlight, and the third has lamplight. So it is with feelings and their causes. In man, feelings are aroused in the human soul; in the donkey, feelings arise in the soul of the donkey, and in the eagle, in the soul of the eagle. These feelings have nothing in common, except that the same term is used for all. Remember this point because it is very important. It is a concept that has been a stumbling block to many philosophers, and has led to erroneous ideas and false conclusions.[3]

THE NUTRITIVE POWER

Returning to the subject of the powers of the soul, I want to say that the nutritive power consists of:

The power of providing nourishment to all parts of the body
The power to retain the food until it is digested

---

[3]One such erroneous belief is that man has no superiority over beast.

The digestion of food
The expulsion of waste substances
The growth and development of the human body
The power of reproduction
The separation of the nutritive juices necessary to sustain life
from the substances that must be expelled

A detailed discussion of these seven features belongs to the science of medicine. In the context of our discussion there is no need to elaborate on their nature and describe how they operate: in which parts of the body they appear, where they are always present,[4] and which disappear after a certain time.[5]

THE POWER OF FEELING

The power of feeling can be enumerated as the five familiar senses of sight, hearing, taste, smell, and touch. Unlike the other four senses, the sense of touch exists over the surface of the entire body; it is not restricted to any specific organ.

THE POWER OF IMAGINATION

Imagination is the power by which one retains impressions that have been received by the mind, after they have vanished from the receptor senses. By means of his imagination, man connects some impressions and separates others. In so doing, he creates new ideas out of images that are stored in his memory, and dreams up visions he has never heard of and could not possibly have perceived. For example, a person may imagine: an iron ship sailing through the air, a man whose head reaches up to heaven and whose feet stand on the ground, an animal with a thousand eyes. Many other such impossible things may all be inventions of man's imagination or fantasies of his dreams. It is in this regard that the Mutakallimun[6]

---

[4]The nourishing functions are ever-present.

[5]The functions of growth and procreation exist for a limited period of time.

[6]The Mutakallimun were a sect of Arab philosophers who tried to harmonize Moslem theology with Aristotelian philosophy. *Kalam* is Ara-

made a serious and disgraceful error. Their false theories form the cornerstone of a philosophy that divides the world into the *necessary,* the *possible,* and the *impossible.* The Mutakallimun believe, or have led others to believe,[7] that everything a person imagines is possible. They do not realize that human imagination has the power to ascribe an existence to things that could never exist.

THE POWER OF DESIRE

The power of desire is the faculty by which a person either intensely desires or detests something. This power motivates man to do all in his power to obtain what is desired or reject what he loathes. The power of desire helps him select what he likes and avoid what he dislikes by stimulating feelings of anger and affection, fear and courage, cruelty and compassion, love and hate in response to various situations. These emotions are then actualized by various parts of the body. For instance, the hand grasps what is desired, the foot walks away from what is despised, the eye lingers on what is adored and avoids what is not pleasing, the heart encourages bravery or contributes to faint-heartedness. Similarly, all parts of the body, whether external or internal, are instruments of the power of desire.

THE POWER OF REASONING

The power of reasoning is peculiar to man. It enables him to understand, consider, and acquire knowledge of the sciences, and to distinguish between good and evil. Some of the functions of the power of reasoning are practical, while others are theoretical. The practical functions, in turn, are either mechanical or intellectual. Through his theoretical power, man knows things as they really are; these are the sciences, which by their very nature are unyield-

---

bic for word, and *Mutakallimun* means sages of the word. In *Moreh Nevuchim* (*The Guide of the Perplexed*) I:71–76, the Rambam vehemently opposes their views and methods.

[7]It is possible that they themselves did not believe this concept, but they led others to believe it through their writings.

ing to his changes.[8] Man's mechanical power is his aptitude to learn a trade or a craft, such as carpentry, farming, medicine, or seamanship. The intellectual power is the faculty by which a person reflects on something he intends to do, and weighs whether it can be done. When he decides that it is feasible, he ponders how it should be done.

I think this is all that needs to be said here about the soul.

THE FORM OF THE SOUL

You should recognize that man's soul, this single entity whose powers and parts we have described, may be compared to matter, and that the power of reasoning is its completed form. As long as the soul lies dormant and does not acquire its form from knowledge, then the nature of the soul is useless and exists in vain. Solomon said, *"A soul without knowledge is surely not good"* (Mishlei 19:2). This means that if a soul has not attained its form and remains without intelligence, its existence is not a good one. But this is not the place for a discussion of the subjects of form, substance, intellect, various kinds of knowledge and how to acquire them, and it is not necessary for what we want to say about the subject of ethics. This discussion is more appropriate to *The Book of Prophecy*, which I mention elsewhere.

Now I end this chapter and begin the next.

---

[8]These include such natural phenomena as the planets, stars, and galaxies, or the laws of nature as they affect man's existence on earth.

Chapter Two

Identification of the Powers of the Soul That Are the Source of Good and Evil Character Traits

TRANSGRESSIONS AND COMMANDMENTS

Rebellion against the laws of the Torah or obedience to its commandments is rooted in only two of the five powers of the soul: the power of feeling and the power of desire. These two powers alone are the source of all transgressions and commandments.

The nutritive power and the power of imagination are not implicated in a person's performing a commandment or committing a transgression because man has no control over these powers and cannot influence them. In other words, man cannot consciously suspend their functions[9] or curtail any of their activities. Proof of this is that the functions of both the nutritive and the imaginative powers continue even during sleep,[10] which is not true of any other powers of the soul.

Regarding the power of reasoning, there is some disagreement among the philosophers,[11] but I say that commandments and transgressions may also originate in the power of reasoning. Thus, for example, a person who believes in a false doctrine commits a transgression, and one who accepts a true principle [like the existence of Hashem] fulfills a commandment. But the belief by itself does not result in an action, and the term mitzvah or transgression

---

[9]The powers of nutrition and imagination are involuntary functions that are beyond man's control.

[10]When a person is asleep, the power of nutrition continues to contribute to the processes of growth and digestion, while the power of imagination produces the person's dreams.

[11]It is unclear whether concrete mitzvos and transgressions can be related to abstract thought and belief.

refers generally to an act. Therefore I can say that only the powers of feeling and of desire result in transgressions and commandments.

VIRTUES AND VICES

As far as the virtues are concerned, there are two kinds: moral[12] and intellectual,[13] with the corresponding classes of vices.

The intellectual virtues, which are part of the soul's reasoning power, include: wisdom, which is the knowledge of the direct and indirect causes, and reason, which consists of (1) inborn, theoretical reason, or axioms,[14] (2) acquired intellect,[15] which we need not discuss here, and (3) brilliance, the ability to understand a subject and grasp an idea quickly or even immediately. The vices connected with this power of the soul are the opposites of these virtues.

Moral virtues belong only to the power of desire. In this connection, the power of feeling acts merely as a helper.[16] A great many virtues are implicit in this power: prudence, by which I mean fear of sin; generosity; honesty; modesty; tolerance; contentedness, which the Sages call wealth, as when they say, "Who is wealthy? He who is happy with his lot" (*Avos* 4:1); courage; faithfulness; and other similar virtues. The vices of this power are revealed when one goes to extremes of too much or too little.

Regarding the powers of nutrition and imagination, you cannot say that they have vices or virtues. All that can be said of them is

---

[12]These include contentment, self-control, generosity, modesty, and the like.

[13]These include wisdom, insight, and discernment.

[14]These fundamental principles are, literally, first impressions. They need no proof and are explained by common sense, for example: two is more than one, the whole is greater than a part, and two things equal to the same thing are equal to each other.

[15]This aspect of reason is acquired through study, self-training, and diligence.

[16]The eye, seeing the distress of a poor man, stirs the soul to compassion and the body to assistance. The ear, hearing the pleas of unfortunate people, prompts the heart to bravery, which drives the individual to rescue the unfortunates from their oppressors speedily. Conversely, when the eye sees a tempting but forbidden object, the heart generates the desire, and the body hurries to fulfill it by committing the transgression.

that they work properly or improperly. For example, you can say that a person's digestion is good or bad, or that one's imagination is confused or clear. This does not mean, however, that these powers have virtues or vices.

That is all I wanted to discuss in this chapter.

Chapter Three

Diseases of the Soul

THE SICK SOUL

The early philosophers said that the soul, like the body, may be healthy or sick. The soul is healthy when its condition and that of its powers is such that it always does what is right and acts properly. The soul is sick when its condition and that of its powers is such that it always does what is wrong and acts improperly.

The science of medicine studies the health of the body. People who are physically ill have distorted tastes and, therefore, think that bitter things taste sweet and sweet things bitter. They imagine that wholesome things are unwholesome, and they have a rapacious appetite and a lust for things such as dust and coal, as well as for very sharp and sour foods, which healthy people loathe and reject because they do not enjoy them and may even find them harmful. In the same way, people whose souls are sick—wicked and corrupt people—think that evil is good and that good is evil.[17] A wicked man constantly craves excess, which is harmful, but he believes it is beneficial because of the illness of his soul.

HEALERS OF THE SOUL

When people who are unfamiliar with the science of medicine realize that they are sick, they consult a physician who tells them what they must do. He warns them not to eat certain things they mistakenly consider to be beneficial, and he prescribes things that they may find unpleasant and bitter. He does this so that their bodies may return to health and they will again choose the good and despise the bad.

---

[17]Compare, "Ah, those who call evil good and good evil; who present darkness as light and light as darkness" (Isaiah 5:20).

Similarly, people whose souls become ill should consult the Sages, who are healers of the soul and will caution them not to indulge in evils that they mistakenly believe are good. In this manner, which I will discuss more fully in the following chapter, they may be cured by the art that heals man's moral qualities. However, if a person who is morally sick does not realize that he is sick but imagines that he is well, or if he is aware that he is sick but does not try to get healed, then his end will be the same as the person who suffers from a physical ailment and who continues to indulge himself and does not seek a cure. He will surely die.

Those who know that they are sick, but nevertheless indulge in their pleasures, are accurately described in the Torah. The pleasure seeker says, *"I will follow my heart's desires. Let me add some moisture to the dry"* (Devarim 29:18), meaning that he intends to satisfy his thirst, [by satisfying his lusts], but thereby intensifies it.

A person who does not realize that he is sick is portrayed by King Solomon, *"The way of a fool is right in his own eyes; but the wise man accepts advice"* (Mishlei 12:15)." Solomon is saying that the one who listens to the advice of the Sage is wise, for the Sage teaches the way that is truly right, not the path that the person wrongly sees as right. Solomon also says, *"A road may seem right to a man, but in the end it is a road to death"* (Mishlei 14:12). Again, regarding those who are morally ill and do not know what is harmful or beneficial, Solomon says, *"The way of the wicked is all darkness; they do not know what will make them stumble"* (Mishlei 4:19).

I will deal with the art of healing the soul in the next chapter.

Chapter Four

Curing Diseases of the Soul

THE MIDDLE ROAD

Good deeds are balanced deeds, occupying a middle ground between two equally bad extremes: *too much,* excess[18] and *too little,* insufficiency.[19]

Virtues are character traits, both inborn and acquired, that lie midway between the two extremes of excess and insufficiency.[20] Good deeds are the direct result of these character traits.

To illustrate: Self-control lies midway between intemperate passion and a total absence of feeling for worldly enjoyment. Self-control is proper behavior, and the character trait that engenders self-control is an ethical one. But immoderate passion, which is at one extreme, and the total absence of feeling for worldly pleasure, at the other extreme, are equally deplorable. The character traits from which these two extremes result—intemperate passion from immoderation and absence of feeling from insensibility—are morally imperfect qualities.

---

[18]An example of excess is a person who squanders his money.

[19]An example of insufficiency is a miser.

[20]The Rambam derived his doctrine of the middle road (also called the Golden Mean) from the Torah, the Prophets, and the Sages of blessed memory, as presented in this discourse. We read in Tanach, for example, *"Do not swerve to the right or the left; keep your feet from evil"* (Mishlei 4:27); *"Do not overdo goodness and don't act the wise man to excess, or you may be dumbfounded. Do not overdo wickedness . . ."* (Koheles 7:16,17); *"Give me neither poverty nor riches, but provide me with my daily bread"* (Mishlei 30:8). The Sages say, "The ways of the Torah may be compared to two roads, one of fire, the other of snow. If the traveler veers to one side, he will be burned to death; if he veers to the other, he will perish in the snow. What is he to do? Let him take the middle road" (*Yerushalmi Chagigah,* 1,1 and *Tosefta Chagigah,* 2).

Similarly, generosity is the middle road between stinginess and wastefulness; courage, between recklessness and cowardice; dignity, between haughtiness and boorishness. Dignity is when one carries himself honorably and does not debase himself, haughtiness is when one seeks honor more than is deserved, boorishness is when one does things that are unbecoming. Friendliness is the middle road between aggressiveness and submissiveness.[21] Humility is the middle course between conceit and self-abasement; contentedness, between greed and laziness; and goodheartedness, between meanness and extravagance. A goodhearted man is one who is intent on doing good to others, providing personal assistance, advice, and money to the best of his ability, but without harming or disgracing himself. This is the middle road. The mean man, at one extreme does not want to help others, even if he himself will not suffer any loss, hardship, or damage through his generosity. The extravagant man, on the other hand, goes to extremes of generosity, even to the extent of personal damage, disgrace, hardship, and loss.

Tolerance is the middle course between anger and indifference. Sensitivity is the middle course between arrogance and timidness. According to our Sages, "A timid person cannot learn" (*Avos* 2:6); they did not say, "A sensitive person cannot learn." They also said, "The sensitive one goes to the Garden of Eden" (*Avos* 5:24) and did not say, "The timid one goes to the Garden of Eden." Therefore, I have made sensitivity the desirable mean and timidness the deplorable extreme. It is the same with the other qualities. We need to define them in terms that everyone agrees on, so that these ideas are clearly understood.

MISCONCEPTIONS

Frequently, people misconstrue these qualities. They think that one of the extremes is good and is a virtue. Sometimes they consider excess a virtue, believing, for example, that daring is noble and people who recklessly risk their lives are heroes. When people see an extremely foolhardy man deliberately run toward danger and

---

[21]The Rambam here uses an old Spanish word that means passivity. This trait stems from indifference and lethargy and is the opposite of aggressiveness, which stems from nervousness and hotheadedness.

intentionally risk his life, escaping only by chance, they praise him to the skies and call him a hero. At other times, the extreme of insufficiency is considered good, and people will say of an apathetic fellow that he is slow to anger or that a lazy man is happy with his lot. A man who is so unemotional that he feels no joy is acclaimed a scrupulous and pious person. In the same way, lavish spending and profuse generosity are wrongly extolled as excellent qualities. This is all a mistake. What should really be praised is the middle road. This is the course that each person should follow, always weighing his actions carefully so that he may achieve the proper middle road.

THE CURE FOR THE DISEASES OF THE SOUL

Good as well as faulty character traits can only be acquired or become embedded in the soul if one repeatedly practices the acts that result from these character traits over a long period of time. If these acts are good, the person acquires a virtue, but if they are bad, the person has a vice.[22] However, no one is born with innate virtues or vices, as I shall explain in Chapter Eight, and everyone's conduct from childhood on is undoubtedly influenced by the behavior of relatives and countrymen.

This being so, a person may have a healthy soul from having followed the middle course in conduct. It is also possible that his actions may be leaning toward one extreme or the other, as we have discussed, in which case his soul is diseased. If that is so, he should seek a cure, just as he would if he were sick in his body. When the balance of one's physical health is disturbed, we must determine which way it is leaning in order to force it in the opposite direction until it returns to its proper condition. When it is straightened, we stop the treatment and feed the patient food that will maintain a physical balance. We must use exactly the same method to adjust an individual's moral equilibrium.

As an illustration, let us take the case of a man who has the trait of stinginess and uses it to deny himself every enjoyment in life. This is a defect of the soul that will result in immoral acts, as we explained. If we want to cure this sick man, it is not enough to order

---

[22]As the Sages put it, "Once a person has committed a sin and repeated it, it becomes to him a permitted act" (*Yoma*, 86b).

him to practice generosity; that would be as ineffective as a physician trying to cure a patient who is consumed by burning fever with mild medicines, which would not serve the purpose at all. Instead, we must encourage the miser to spend his money liberally, over and over again, until the tendency that brought on his avarice has totally disappeared. Then, when he reaches the point of almost becoming a spendthrift, we must put a stop to his wasteful spending and order him to continue with acts of generosity, watching him carefully all the while to make sure that he does not lapse either into extravagance or stinginess.

On the other hand, if a person is a spendthrift, we must order him to save money and repeat acts of miserliness. It is not necessary, however, for him to perform acts of avarice as many times as the stingy man should perform acts of wasteful spending. This novel idea, which is an established rule and secret of the science of healing the soul, tells us that it is easier for a spendthrift to become a generous donor than it is for a miser to adopt the habit of generosity. Likewise, it is easier for a person who is indifferent to pleasure to become pious and abstain from sin than it is for a man burning with passion to curb his desires. Therefore, the pleasure-seeker must be induced to practice restraint more than the indifferent man should be persuaded to indulge his passions. Similarly, the coward must be exposed to danger more frequently than the reckless man should be forced to practice restraint. The mean man needs to practice kindness to a greater degree than the overly generous person must practice meanness. This is a fundamental rule of the science of healing faulty character traits.

THE WAY OF THE PIOUS

Pious men did not keep their character traits exactly on a even keel but rather let them swing to excess or to insufficiency, as a precaution and a protection against becoming too much of either. So, for example, in practicing abstinence, they would swing toward excessive denial of all pleasures; when it came to bravery, they would tend to recklessness; their generosity would border on lavishness; their modesty tended to self-effacing humility, and so on. This is what the Rabbis hinted at when they said, "Do more than the strict letter of the law demands" (*Bava Metzia* 35a).

When some of these pious men occasionally went to an extreme by fasting, staying up all night, refraining from eating meat and drinking wine, abstaining from marital relations, wearing woolen and hairy garments, dwelling in the mountains, and secluding themselves in the wilderness, they did so only to counter the opposite urge and restore the health of their souls, as I mentioned above. They also felt that they would be influenced by the immorality of their townspeople. When pious people saw that they might be corrupted by associating with evil people and accepting their actions, they fled to the wilderness. Fearing that their own morals might be tainted by those around them, they removed themselves from bad people, as the prophet Yirmiyah said, *"Oh, to be in the desert, at an encampment for wayfarers! Oh, to leave my people, to go away from them. For they are all adulterers, a band of rogues"* (Yirmiyah 9:1).

When ignorant people tried to emulate these saintly men, they did not perceive the acts of excess as a form of therapy for the soul; rather, they considered the deeds virtuous in themselves and blindly imitated the acts, believing that their imitative behavior would turn them into saintly men. They tormented their bodies with all kinds of afflictions, thinking thus to achieve perfection and moral stature and so come closer to Hashem, as if He hates the human body and wants to destroy it. It never dawned on them that these actions were bad and caused moral imperfection of the soul. Such men can only be compared with one ignorant of the science of medicine who sees skillful physicians ministering to persons who lie near death's door, giving them such medicines as colocynth, scammony, aloe, and the like, and denying them food, a treatment that effectively cures the patients. The fool concludes that since these things cure sickness, then surely they must work wonders in preserving health or prolonging life. But if a person should take these things constantly and treat himself like a sick person, then he would really become ill. In the same way, those who are spiritually well but take extreme remedies unnecessarily become morally ill.

THE IDEAL OF MODERATION

The Torah, which is perfect, leads us to perfection, as one who knew it well testified, *"The Torah of Hashem is perfect, restoring the*

soul; the testimony of Hashem is trustworthy, making the simple one wise"
(Tehillim 19:8). But the Torah makes no mention of excess, such as
self-torture or affliction, except on Yom Kippur. On the contrary, its
commandments and prohibitions are designed for man to live a life
of moderation, in harmony with nature. One should eat and drink
in moderation, be moderate in permissible marital relations, and
live with sober moderation in the world, dealing honestly and fairly
with men. One should not live in the wilderness or in the mountains, wear garments of wool and hair, or otherwise torture his
body. As a matter of fact, the Torah, as interpreted by the Sages in
the chapter dealing with the laws of the nazir[23] warns us against
such practices. It says, *"The [kohen] shall make an atonement for [the
nazir] because he has sinned against the soul"* (Bamidbar 6:11). The
Rabbis argue, "Against what soul has he sinned? Against his own
soul, because he has denied himself the enjoyment of wine. We can
draw a logical inference (*kal va-chomer*) from this: If a person who
deprived himself of wine must bring an atonement, then surely
must one who denies himself every enjoyment" (*Nedarim* 10a).

The words of our prophets and Sages show that they aimed for
moderation in the care of their souls and bodies, according to the
dictates of the Torah. Hashem addressed this issue through His
prophet Zachariah, responding to those who asked whether the
once-a-year fast should continue or not.[24] They asked Zachariah,
*"Shall I weep and practice abstinence in the fifth month (Av), as I have been
doing all these years?* (Zachariah 7:3). The answer was, *"When you
fasted and lamented in the fifth and seventh months all these seventy years,
did you fast for My benefit? And when you eat and drink, who but you does
the eating, and who but you does the drinking?"* (Zachariah 7:5,6). After
that he urged them to practice justice and morality, rather than
fasting. *"Thus said the Lord of Hosts, 'Execute true justice; deal loyally
and compassionately with one another. Do not defraud the widow, the
orphan, the stranger, and the poor; and do not plot evil against one
another' "* (Zachariah 7:9, 10). *"Thus said the Lord of Hosts, 'The fast of
the fourth month, the fast of the fifth month, the fast of the seventh month,*

---

[23]A nazir is one who takes a vow not to drink wine or eat grapes or
raisins. He may not cut his hair, and he may not have any contact with the
dead for the duration of his vow.

[24]This is the fast of *Tish'a be-Av.* When the Jews returned to Jerusalem
and rebuilt the Second Temple, they asked whether they should continue
fasting on the days commemorating the destruction of the First Temple.

and the fast of the tenth month shall become occasions for joy and gladness,
happy festivals to the House of Judah; but you must love truth and peace' "
(Zachariah 8:19).

Note that truth refers to the intellectual virtues, because they
are unalterably true, as I explained in Chapter Two, and peace
reflects the moral virtues, for on them depends the peace of
the world.

To return to our theme: If those of our fellow Jews who imitate
the non-Jews—and it is of them alone I speak—claim to torment their
bodies and deny themselves every pleasure merely to train the
powers of their souls by tending a little to the extreme, as is proper
and as I recommended in this chapter,[25] I reply that they are in error,
as I will now explain. The Torah gave us commandments and prohibitions in order to condition us to one side of the center. Therefore,
we were given the prohibition of forbidden foods, of illicit intercourse, of prostitution, and given the requirement of a marriage
ceremony. Intercourse is not permitted at all times, as, for example,
during menstruation and after childbirth. The Sages additionally,
restricted intercourse and disallowed it altogether during the day, as I
explained in the Tractate Sanhedrin.[26] Hashem gave us many commandments to restrain our indulging too much in sensuous desire
and even to force us somewhat in the direction of self-denial, so that
the trait of moderation would be firmly anchored in our souls.

COMMANDMENTS TEACHING MODERATION

The same holds true for all the commandments in the Torah,[27] such
as the giving of tithes (*maaseros*) and the prohibition against harvesting single stalks that fall during the reaping (*leket*), forgotten
sheaves (*shik'chah*), single fallen grapes (*peret*), and incompletely
formed grape clusters (*alelos*). Also included are the laws of the

---

[25]The Sages who went to one extreme did so because they saw in
themselves a tendency toward the other. Had they not seen such a flaw in
their character, they would not have gone to an extreme. To those who
claim that they torment their bodies so as to veer slightly to one side
rather than because they have faults, the Rambam says that the Torah has
already guided us off center.

[26]See the Rambam's Commentary on the Mishnah, *Sanhedrin* 7:4.

[27]The commandments relating to the giving of dues to Hashem and
to the poor.

Sabbatical year (*shemittah*) and the Jubilee (*yovel*) and the law of giving charity according to the wants of the needy person. All these commandments tend to excessive magnanimity and should be practiced so that we avoid the other extreme of stinginess. By thus encouraging our generosity, we may reach the point where the quality becomes firmly ingrained in our character.

Consider most of the commandments from this perspective, and you will find that they are all designed to discipline and adjust the powers of the soul. Thus, the Torah forbids taking revenge, bearing a grudge, becoming a blood-avenger, stating, "*Do not take revenge or bear a grudge against your countrymen*" (Vayikra 19:18); "*You must make every effort to help him [unload his donkey]*" (Shemos 23:5); "*You must help [your brother] load [his donkey]*" (Devarim 22:4). These commandments are meant to weaken the force of rage and anger. Similarly, the commandment, "*You must return [the lost ox or sheep] to your brother* (Devarim 22:1) is designed to remove the trait of niggardliness. Also, the commandments, "*Stand up for a greybeard, and give respect to the old*" (Vayikra 19:32), "*Honor your father and mother*" (Shemos 20:12), and, "*Do not stray from the word that they declare to you*" (Devarim 17:11) are intended to displace impudence and strengthen modesty.

To counter excessive bashfulness, the Torah instructs us in actions that will remove this trait and help us remain on the middle course, "*You must admonish your neighbor*" (Vayikra 19:17), and "*Do not be impressed by any man*" (Devarim 1:17).

However, if someone, likely a fool, tries to embellish these laws with additional strictness—forgoing food and drink more than the Torah demands, restricting marital relations more than is required, distributing to the poor more than he can afford, or dedicating more money for sacred purposes than the Torah requires—then he would unwittingly commit wrongful acts. He would be going to an extreme and abandoning the middle road. In this connection, I have never heard anything more to the point than this passage from the Talmud (Yerushalmi, *Nedarim* 9), where the Rabbis castigate those who assume oaths and vows to the extent that they become prisoners of their commitments. The Rabbis reproach them as follows, "Said Rabbi Idi in the name of Rabbi Yitzchak, 'Isn't what the Torah prohibits enough for you, but you must take on additional prohibitions?' " This poignant phrase succinctly presents the idea I have been trying to convey.

From all that I have stated in this chapter, it is clear that a person should aim for the middle road in all his actions and not swerve to one extreme or the other. Only when he has to heal his soul should he incline to the opposite trait from which his soul is suffering. A man who is familiar with the science of medicine and notices a slight change for the worse in his health would not remain indifferent and let his health deteriorate to the point that he would need very potent medicine. Similarly, a man who notices a disorder in one of his limbs would nurse it carefully and abstain from things that will be harmful to it. He will apply every remedy that will heal the sick limb or at least prevent its worsening. In the same way, the moral man should constantly examine his moral qualities, weigh his actions, and probe the characteristics of his soul each and every day. If, at any time, he finds his soul veering to one extreme or the other, he should quickly apply the proper remedy. He should not allow an evil trait to acquire potency through repetition. He should also be mindful of the flaws in his character and do his best to cure them, as I have said above, for it is impossible for any man to be free of all faults. Philosophers tell us that it is very difficult and rare to find a man who is perfect by nature in all his qualities, both moral and intellectual. This thought is often expressed in the prophets, *"He cannot trust His own servants and casts reproach on His angels"* (Iyov 4:18); *"How can man be right before Hashem? How can one born of woman be cleared of guilt?"* (Iyov 25:4). Solomon says it plainly, *"For there is not a righteous man on earth who always does good and does not sin"* (Koheles 7:20).

You know also that Hashem said to Moshe Rabbenu,[28] the master of all authorities, *"Because you did not have enough faith in Me to sanctify Me in the presence of the children of Israel"* (Bamidbar 20:12); *"Because you rebelled against My word at the waters of Meribah"* (Bamidbar 20:24); *"Because you did not sanctify Me among the children of Israel"* (Devarim 32:51). Moses' sin was that he deviated from the mean of

---

[28]The Rambam argues that even Moshe Rabbeinu exhibited bad character traits. For example, when the Jews had no water in the desert, they complained to Moses, who prayed to Hashem. Hashem directed Moses to speak to a rock and it would spout water. Instead Moses struck the rock with his staff and consequently was chastised severely. The commentators are puzzled to understand Moses' sin in this matter. The Rambam contends that his sin was the display of unwarranted anger, which caused him to strike the rock instead of simply speaking to it.

patience to the extreme of anger when he shouted, *"Listen now, you rebels!"* (Bamidbar 20:10). Hashem found fault that a man such as he would show anger in front of all Israel when it was unwarranted. It was a *Chillul Hashem* (desecration of Hashem's Name) because people emulated Moses and imitated his conduct and words in the hope of attaining happiness in this world and the one to come. They would be unable to conceive how Moses could display anger, a harmful character trait that stems from an evil disposition of the soul. Thus, Hashem's words, "You rebelled against My word" may be explained as follows: Moses was not speaking to ignorant and unworthy people, but to an assembly, the least of whose women, as our Sages say, was on the level of the prophet Ezekiel ben Buzi (*Mechilta, Shemos* 25:2). When Moses said or did anything, everyone carefully examined his words and actions, and when they saw that he became enraged, they said, "He certainly has no moral shortcoming. Unless he knew that Hashem was angry with us for demanding water and that we had aroused Hashem's fury, he would not have been angry with us." However, we do not find that Hashem was angry when he spoke to Moses about this matter, but rather He said, *"Take the staff and assemble the community . . . and allow the community and their livestock to drink"* (Bamidbar 20:8).

I have digressed from the main theme of this chapter in order to solve one of the most difficult passages that has been the subject of numerous commentators who asked, "What was the sin that Moses committed?" Compare what others have said with my opinion, and the true interpretation will surely prevail.

To return to our subject. If a person will always carefully weigh his actions and aim for the middle course, he will reach the highest level of perfection possible to a human being. In this ideal way he will come close to Hashem and enjoy His bliss. The Sages had this in mind when they wrote (*Sotah* 5b), "He who weighs his course is worthy of seeing the salvation of Hashem," as it says, *"Ve-sam—To him that sets a course—I will show the salvation of Hashem"* (Tehillim 50:23). Do not read *ve-sam* but *ve-sham*—he who estimates and weighs. This is exactly the idea that I have explained in this chapter.

I think this is all that needs to be said about this subject.

Chapter Five

Deals with the Application of Man's Powers of the Soul Toward the Attainment of the One Ultimate Goal

THE ULTIMATE GOAL

You must let the powers of your soul be ruled by your intellect, as we have discussed in the previous chapter. Focus your thoughts constantly on one single goal: attaining the knowledge of Hashem, as far as it is possible for any human being to know Him. All of man's actions and words, whether at work or at leisure, should be aimed at this goal so that no action is senseless and pointless. Whether one eats, drinks, has marital relations, sleeps, is awake, moves around, or rests, the primary goal should be to preserve one's physical health. And the purpose of keeping one's health is to create a wholesome environment for the soul, so that one can acquire wisdom, good character traits, and a sound intellect, all directed at the ultimate goal.[29]

Accordingly, you should not concentrate simply on bodily pleasure, choosing food and drink and other things just because you enjoy them. You should rather select the most healthful food, and if it happens to be palatable, so much the better. But if it happens to taste bad, you should still eat it. There are times, however, when a tasty dish may promote a cure; for example, when a person suffers loss of appetite, highly seasoned delicacies and savory morsels may stimulate his appetite. Similarly, a person who suffers from depression may counter it by listening to singing or beautiful music, by strolling through beautiful parks or magnificent

---

[29]The ultimate goal is to know Hashem.

buildings, by viewing beautiful paintings or other things that excite the mind and dispel a gloomy mood. The purpose of all this is to restore one's health, but the primary goal of maintaining good health is to acquire wisdom. In the same way, when it comes to wealth, you should spend on charitable causes as well as to keep your body in good health, so that you may live a long life and obtain as much knowledge of Hashem as you can.

A HEALTHY SOUL IN A HEALTHY BODY

When viewed from this vantage point, the science of medicine is important in helping us acquire the proper mental and moral attitudes for knowing Hashem and for attaining true spiritual happiness. Therefore, the medical profession and the study of medicine are lofty religious pursuits and should not be ranked with the crafts of weaving or carpentry. Through the science of medicine, a person learns to weigh his deeds and turn them to virtuous, humane acts. A man who insists on indulging in delectable, tasty, sweet-smelling food, although it may be harmful to his health and even lead to serious illness or sudden death, is, in my opinion, like an animal. He is not acting like a human being, for a human being is endowed with understanding. He behaves like an animal, as it says, *"He is like the dumb animals"* (Tehillim 49:13). Man acts like a human being only when he eats wholesome food, even avoiding enjoyable dishes and eating unappealing fare if his health demands it. Such a person is guided by reason and thus distinguishes himself from other creatures. In the same way, if a man has marital relations whenever he has the desire, without regard to harmful or beneficial effects, he acts like a beast and not like a human being.

It is possible for one's conduct to be guided solely by the practical and pragmatic consideration of maintaining physical health or guarding against disease. However, such a person does not deserve to be called a pious man. Just as he is single-minded in his desire to enjoy good health, someone else may be similarly fixated upon the joys of eating or of marital relations. But none of these actions lead toward the true goal. They are only correct if your interest in maintaining your health and extending your life span is to preserve the instruments of your soul. The body must be in perfect condition, so that your soul will not be hindered in its pursuit of moral and intellectual virtues.

So, too, must you use all the sciences and knowledge you acquire. Some lead directly to the higher purpose. Other areas of knowledge, such as mathematics, conic sections,[30] mechanics, geometry, and hydraulics, do not lead directly to a higher purpose, but should be studied to sharpen the mind and train the intellect. You will acquire thereby the skills of inductive reasoning and logic, and these will ultimately lead toward understanding the essence of Hashem.

The same applies to conversation. A noble person is one who speaks only of those things that benefit his soul or body or keep him away from harm. These may include discussions of science or virtue, praise of virtue or a virtuous man, or expressions of contempt for vice or scorn for a shameful person. To reject people who behave disgracefully and to discredit their conduct is a duty and a commendable deed—if it is done to disparage them in the eyes of other people who will therefore avoid such conduct. As the Torah tells us, *"Do not follow the ways of Egypt where you once lived"* (Vayikra 18:3). The story of the people of Sodom (Bereishis 13:13) and other passages in the Torah that discredit the corrupt and praise the good have only one purpose, as I have mentioned: to encourage people to emulate the righteous and to shun the ways of the wicked.

ENHANCING LIFE

If you keep the pursuit of wisdom in mind, you will abandon your customary activities and talk much less.[31] Whoever follows these precepts will not decorate his walls with golden ornaments or trim his garments with golden fringes, unless such luxuries are intended to cheer the soul and banish its sickness so that it will become clear and pure and once again be receptive to wisdom.

This is what the Sages had in mind when they said, "It is proper that a Torah scholar should have a beautiful dwelling, a beautiful wife and the comforts of home" (*Shabbos* 25b), for a person

---

[30]These were described by Appolonius, a Greek mathematician who lived 400 B.C.E.

[31]See Hilchos De'os, 2:4,5, for more on this subject.

becomes tired and his mind dulled by continual mental concentration on difficult problems. Just as the body becomes exhausted from hard labor and needs revitalization through rest and leisure, so too the mind needs to relax by contemplating works of art and other beautiful objects. In this vein, it is written, "When the Rabbis became exhausted from studying, they would engage in lighthearted conversation" (*Shabbos* 25b). From this perspective, we may say that pictures and embroideries are not immoral or unnecessary when they serve to enhance a person's home, furniture, and clothing.

STRIVING FOR A LOFTY GOAL

To live according to this standard represents a very high level of perfection, one that is very difficult to reach. Only a few have attained this state and then only after persistent effort. Such achievement requires that a man use all the powers of his soul to the single ideal of knowing Hashem. Whatever he does, whether great or small, and whatever he says, must be geared, directly or indirectly, to a higher, spiritual purpose. Such a man considers before he acts or commits a single deed whether it will bring him closer to that goal and proceeds to act only if the answer is that it will. If there exists a man who has attained such a level of commitment, I would consider him on a par with the prophets.

Such striving is what the Almighty demands of us when He says, *"Love Hashem, your God, with all your heart, with all your soul, and with all your might"* (Devarim 6:5), meaning with all the powers of your soul. In other words, infuse each faculty of your soul with the love of Hashem. The prophets similarly urge us to this goal saying, *"In all your ways know Him"* (Mishlei 3:6), to which the Sages add this explanation, "even if you have to commit a transgression" (*Berachos* 63a).[32] The Sages meant that you should set the goal of truth for your every action, even though it may involve a transgression.

Our Sages summed up the idea briefly, concisely, and clearly with this ethical precept, "Let all your deeds be for the sake of

---

[32]Elijah transgressed when he erected an altar and brought a sacrifice outside the Temple in order to convince the people that Hashem is the true God (I Melachim, 18:20–40).

Heaven" (*Avos* 12:17). When you consider how they have encapsulated a great and momentous idea with a few words, while others have written books without adequately explaining it, you recognize that the Sages undoubtedly spoke with divine inspiration.

What I have expounded in the present chapter is sufficient to serve as an introduction.

Chapter Six

The Difference between a True Saint and a Person Who Has Subdued His Natural Inclinations and Practices Self-restraint

THE VIEW OF KING SOLOMON

Philosophers maintain that a person who controls his base instincts is someone who inwardly craves the immoral even though he may perform many commendable acts. He overcomes his passion by actively grappling with the urges stirred by his emotions, desires, and natural inclination. But even while he is acting in a moral fashion, he is being tormented by his inner conflict. A saintly man, however, is guided in his actions by his innate disposition to do good. His urgings and desires are to do good things.

Philosophers unanimously agree that a saintly man is better and more perfect than a person who has to curb his passions, although the two are equal in many things. In general, a person who has to subdue his cravings must necessarily be rated lower than a saintly man because the desire to do evil lurks in his heart. And although he does not actually do evil, his fondness for evil indicates that his soul is flawed.

King Solomon expressed a similar idea when he said, *"The soul of the wicked desires evil"* (Mishlei 21:10). Speaking of the joy a saintly man experiences when he is doing good and the torment felt by one who acts virtuously but is not innately righteous, King Solomon says, *"It is a joy to the righteous to do justice but a torment to evildoers"* (Mishlei 21:15). The sayings of *Tanach* accord with the tenets of philosophers.

194

THE OPINION OF THE RABBIS

In studying the works of the Rabbis on this subject, we find that they value the person who controls his impulse to sin more than one who has no urge to sin and, therefore, does not struggle to refrain from evil. They even go so far as to say that the more praiseworthy and perfect a man is, the greater is his desire to transgress and the stronger his turmoil when he controls his urge to sin. "The greater a man, the stronger his evil inclination" (*Sukkah* 52a). And, if this were not enough, they add that the reward of the person who overcomes his evil inclination is commensurate with the anguish he suffers because of his resistance. In the words of the Rabbis, "The reward is in proportion to the suffering" (*Avos* 5:26). Even further, they command you to acknowledge your desire and your need to conquer it, forbidding you to say, "Even if the Torah did not prohibit it, my nature is such that I have no desire to commit such-and-such transgression." Rabbi Shimon ben Gamliel put it like this, "You should not say, 'I do not desire to eat meat together with milk; I do not desire to wear clothes made of a mixture of wool and linen; I do not desire to enter into an illicit marriage,' but you should say, 'I do indeed desire to perform these acts, but my hands are tied, for my Father in Heaven has forbidden it.' "

RECONCILIATION OF OPPOSING VIEWS

If we compare the sayings of the philosophers with those of the Rabbis, they might seem to contradict each other. However, this is not so. Not only are both correct; there is not the slightest disagreement between them. When the philosophers describe a person who has no longing for evil as superior to one who desires evil but conquers his passion, the evils they speak of are those that all commonly agree are immoral, such as murder, theft, robbery, fraud, causing injury to one who has done no harm, repaying benevolence with malice, contempt for parents, and the like. Of these commandments the Rabbis said, "If they had not already been written in the Torah, it would have been proper to include them" (*Yoma* 67b). Some of our later Sages who were infected with the erroneous theories of the Mutakallimun[33] called these *sichliyos* (rational commandments).[34]

Clearly, a soul that lusts to perform these misdeeds is flawed. A noble soul has absolutely no desire to commit any of these crimes and is not disturbed in abstaining from them. However, when the Rabbis praise one who overcomes his desire as more worthy and entitled to a greater reward than one who has no such battle, they are referring only to the revealed laws.[35] This is so because if it were not for the Torah, these would not be considered transgressions at all. Therefore, the Rabbis say that you should allow your soul to yearn for them, knowing that the Torah alone restrains you from these actions. Consider the wisdom of the Sages. They did not state, "One should not say, 'I have no desire to kill, to steal and to lie,' rather say, 'I have a desire for these things, but what can I do, my Father in Heaven forbids it!' " The examples they do cite are all from the *mitzvos shim'iyos*, the revealed commandments, such as eating meat and milk together, wearing clothes made of wool and linen, and entering into forbidden marriages. These and similar commandments are what the Torah called *chukkim*, statutes. The Rabbis explained that *chukkim* are "statutes which I (Hashem) enacted for you, which you have no right to criticize." *Chukkim* are laws that the nations of the world attack and that Satan condemns; for instance, the statutes concerning the red cow, the scapegoat, and so forth (*Yoma* 67b). The transgressions that the later authorities[36] called *sichliyos*, rational laws, are referred to in the Torah as mitzvos, as the Rabbis explained (*Makkos* 23b).

From this discussion you should now understand those transgressions which the more noble person does not covet and the less noble person needs particularly to resist. It should also be clear

---

[33]The Rambam consistently took issue with the Mutakallimun, Moslem philosophers who tried to harmonize their theology with Aristotelian philosophy.

[34]Rabbeinu Saadiah Gaon divides the commandments into *sichliyos* (rational) and *shim'iyos* (revealed) (*Emunos ve-De'os* 3:2). According to the Rambam, moral acts are mitzvos and the revealed laws are *chukkim*.

[35]These are the mitzvos *shim'iyos*, commandments that had to be revealed because man could not have discovered them with his intellect and his sense of ethics.

[36]Rabbeinu Saadiah Gaon, 882–942.

which transgressions are their opposite. It is astounding that these two discourses[37] are, in fact, compatible with each other, and the text bears out the truth of our explanation.

This ends the discussion of the subject matter of this chapter.

---

[37]The discussions of the philosophers and the Rabbis.

Chapter Seven

Deals with the Barriers between Hashem and Man and Their Significance

BARRIERS TO KNOWING HASHEM

Many passages in the Midrash, the Aggadah, and the Gemara describe how the prophets beheld the Almighty through some type of obstruction[38] that was dense or transparent, depending on the closeness of the prophet to Hashem and the degree of his prophetic power. The Rabbis said that Moshe Rabbenu saw Hashem through a single clear, transparent partition. As they put it, "He looked through an *aspeklaria hame'irah*, a translucent glass" (*Yevamos* 49b). *Aspeklaria* is the term for a mirror made of a transparent substance like crystal or glass, as explained at the end of Tractate *Kelim* (30:2).

What follows is my explanation of this subject. I discussed in Chapter Two that virtues can be classified as intellectual or moral. Similarly, vices can be intellectual—foolishness, ignorance, and stupidity—or they can be moral—excessive sensuality, pride, hostility, anger, impudence, greed, and many other such. I have identified and listed them in Chapter Four. Each of these shortcomings is an obstruction between man and Hashem, blessed be His Name. This is what the prophet had in mind when he said, *"But your iniquities have been a barrier between you and your God"* (Yeshayah 59:2); our sins, which are these vices, are what separate us from Hashem.

QUALIFICATIONS OF A PROPHET

Note well that no prophet received the gift of prophecy unless he had all the intellectual virtues and most of the moral ones. As the

---

[38]The prophet beheld Hashem through layers that made his vision unclear and shadowy.

198

Rabbis said, "Prophecy rests only on one who is wise, strong and rich" (*Shabbos* 92a). They use the term *wise* to signify one who has all the intellectual qualities and *rich* to encompass the moral quality of contentment because they call a contented man rich. Indeed, when defining the word *rich* they say, "Who is rich? He who is contented with his lot" (*Avos* 4:1), meaning someone who is satisfied with what fortune brings him and who is not upset with what he does not have. Similarly, strong is a moral character trait, and a strong man is one who lets his desires be guided by intelligence and reason, as I explained in Chapter Five. The Rabbis say, "Who is strong? He who subdues his personal desires" (*Avos* 4:1).

It is not essential that a prophet have all the moral qualities and be entirely free of any shortcomings. After all, there is a passage that shows King Solomon was a prophet, *"Hashem appeared to Solomon in Gibeon"* (I Melachim 3:5); yet, we know from his having taken so many wives that his moral failing was lust, a weakness that stems from an excessive desire for pleasure. And Scripture unequivocally states, *"It was just in such things that King Solomon of Israel sinned!"* (Nehemiah 13:26).

Similarly, David the prophet who said, *"To me spoke the Rock of Israel"* (II Shmuel 3:3) had the character trait of cruelty. Although David used his cruelty to destroy idol worshipers and nonbelievers and was merciful toward Israel, nevertheless, it says clearly in Chronicles that Hashem did not allow him to build the Temple. This would not have been appropriate, since David had caused so many people to be killed. Hashem said to him, *"You shall not build a House for My name for you have shed much blood on the earth in My sight"* (II Divrei Hayamim 22:8).

We find that Elijah was prone to anger. Although he vented his anger only against nonbelievers, our Sages say that Hashem removed him from the world, saying that he was unfit to lead men and serve as their priest, for "Whoever has as much zeal as you have will destroy them."[39] Likewise, we find that Samuel was afraid of Saul[40] and that Jacob was afraid to meet Esau.[41]

These and similar character traits were barriers between Hashem and the prophets. Any prophet who strayed from the

---

[39]*Tanna de Bei Elijah Zuta* 8; *Yalkut Shim'oni Melachim* 217, *Sanhedrin* 113a.

[40]When Hashem sent him to anoint David as king, Samuel said, *"How can I go? If Saul hears of it he will kill me"* (I Shmuel 16:2).

[41]*"Jacob was very frightened"* (Bereishis 32:8), and fear is a character flaw.

medium course because of two or three qualities, as I explained in Chapter Four, is said to have seen Hashem obliquely.

Do not be surprised to learn that a few moral shortcomings lessen the degree of prophetic inspiration. In fact, we find that some moral defects inhibit prophecy altogether. Anger may do this, as our Sages say, "If a prophet becomes enraged, his prophecy leaves him" (*Pesachim* 66b). Their proof is the case of Elisha, whose prophecy departed from him when he became furious.[42] It did not return until his anger was stilled, and he exclaimed, *"And now bring me a musician"* (II Melachim 3:15).

Grief and anxiety may also prevent prophecy, as it did for our father Jacob. During the days that he mourned for Joseph, the *ruach hakodesh* (Holy Spirit) withdrew from him until he received the news that his son lived. Only then *"The spirit of their father Jacob was revived"* (Bereishis 45:27), which Targum Onkelos translates, *"And the spirit of prophecy came to rest on their father Jacob."*

Also, the Rabbis say, "The spirit of prophecy does not rest on one who is lazy, nor on one who is sad, but only on a person who is rejoicing" (*Shabbos* 30b; *Pesachim* 117a).

MOSES THE PROPHET

When Moshe Rabbenu discovered that there was no barrier between him and Hashem and that he had reached perfection by attaining every possible moral and intellectual virtue, he tried to comprehend the essence of Hashem. Thus he prayed, *"Please let me have a vision of Your Glory"* (Shemos 33:18). But Hashem let him know that this was impossible; because he was a human being, his intellect was still bound to physical matter. Hashem said, in fact, *"A man cannot have a vision of Me and live"* (Shemos 33:20). And so, there remained one transparent barrier separating Moses from his grasp of the true essence of Hashem, and this barrier was his human intellect that was still connected to physical matter. Hashem did, however, grant Moses' request by giving him more knowledge of the Divine than he had previously possessed, although the ultimate goal he sought was beyond his human reach.

---

[42]He was angry with Jehoram the son of Ahab (II Melachim 3:14).

The true comprehension of His essence is termed, *beholding the divine face,*[43] because when you see the features of a face they are imprinted on your mind so you will never confuse this face with another. But if you see only the back, you may or may not be able to recognize or distinguish this back from another. Similarly, the true comprehension of Hashem lies in understanding the reality of His existence, which is not possible for any being. It is impossible even for man to attain this high degree of understanding, although Moses came close. This is what is meant by the phrase, *"You will see My back"* (Shemos 33:23). I intend to discuss this subject at greater length in *The Book of Prophecy.*

The Sages knew that these two classes of vices—intellectual and moral failings—separate man from the Almighty and determine the level of prophetic inspiration. Therefore, the Sages said of colleagues who evidenced wisdom and good qualities, "They deserve that the *Shechinah* (Divine Presence) should rest on them as it did on Moshe Rabbenu" (*Sukkah* 28a, *Bava Batra* 134a). But do not be confounded by this equation. The Sages did find their colleagues comparable to Moses in some respects, but they did not consider them Moses' *equals.*[44] In the same way, they likened other Rabbis to Joshua.

This is what I intended to explain in this chapter.

---

[43]*"My face, however, will not be seen"* (Shemos 33:23).

[44]The Torah states, *"No other prophet like Moses has arisen in Israel"* (Devarim 34:10).

Chapter Eight

Deals with the Inborn Nature of Man

HABIT BECOMES SECOND NATURE

It is as impossible for one to be born with good or bad traits, as it is for one to be an accomplished craftsman from birth. However, a person may have a natural inclination to a particular virtue or vice from birth, so that one type of activity comes easier than another. For example, it is easier for a person whose brain matter is clear and contains only a small amount of fluid[45] to learn, remember, and understand things than a phlegmatic man whose brain is overloaded with fluids. But, if one who has this natural gift fails to stimulate his talent, he surely will remain ignorant. On the other hand, if an inherently dull and phlegmatic person is taught and enlightened, he will gain knowledge and understanding, albeit with great difficulty. In exactly the same way, a person whose blood is warmer than normal has the potential to become a brave man. If this man is trained to be brave, he will become boldly daring in short order. Someone else whose temperament is colder than normal would be naturally inclined to cowardice and fear. If he is taught to be fearful, he will quickly become a coward. But if he is conditioned to be fearless, he will eventually learn to be valiant, although it will take a great deal of hard work. In spite of his predisposition, he can achieve heroism if he receives the proper training.

---

[45]Galen, a Greek physician of the 2nd century developed a theory that human personality was determined by four basic body fluids or humors: blood, phlegm, black bile, and yellow bile. The dominance of one over another made a person sanguine (warm, pleasant), phlegmatic (slow-moving, apathetic), melancholic (depressed, sad), and choleric (hot tempered).

THE FALSE THEORY OF PREDETERMINATION

I have elaborated on this subject, so that you will not believe the nonsense astrologers try to foist on people. They falsely maintain that the ascendancy of a constellation at the time of someone's birth determines whether he will have good or bad character traits; thus, a person's actions are predetermined. We, on the other hand, believe in a principle, which is advanced by both the Torah and Greek philosophy and has been substantiated by reliable proofs: that man's conduct is entirely in his own hands and that no external compulsion forces him to be good or bad.

The only exception to this principle is that a person may be predisposed to certain things by his innate temperament, as I have explained, and therefore may find it easy or difficult, as the case may be, to do a certain thing. But it is absolutely untrue that an external force compels him to act or to refrain from action. If the stars can make a person act, then the commandments and prohibitions of the Torah would be meaningless, and the Torah would be completely false; man would have no freedom of choice in what he does. By the same token, it would be useless, in fact absolutely futile and pointless, for a person to study, teach, or acquire a craft because the external force that controls him might make it impossible for him to succeed. Reward and punishment, too, would be unjust, both in terms of society punishing a criminal and Hashem punishing man. Take, for example, the case where Simon killed Reuben. Why should Simon be punished, since he was compelled to do the killing and Reuben was destined to be killed? How could Hashem the Blessed One, who is just and righteous, penalize Simon for a deed that he could not avoid, no matter how hard he tried?[46]

If this theory were true, all preparatory measures, such as building houses, earning money, fleeing from danger, and so on, would be absolutely useless because whatever is destined to happen will inevitably happen. The doctrine of predestination is completely false, flies in the face of common sense, and contradicts our

---

[46]On the contrary, he would deserve a reward for doing what he was commanded to do. This may be compared with the case of a man who hired two workers, one to build a house, the other to demolish it. The contractor would have to pay both, the one who built and the one who demolished (Rabbenu Saadiah Gaon, *Emunos ve De'os* 4:4).

own experience.[47] It denies the fundamental principles of the Torah and attributes injustice to Hashem, the Blessed One, far be it from Him!

THE TRUE DOCTRINE

The truth of the matter is that man is in full control of all his actions. If he wants to do something, he does it; if he does not want to do it, he does not do it, without any external force compelling him one way or the other. Therefore, it is appropriate for Hashem to command man, *"See! Today I have set before you two choices, life and good and death and evil . . . You must choose life* (Devarim 30:15,19). He gives us the freedom to choose, and our consequences result from that choice. Punishment is meted out to those who disobey, and rewards are showered on the obedient, as it says, *"Blessed are those who obey"* and, *"Cursed are those who do not obey"* (Devarim 11:27,28).

Learning and teaching are necessary, as all the passages that deal with the study of the commandments affirm, *"Teach your children"* (Devarim 11:19) and *"Learn and safeguard the rules and laws"* (Devarim 5:1). The Torah also requires that man take precautions, as it says, *"When you build a new house, place a guard-rail around your roof. Do not allow a dangerous situation to remain in your house where someone can fall"* and *"So that he will not die in war"* (Devarim 20:5);[48] *"With what shall he sleep?"*[49] and, *"Do not take an upper or lower millstone as security for a loan"* (Devarim 24:6). There are many more passages regarding precautions in the Torah and in the Prophets.

---

[47]A person knows that he controls his actions. He can speak at will or remain silent, and he can give or take, if he so desires. Says Rabbenu Saadiah Gaon: Hashem does not interfere in man's actions. He does not force him either to worship or to rebel (*Emunos ve De'os* 4:4).

[48]The reference is to a soldier who has built a house, planted a vineyard, or betrothed a woman. Before a battle, he is told to return home *"lest he die in the war and have another man live in his house . . ."* If it was preordained that he would not live in his house or marry his betrothed, this injunction would make no sense. If he was fated to die, he would die anyhow, and if he was destined to live, he would return home unscathed from the battlefield.

[49]This refers to security against a loan, *"If you take your neighbor's garment as security, you must return it to him before sunset."*

ALL IN THE HANDS OF HEAVEN

What the Rabbis have said, "All is in the hands of Heaven except for the fear of Heaven" (Megillah 25a) is true and agrees with what I have said about man's freedom of choice. However, people often mistakenly derive from this passage the belief that actions, which they have freely chosen, have actually been forced on them, such as marrying a certain woman or earning a certain amount of money. This assumption is absolutely untrue.

If a man marries a certain woman with a contract and ceremony, she becomes his lawful wife, and he has thus fulfilled the commandment to *"be fruitful and multiply."* Hashem does not preordain that a person fulfill a commandment. Conversely, if a man enters into a marriage that is a forbidden union, he has committed a transgression. But Hashem does not decree that the man shall sin. Continuing, suppose a man robs another's money by cheating him or stealing from him and then denies his actions under oath. If we say that Hashem had predestined that this money should pass from the one to the other, we would be saying that Hashem had foreordained a sinful act. This is not possible. The truth is rather that all of man's actions are under his control and subject to his free will. And these actions include the commandments and the transgressions; for, as I explained in Chapter Two, the commandments and prohibitions of the Torah relate only to those actions over which man has absolute freedom of choice.

The fear of Heaven is an attribute of the soul's power of desire. It is not controlled by Hashem, but rather is entirely subject to man's free will. This being so, what is meant by, "All is in the hands of Heaven?" By using the word *hakol* (all), the Sages intend only those natural phenomena that are not influenced by the will of man, such as a person's height (whether one is tall or short), the weather (if it rains or is dry), the environment (whether the air is polluted or clear), and all other such events in the world that have nothing to do with a person's behavior.

THE REMEDY OF TESHUVAH

When the Rabbis stated that obedience or disobedience to the commandments depends not on the will of Hashem but on man's free will, they echoed Jeremiah, who said, *"Out of the mouth of the Most High there comes neither the bad nor the good"* (Eichah 3:38). By *the bad* he meant *vice,* and by *the good* he intended *virtue,* meaning that Hashem does not predetermine any person as bad or good. Since this is so, a person owes it to himself to mourn his sins and transgressions, since he has committed them of his own free will, as Jeremiah says, *"For what should a living man mourn? Let every man mourn because of his sins"* (Eichah 3:39). Jeremiah answers his question positively, telling us that the remedy for our disease lies with us. Just as our failings stemmed from our own free will, so do we have the power to repent of our evil deeds. He goes on to say, *"Let us search and examine our ways, and turn back to Hashem. Let us lift up our hearts with our hands to God in Heaven"* (Eichah 3:40,41).

MIRACLES AND THE LAWS OF NATURE

There is a widespread belief, reflected also in the sayings of the Sages and prophets, that a man's sitting down and getting up, that all his movements, in fact, are determined by the will and desire of Hashem.[50] This is true in a limited sense. When a stone is thrown into the air and falls down, it is correct to say that the stone fell according to the will of Hashem because Hashem decreed that the earth and all upon it should be drawn to the center. In the same way, sparks of fire rise upward according to Hashem's will that fire should ascend. But this does not mean that when something is thrown upward, Hashem instantly wills the moment of its falling. The Mutakallimun disagree on this point, for I have heard them say that the will of Hashem is constantly at work, creating new things and situations every moment. We do not agree with them.

We believe that the Divine Will decreed during the six days of Creation that all things are forever regulated by the laws of nature and will always operate by these rules, as Solomon says, *"As it was, so it will be forever; as it was, so it continues, and there is nothing new beneath the sun!"* (Koheles 1:9). The Sages interpreted this to mean that all miracles that are exceptions to the natural order, whether they have already occurred or have yet to occur according to promise, were foreordained by the Divine Will during the six days of

[50]For example, "A man does not bruise his finger in the world below unless it was so ordained in Heaven above" (*Chullin* 7b).

Creation. At that time, when the laws of nature were established, provisions were made in nature for future miracles, and when a miracle occurred at its proper time, people have regarded it as a supernatural occurrence. In reality it was no such thing.[51]

The Rabbis elaborate on this subject in Midrash Koheles and other places. They say, for example, "The world follows its natural course" (*Avodah Zarah* 54b). You will find that the Sages always avoided attributing a time-related event to the Divine will. When they said that a person gets up and sits down in accordance with the will of Hashem, they meant that man's nature was such that he would always have the free choice of getting up and sitting down. They did not mean that Hashem wills the moment when a person gets up or remains seated, any more than He determines at any given moment that a stone should fall to the ground.

To summarize: We believe that just as Hashem wished man to stand erect, be broad-chested, and have fingers, so did He want man to move about or rest of his own accord. That man is free to act of his own free will, without any outside force compelling him or preventing him from doing as he chooses, the truthful Torah makes clear in the following verse, *"Man has now become like one of us in knowing good and evil"* (Bereishis 3:22). Targum Onkelos interprets the phrase *mimenu lada'at tov ve-ra* to mean *knowing by himself good and evil.* He considers Adam unique in the world. There was no other being that shared his inborn characteristic of knowing good and evil *mimenu* (by himself) and through his soul, choosing whichever he wished without restraint. This being so, *"he may put forth his hand and take from the Tree of Life and live forever"* (Bereishis 3:22).

Since the reality of man's nature is such that he has the free choice to do good or evil at will, he must be taught the consequences of both. He must be instructed to obey the commandments and cautioned against violating the prohibitions. He must be enlightened regarding the punishment that is meted out for rebellion and the reward that awaits those who obey the Torah, since each of these choices will have been justly deserved. In addition, man should train himself to perform good deeds, so that goodness will

---

[51]The Midrash Rabba, Shemos 21:6, says "When Hashem created the world He made a compact that the sea would divide (referring to the parting of the Red Sea), the fire not hurt (the incident with Hananiah, Mishael, and Azariah in the furnace) and the lions not harm (Daniel in the lions den) . . ."

become second nature to him. Similarly, by avoiding wrongdoing, he will find that his shortcomings disappear. He should never say that his failings have become so ingrained that they cannot be changed because every character trait can be changed from good to bad or vice versa; it all depends on one's free will.

This is all I intended to say on the subject of commandments and transgressions.

MISUNDERSTOOD SCRIPTURES

There remains one issue to explain, concerning a number of Scriptures about which people are confused. They mistakenly infer from certain Biblical verses that Hashem has preordained some to rebel against Him and that He compels their transgression. This is incorrect, and I feel that I must set the record straight because many people are bewildered by these passages. One of these involves the promise Hashem made to Abraham, *"Know for sure that your descendants will be foreign in a land that is not theirs. They will be enslaved and oppressed for 400 years"* (Bereishis 5:13). Pointing to this verse, some people pose this challenge. "It says here that Hashem ordered the Egyptians to oppress Abraham's descendants. Why then did He punish them? After all, by enslaving Abraham's offspring, the Egyptians were simply carrying out Hashem's will."

We answer with an analogy: If Hashem had decreed, "Let mankind be composed of lawbreakers and wicked people on the one hand and devout and pious people on the other,"[52] this pronouncement would not compel one to be evil, any more than it would force another to be virtuous. If a person wants to be wicked, he will be wicked by his own free choice, and if he chooses to be righteous, he has the option to do so, and no one can stand in his way. Similarly, if a righteous man elects to be corrupt, no one can prevent it. Hashem did not particularize His declaration saying, "So-and-so is destined to be wicked"; rather He spoke of mankind in general, which in no way affects the individual's inborn free will. In the same way, each and every Egyptian who oppressed and tyrannized the Jews had the free will to choose not to be an op-

---

[52] In fact, Hashem decreed that mankind should include these two types.

pressor because Hashem did not command any specific Egyptian to persecute the Jews.

The same reply can be given to those who are perplexed by this passage in the Torah, *"Behold, when you (Moses) go and lie with your ancestors, this nation shall rise up and stray after the alien gods of the land"* (Devarim 31:16).[53] Similarly the statement, "Whoever worships idols will receive such-and-such punishment" simply points to the consequences of the transgression. If no one transgresses, the statement remains an unrealized threat.

We cannot say that because the Torah instituted stoning as capital punishment for someone who desecrates the Shabbos that this individual was, therefore, preordained to violate it. This is no more true than to say that because certain curses occur in the Torah those who were cursed, such as idol worshippers, were, therefore, predestined to commit a particular sin. On the contrary, anyone who practiced idol worship did so freely and deserved the punishment that was decreed, as it says, *"Just as they have chosen their ways and take pleasure in their abominations, so will I choose to mock them, to bring on them the very things they dread"* (Yeshayah 66:3,4).

PHARAOH'S PUNISHMENT

However, regarding the apparent contradiction of Hashem saying, *"I will harden Pharaoh's heart"* (Shemos 14:4) and then punishing him with death, I have much to say because there is an important principle of Divine Providence at issue here. Pay close attention to what I say on this matter, ponder it, compare it with the words of others, and select that which is the best.

My opinion is this: If Pharaoh and his advisers had committed no other sin than that of not letting Israel leave as they were commanded, I admit that the matter would give rise to serious doubt, for Hashem did indeed prevent the Egyptians from releasing the Jews, as it is written, *"I have made him and his advisors stubborn"* (Shemos 10:1). This being so, how could He demand that Pharaoh send them away while Pharaoh was being compelled to do the opposite? And how could He then punish Pharaoh for not letting them leave? This would undoubtedly be unjust and completely

---

[53]Again, the implication seems to be that Hashem preordained the Jewish worship of alien gods.

contradict all that we have previously said.[54] But this was not what happened. Pharaoh and his advisers, of their own free will and without any coercion, oppressed those who lived among them, committing terrible atrocities, as the Torah plainly states, *"He said to his people, 'The Israelites are becoming too numerous and strong for us. We must deal wisely with them . . .'"* (Shemos 1:9,10). They acted on their own evil initiative and drew on their innate wickedness without any outside interference. The punishment Hashem brought on them was His withholding the power of repentance, so that the retribution they so justly deserved would not be reversed. The fact that they were prevented from repenting is apparent in Pharaoh's refusal to let the Israelites go. Hashem explained to Pharaoh that if He had merely wanted to set the Israelites free He would simply have destroyed Pharaoh and his advisers without delay and so freed the Israelites. But Hashem wanted not only to redeem His people but also to punish Pharaoh because of his oppression of them, as He had promised Abraham, saying, *"But I will finally bring judgment against the nation who enslaves them, and they will then leave with great wealth"* (Bereishis 15:14). Because Hashem never could have punished the Egyptians if they had repented, they were barred from repentance. And they continued to keep the children of Israel in slavery, as it says, *"I could have unleashed My power, killing you and your people with the epidemic, and you would have been obliterated from the world. The only reason I let you survive was to show you My strength, so that My name will be recounted all over the world"* (Shemos 9:15,16).

You cannot challenge my saying that Hashem sometimes punishes a person by withholding repentance and not allowing him to choose to repent because Hashem knows the sinners and metes out their punishment with wisdom and fairness. Sometimes He punishes only in this world, sometimes only in the World to Come, and sometimes in both. Also his punishments in this world differ, sometimes affecting the sinner's body, sometimes his finances, and sometimes both at once. Sometimes a person's actions that are usually subject to his own free will are impaired by way of punishment; for example, his hand is disabled so that he cannot do anything with it, as happened to Jeroboam ben Nebat (I Melachim

---

[54]Man is born with free will, and no external power can force him to act or to refrain from action.

13:4),[55] or he is struck blind, like the people of Sodom who gathered in front of Lot's door (Bereishis 9:11). In the same way Hashem withholds a person's ability to use his free will for repentance, so that the thought of repentance does not even come to mind and the sinner dies in his sinfulness. We cannot comprehend Hashem's wisdom in punishing a certain individual with one punishment and no other, any more than we know why a certain species has one form and not another. And there is no need for us to understand. It is enough if we remember one general principle, that Hashem is just in all His ways, that He punishes sinners according to their sins, and that he rewards the virtuous according to their goodness.

You may wonder why Hashem repeatedly asked Pharaoh to set Israel free, something Pharaoh was unable to do since Hashem had taken away his freedom of will. And why did Hashem threaten Pharaoh with the plagues? The plagues, after all, were inevitable, given Pharaoh's inability to change. If these events were predestined, why did Hashem have Moses request Pharaoh's cooperation and threaten him when he did not comply?[56] But this was part of Hashem's wisdom. He wanted to teach Pharaoh that Hashem can take away freedom of will by showing him how he would no longer be in control of events even if he wanted to change his mind. Hashem told Pharaoh (through Moses), "I want you to give them their freedom, and if you let them go you will be saved, but I know that you will not let them go, so that you should die."

It would have made sense for Pharaoh to release the Israelites immediately. Thus would he have falsified the words of Moses, who said that Pharaoh was incapable of obeying. But Pharaoh did not have the power to change, and his inability to do the one thing that would have saved his life was the wonder, as it says, ". . . so that My name will be recounted all over the world" (Shemos 9:16). People have marveled at Hashem's unique punishment of Pharaoh that deprived him of any choice in the situation and even alerted him to the limits set on his free will.

Exactly the same thing happened to Sihon, King of Heshbon. As a punishment for earlier sins, Hashem prevented him from

---

[55]When he ordered his soldiers to arrest the prophet, his arm became immovable.

[56]The translation here follows the commentary by Rabbi Avraham Horowitz (Chesed Avraham), the father of the Shelah, Rabbi Yeshayah Horowitz.

allowing Israel to pass through his land. As a result, Israel marched against him, and he was killed, as it says, *"But Sihon, King of Heshbon, would not let us pass through his land. Hashem had hardened his spirit and made his heart firm"* (Devarim 2:30). Most commentators have misinterpreted this difficult passage, assuming that Sihon was punished for not permitting Israel to pass through his land, just as they assumed that Pharaoh and his people were punished for not allowing the children of Israel to leave. Therefore they ask, "How could he (Sichon) rightfully be punished? After all he had no choice in the matter since Hashem had hardened his spirit and made his heart firm." These assumptions are incorrect, and the matter is rather as I have explained it.[57]

THE REPEAL OF FREE WILL

Through the prophet Isaiah, Hashem has clearly stated that He punishes some transgressors by making it impossible for them to repent. He does this by denying them their free will, as it says, *"Dull that people's mind, stop its ears and seal its eyes — lest, seeing with its eyes and hearing with its ears, it will grasp with its mind, and repent and heal itself"* (Yeshayah 6:10). The meaning of these words is so clear that no explanation is required, and they open many doors. This same principle is the basis of Elijah's words, who, when speaking of the unbelievers of his time, said, *"You have turned their hearts backward"* (I Melachim 18:37). He meant that Hashem punished them for the sins they had freely committed by making them incapable of repentance. Because they could not exercise their free will to repent, they would not stop sinning; they would remain unbelievers. As the prophet says, *"Ephraim is addicted to idols, let him be"* (Hoshea 4:17), meaning that since Ephraim freely chose to worship idols, his punishment would be his inability to overcome his addiction to idolatry. A person who appreciates subtle ideas will find this an excellent explanation.

---

[57]Pharaoh and the Egyptians were punished because of their oppression of Israel, and Sichon was punished because of earlier acts of injustice.

ISAIAH'S PRAYER

Very different is Isaiah's meaning when he said, *"Why, Hashem, do You make us stray from Your ways, and turn our hearts from revering You?"* (Yeshayah 63:17). These words have no relation to the above explanations; their meaning is derived from context. The prophet bemoans our exile and our life as strangers in a strange land, as well as the end to Israel's kingdom, and Israel's subjugation to other nations. His words are a prayer, *"O Hashem, God of Israel, if Israel continues to see the power of the unbelievers, they will stray from the path of truth and their hearts will drift away from Your fear, and it will be as if You caused those ignorant people to abandon the path of truth."* This statement is similar to Moses' when he says, *"The nations who will hear this news about You will say, 'Hashem was not able to bring this nation to the land that He swore to them, so He slaughtered them in the desert' "* (Bamidbar 14:15,16). Isaiah ends by asking that Hashem not allow His name to be desecrated, *"Relent for the sake of Your servants, the tribes that are Your very own!"* (Yeshayah 63:17).

Malachi, one of the Twelve Minor Prophets, quotes the words of those who are affected by the apparent success of the wicked, *"All who do evil are good in the eyes of Hashem, and in them He delights, or else where is the God of justice?"* (Malachi 2:17). Commenting on the length of the exile, the prophet says, *"You have said, 'It is useless to serve God. What have we gained by keeping His charge and walking in abject awe of the Lord of Hosts?' And now we call the arrogant happy"* (Malachi 3:14,15). But the time will come when Hashem will reveal the truth, as the prophet says, *"And you shall come to see the difference between the righteous and the wicked, between him who has served Hashem and him who has not served Him"* (Malachi 3:18).

These are the puzzling passages in the Torah and the rest of Tanach from which it might appear that Hashem forces man to transgress. I have clearly explained the meaning of these verses, eliminating any ambiguities. If you examine the explanation closely, you will find it truthful.

I, therefore, maintain my original position, which is that observance or transgression of the commandments depends entirely on man's free will. Man is the master of his actions, and the choice is up to him to act or not act; however, Hashem may punish him for a past sin by taking away his free will, as I have explained. It is also entirely within man's power to acquire good or bad character traits.

Therefore he should do his utmost to acquire good qualities, which he alone can attain, as the Sages in their ethical teachings say, "If I am not for myself, who will be for me?" (*Avos* 1:14).

DIVINE FOREKNOWLEDGE

I have one more thing to say about this issue, which will complete the subject matter of this chapter. Although initially I did not consider mentioning this topic, I feel it necessary to do so. The subject is foreknowledge of Hashem because this is often used against us by those who believe that man is predestined to do good or evil. They assert that man has no freedom of action, since his choice is predetermined by Hashem's foreknowledge. They base their belief on the following question: "Does Hashem know or does He not know that a certain individual will be good or bad?" If you answer, "He knows," then it necessarily follows that man is forced to act according to Hashem's knowledge; otherwise, that knowledge would be imperfect. If you argue that Hashem does not know the future, that is an absurdity that would undermine the foundation of religion. Therefore, listen to what I have to say, for, undoubtedly, it is the truth.

THOUGHTS ON METAPHYSICS

It is a fundamental doctrine of the science of the Divine – by which I mean metaphysics – that the terms *knowledge* and *life,* when applied to Hashem mean something different than they do when applied to man. Man exists apart from knowledge, and knowledge exists separate from man; therefore, they are two entities. But this definition when applied to Hashem would make Him a plurality and multiply his divinity. Each of his attributes would become a Divine object; there would be Hashem, His knowledge, His life, His power, and His strength.

I will mention only one simple proof that is plain to understand and easy to explain, although there are many strong and convincing arguments that resolve this problem. It is indisputable that Hashem is identical with His attributes and His attributes with Him. He is the knowledge, the knower, and the known; He is the life, the living, and the source of His own life. The same may be said of all His other attributes. Because this idea is hard to grasp, you should not hope to understand it completely by reading two or three lines in this discourse.

As a logical outcome of this important principle (that Hashem and His attributes are identical), the Hebrew language does not allow you to say *chei Hashem*[58] (the life of Hashem) as you can say *chei Far'oh* (the life of Pharaoh) (Bereishis 42:15), where the word *chei* is a construct form[59] combining two different thoughts. But a construct cannot be used to combine a thing with itself. Since the life of Hashem is His essence and His essence is His life and the two are not separate and distinct from each other, the word *chai* cannot be used in its construct form *(chei)*. Instead the expression, *chai Hashem,*[60] (the living God) is appropriate (I Melachim 18:15). It also appears in Jeremiah, *"As Hashem lives (chai Hashem) who has made us this soul"* (Yirmiyah 38:16). The meaning of the phrase *chai Hashem* is that Hashem and His life are one and the same.

Metaphysics[61] expounds on this idea, stating that the human intellect cannot fully fathom the true essence of Hashem. This is so because His essence is perfect and man's intellect is imperfect, and His essence cannot be known as we understand knowledge.[62] Our intellect is as incapable of comprehending Him as our eyes are incapable of gazing directly into the sun. The inability is not due to

---

[58]*Chei* is written with a *tzere,* the vowel "e."

[59]This forms a compound of two nouns. For example, *banim* (sons) combines with *Yaakov* to form *bnei Yaakov* (the children of Jacob); *bayis* (house) combines with *hamelech* to form *beis hamelech* (the house of the king); *ishah* (woman), and *chayil* (valor) combine to form *eshet chayil* (woman of valor).

[60]*Chai* is written with a *patach,* the vowel "a."

[61]Written by Aristotle (384–322 B.C.E.). The Rambam's generation was strongly influenced by Aristotle's philosophy, and many were confused by seeming contradictions between the Torah and this philosophy. The Rambam tried to prove that Torah and philosophy agreed on many points; nevertheless, there were some issues of disagreement. In his *Moreh Nevuchim,* the Rambam presents these issues: that the world was created *ex nihilo,* that Hashem exercises close supervision over each person *(hashgachah peratis),* that man has a free will, and that Hashem's foreknowledge does not preclude man's free determination.

[62]We understand the essence of a being by studying its direct and indirect causes. Since Hashem has no cause—He is, in fact, the initial Cause, the Cause of all causes—we cannot conceive His essence.

any deficiency in the light from the sun, but rather to the unbeliev-able power of the sun, which engulfs the capacity of our eyesight. The Sages spoke a great deal about this subject, and everything they said is absolutely true. From what we have said it follows that we cannot grasp His knowledge because He is His knowledge, and His knowledge is He.

The people who question Hashem's knowledge of the future and man's free will, do not understand this remarkable idea. They admit that the true essence of Hashem is beyond comprehension; yet, they continue trying to understand Hashem's knowledge and imagine that they can attain it. This is, of course, impossible. If the human mind could grasp His knowledge, it would be able also to understand His essence since both are one and the same. Perfect knowledge of Hashem means understanding Him in His essence, which means encompassing His knowledge, His power, His will, His life, and all His other Divine attributes.

To summarize, I have made it clear that trying to fathom Hashem's knowledge is utter foolishness. All that we can grasp is that we know that Hashem exists and, therefore, are aware that He knows. If someone asked, "What is the nature of His knowledge?" we must respond that we do not know, any more than we know the nature of His existence. Those who attempt to grasp Hashem's existence are reproached in the following Scripture, *"Would you discover the mystery of God? Would you discover the limit of the Almighty?"* (Iyov 11:7).

Consider all that I have said, namely, that man has control over his actions and that it is up to him to do right or wrong without Hashem compelling one or the other. Therefore, it is right that he is commanded to perform commandments and that he is rewarded and punished for his actions. There is no doubt about any of this. As far as understanding Hashem's knowledge and how He knows everything, this is beyond our comprehension, as I have explained.

This is all that I intended to say in this chapter. It is time to end this introduction and begin the commentary to this Tractate.

•5•

Discourse on the World to Come

Introduction to the First Mishnah of the Tenth Chapter (Perek Chelek) of Sanhedrin

Discourse on the World to Come

REWARD AND PUNISHMENT

Here, I see fit to discuss some fundamental principles of faith that are extremely important.

You should be aware that Torah scholars are not in agreement about the reward for fulfilling the mitzvos that Hashem commanded through Moshe Rabbenu and the punishment for violating them. Opinions are so confused that it is almost impossible to find someone who clearly understands the matter. Because of errors in the arguments, no one can say anything with certainty.

According to one group, reward is the Garden of Eden, a place where people eat and drink without physical exertion and hard work. This group believes that people in the Garden of Eden have houses made of precious stones and beds covered with silk, that rivers there flow with wine and fragrant oils, and many other things like that. This group further believes that evil is punished in Gehenna, a place of blazing fires where bodies burn and people suffer all sorts of agonies and torments that would take too long to enumerate. The members of this group support their beliefs with statements from our Sages and from Scripture, whose plain meaning seems to confirm all or most of what they are saying.

The second group believes that the reward for observance is the coming of the Messiah, may he soon appear, when all human beings will be transformed into angels, becoming numerous, powerful, and immortal. According to these thinkers, the Messiah will live forever with the help of Hashem, and in this messianic time the earth will produce ready-made clothes and ready-baked bread and other such impossible things. Evildoers, according to these thinkers, will not live to see this because they are unworthy. These thinkers also support their assertions with many statements from the Sages and Scripture, whose plain meaning seems to prove their arguments in whole or part.

The third group imagines that the hoped-for good is the resurrection of the dead, when one returns to life and rejoins his family to eat and drink and never again die. Evildoers are punished by never returning to life. These thinkers also advance proofs from the Sages and Scripture, whose plain meaning seems to bolster all or part of their claims.

The fourth group believes that the reward for fulfilling the commandments is physical contentment, marked by our achieving in this world all worldly desires such as fertile land, abundant wealth, many children, good physical health, peace, security, government by a Jewish king, and domination of our enemies. They describe the punishment for disavowing the Torah as the opposite of these things, such as we are experiencing in our present exile. To prove their ideas, they point to the curses in the Torah, to Scriptures, and to various stories in the Bible.

The fifth group, and they are the majority, combine these various opinions. They say that our reward is the Messiah, who will resurrect the dead to inhabit the Garden of Eden, where they will eat and drink and live in good health forever.

The remarkable point that few describe is the World to Come. They give it little thought and do not speculate what the term really means and whether it refers to the ultimate reward or whether one of the above-mentioned opinions represents the final reward. Few distinguish between the ultimate goal and the circumstances[1] that lead to this ultimate goal. Instead, all people—simple folk and intellectuals alike—ask, "How will the dead come back to life? Naked or clothed? Will they arise in the same garments in which they were buried, with their embroideries, designs, and beautiful stitching, or will they appear in clothes that will just serve to cover their nakedness? And when the Messiah comes, will there be rich and poor? Will there be strong and weak?" Many such questions are asked all the time.

---

[1]The Rambam later explains that all other rewards are only preparatory to the ultimate reward of the World to Come.

AN APT ANALOGY

You who are studying these pages should understand the analogy I am going to make, so that you will get a clear idea of what I am going to say about this subject. Imagine a young boy who is brought to a teacher to learn Torah. It is of great benefit to him because it will enable him to attain perfection. However, because he is young and lacks sufficient thinking power, he cannot appreciate the value of that benefit or contemplate the perfection it will help him achieve. Therefore, the teacher, who is closer to perfection than the young boy, must encourage the boy to learn by offering him things that a child loves. So, the teacher might say, "If you study I'll give you nuts or figs," or "I'll give you a bit of honey."

With such encouragement, the boy studies and does his best, not for the sake of the learning itself, because he does not understand its importance, but to get the treat. He enjoys eating the treat more than studying. He considers learning drudgery and hard work, but he applies himself in order to obtain through his toil the goal he desires, the nut, or the piece of candy.

As he grows older and his mind develops, he no longer values the things he once craved; he begins to desire other things. Now the teacher must tempt him with different things, saying, "If you study, I'll buy you a beautiful pair of shoes or a good-looking suit." Again, the student applies himself, not for the sake of studying but for the suit which he values more than Torah study. To him, the suit is the ultimate goal of his learning.

And when the student becomes intellectually more mature, he spurns even this object and desires something more valuable. His teacher then says, "If you learn this portion or this chapter, I'll pay you a dinar or two." Then, he will learn and apply himself in order to receive the money. The money is more precious to him than the learning because the purpose of his learning is to get the money he was promised.

When he becomes still more mature and looks with disdain even on the money, recognizing that it is of little value, the teacher tells him, "If you study you may become a rabbi or a judge; people will honor you and rise before you, as they do with so-and-so." Then the student will study and apply himself in order to attain that distinguished status. His ultimate purpose is that people should honor him, place him on a pedestal, and praise him.

STUDY TORAH FOR ITS OWN SAKE

Although this approach is deplorable, a person must sometimes make the ultimate aim of learning something other than wisdom itself because the human mind is weak. So he says to himself, "Why am I learning? Only to gain respect." In truth this is farcical; it is the kind of learning the Sages term, "not for its own sake," which means that a person fulfills the mitzvos, studies Torah, and applies himself, not for the sake of Torah itself but for some ulterior motive. The Sages cautioned against this, saying, "Do not make the Torah a crown for self-glorification, nor a spade with which to dig" (*Avos* 4:7). They allude to what I have just explained to you, that the ultimate goal of learning should not be honors or money. You should not engage in studying the Almighty's Torah as a means to a livelihood. The only motive for learning should be the acquisition of knowledge. Similarly, the only purpose for studying the truth is to know that it is the truth. The Torah is truth, and the purpose of studying the Torah is to perform its commandments.

The mature man is forbidden to say, "What reward will I get if I fulfill the mitzvos, live according to the rules of ethics, and avoid the transgressions and vices that Hashem prohibited?" This attitude is like that of the little boy who says, "What will you give me if I study?" and the teacher answers, "I'll give you this or that." When we see an immature mind that is unable to grasp the magnitude of this matter, requiring some reward other than the ultimate, we respond to this childishness in kind, as it says, *"Answer a fool according to his foolishness"* (Mishlei 26:5).

The Sages have cautioned us not to serve Hashem and fulfill His mitzvos for ulterior motives. This is what Antigonus of Socho, that perfect man who understood the truth of all things, had in mind when he said, "Do not be like servants who serve their master for the sake of receiving a reward; instead be like servants who serve their master not for the sake of receiving a reward" (*Avos* 1:3). He meant that you should believe in truth for truth's sake. The Sages say of such a person that he serves Hashem out of love, *"He is ardently devoted to His commandments"* (Tehillim 112:1). Rabbi Eliezer expounds as follows, "devoted to His commandments and not to the reward for [performing] His commandments" (*Avodah Zarah* 19a). This is certainly very clear and offers convincing proof of what we have said in this discourse.

A stronger proof is this, "You may say, 'Well, I will study Torah to become rich, or to be called rabbi, or to receive a reward in the World to Come'; therefore, the Torah says, *'to love Hashem your God'* (Devarim 11:13). Whatever you do, do it only out of love for Hashem" (*Nedarim* 62a).

Now we have explained this idea of serving Hashem out of love and have shown that this is what the Torah intended and what the Sages believed. Only a crazy fool who is misled by his idiotic thoughts and mixed-up imagination is blind to this fact. The greatness of our father Abraham was that he served Hashem out of love, and his conduct should inspire you to follow in his footsteps.

But the Sages knew that this ideal is beyond the reach of most. And even someone with the potential to attain this ideal will not fully appreciate it at the beginning and may not consider it a principle of faith. For man only does something in order to derive some benefit from it or to avoid harm; otherwise, he considers his act futile and useless. This being so, how can you tell a Torah scholar, "Do these things, but do not do them for fear of Divine punishment nor in expectation of reward." This is an extremely difficult thing, because not everyone can perceive the truth and become like our father Abraham. Therefore, in order to keep the faith of the masses intact, the Sages permitted people to perform mitzvos with the hope of reward and to avoid transgressions for fear of punishment. They urge and support these attitudes. At the same time, they hope that some who have keen minds will recognize the truth and realize the way of perfection. This is the same approach we use to encourage a child to study, in line with the example I mentioned above.

Indeed, the Sages criticized Antigonus of Socho because he revealed the precept, "Do not serve Hashem for the purpose of receiving a reward," to the masses. They admonished him, saying, "Scholars, be cautious with your words" (*Avos* 1:11).

The public at large does not lose anything by fulfilling the mitzvos for fear of punishment or hope of reward. It is true that this is not the perfect way, but it is good because it provides training and makes them eager to fulfill the mitzvos of the Torah. As a result, they will be inspired to know the truth and reach the stage where they serve Hashem out of love. This is what the Sages meant when they said, "A person should always occupy himself with Torah and performing good deeds, even if his motives are not pure, because doing good with an ulterior motive will lead to doing good for its own sake" (*Pesachim* 50b).

THREE APPROACHES TO *AGGADAH*[2]

It is important to know that there are three differing interpretations of the Aggadic passages in the Talmud.

Most of the thinkers I have met personally and whose essays I have read or heard about belong to the first group. They take the *Aggados* literally and do not attribute any figurative meaning to them at all. To them, any impossible thing is possible. They believe this because they do not understand science and are ignorant of the various branches of knowledge. Their intellect is not sufficiently developed to spur them to a deeper understanding, nor have they found someone who would stimulate them to think deeply. They believe that the intent of the Sages in all their correct and lucid sayings is only what they themselves can understand, and they believe that these sayings should be taken literally. This they assert, despite the fact that the words of the Sages, when taken literally, tend to be so slanderous and irrational that even ordinary people — and surely those who are learned — would be amazed enough to exclaim, "How is it possible that anyone in the world could think like this or believe that this is true, much less approve of it!"

You should pity this group of ignoramuses who think that they are honoring and exalting the Sages, when, in fact, they are reducing them to the lowest levels. They do not understand what they do. As God lives, this group of thinkers destroys the glory of the Torah and darkens its brightness. They distort the meaning of the Almighty's Torah and pervert its intent, so that it seems to say the opposite of what is intended. Hashem said in His perfect Torah, *"For this is your wisdom and understanding in the eyes of the nations. They will hear all these rules and say, 'This great nation is certainly a wise and understanding people'"* (Devarim 4:6). But this group maintains the literal words of the Sages so that when the other nations hear

---

[2]*Aggadah* enhances the legal part of the Talmud with ethical and inspirational meaning. The *Aggadah* sparkles with profound words of wisdom, similes, and proverbs, as well as with edifying tales and parables. It should be noted that *Perek Chelek*, the chapter to which this introduction pertains, is composed almost entirely of *Aggadah*.

them they say, "What a foolish and degraded nation is this small people." In fact, these preachers are explaining passages that they themselves do not understand. I wish they would keep quiet, since they neither know nor understand what they preach, as it is stated, *"If you would only keep silent, it would be considered wisdom on your part"* (Iyov 13:5). Or they might at least say, "We do not understand what the Sages had in mind with this statement, nor do we know how to interpret it." But they think that they do understand, and they try to explain their limited understanding but do not convey what the Sages actually said. They lecture to the masses on such topics as Maseches Berachos, Perek Chelek, and similar tractates,[3] translating them literally, word for word.

The second group—and there are many of them—comprises those who understand the words of the Sages only in their literal sense. They think that the Sages intended nothing more than this literal meaning and, therefore, ridicule and denigrate their words. They slander that which should not be slandered and mock the sayings of the Sages. These people imagine that they are brighter than the Rabbis, whom they dismiss as dimwitted morons, ignorant of all things and totally incapable of understanding any sensible matter.

Many who fall into this erroneous belief are practicing physicians and students of astrology. They regard themselves as thinkers, scholars, and learned philosophers. But how far removed they are from humanity in comparison with true sages and philosophers! This group is even more stupid and foolish than the first. They are a cursed clique because they talk against distinguished, eminent men whose wisdom has been confirmed by scholars. If only these fools would study the sciences, they would understand the methodology needed to write on theology and related matters for the masses and the scholars. If they understood the practical application of philosophy, they would discern whether the Sages were indeed wise men. Then the words of the Sages would become clear to them.

The third group comprises so few, as God lives, that you can hardly call them a group, except in the sense that we call the sun a species, although there is only one of its kind. These individuals have a clear understanding of the greatness of the Sages. They appreciate

---

[3]All of these contain Aggadic passages.

the intellectual excellence of the Rabbis as evidenced in all their statements about concepts relating to the absolute truth. Although these individuals are few and far between, their writings demonstrate a degree of perfection that proves they have attained the truth.

They know full well that the impossible is indeed not possible and that existence cannot be denied. They realize that the Sages do not say meaningless things, that their words have a superficial as well as a hidden, metaphoric meaning. When the Sages mention impossible things, they are speaking metaphorically, for this is the way great Sages speak. That is why Solomon, the greatest of the Sages, began his work by stating, *"To understand proverb and epigram, the words of the wise and their riddles"* (Mishlei 1:6).

Language experts know that a riddle is a form of speech that points at a hidden meaning, not an obvious one, as it says, *"Let me pose you a riddle"* (Shoftim 14:12). Since the Sages deal with lofty matters relating to the purpose of life, they speak in the form of riddle or allegory. How can we criticize the Sages for concealing wisdom with parable and employing comparisons with the ordinary and commonplace? After all, we see that the wisest of all men did so with Divine inspiration. I have in mind Solomon in these works: Mishlei, Shir Hashirim, and parts of Koheles.

Why is it so difficult for us to explain the words of the Sages by stripping away their literal meaning so that they make sense and agree with the truth and the Holy Scriptures? The Sages themselves interpret Scripture figuratively. This is the truth! For example, they say that this passage, *"He (Benaiah) struck the two altar-fires of Moab"* (II Shmuel 23:20), must be taken figuratively.[4] Similarly, this passage, *"Once on a snowy day, he went down into a pit and slew a lion,"* is considered a parable.[5] Likewise, the verse, *"David said, 'If only I could drink water from the cistern which is by the gate of Beth-*

---

[4]*Ariel,* translated here as *the two altar-fires of Moab,* symbolizes the two Temples. *Ari* (lion) represents the Sanctuary, which, like a lion, is wide in the front and narrow in the back (Rashi, Yeshayah 29:1). The reference to Moab alludes to David and Solomon, who are descendants of Ruth the Moabite (*Berachos* 18b).

[5]One opinion in Talmud in *Berachos* 18b interprets this phrase to mean that Benaiah broke off chunks of ice and went down and immersed himself to study Torah in purity; according to another opinion, the verse means that he studied the entire Midrash on Leviticus in one short winter's day.

lehem' " (II Shmuel 23:15), and the rest of the story is a parable.[6] In the same way, one of the Sages considers the entire book of Job a parable (*Bava Basra* 15a), but he does not explain the moral lesson of the parable. Ezekiel's story of the dry bones (Yechezkel 37) is also a parable, according to Rabbi Yehudah (*Sanhedrin* 92b). Many similar instances can be cited.

If you, the reader, belong to one of the first two groups, you will not pay any attention to my words regarding this matter because you will not agree with anything I say. Not only that, but my words will hurt you, and you will hate them. After all, how can you expect a small portion of light and nutritious food to be pleasing if you are accustomed to bad food? The truth is that good food would actually harm you, and you would despise it. Recall what those who were used to eating onions, garlic, and fish said of the manna, *"We are getting disgusted with this weightless food"* (Bamidbar 21:5).

But if you belong to the third group, whenever you come upon a saying of the Rabbis that seems to defy reason, you consider it and realize that it is a riddle or parable. You go to sleep exasperated and preoccupied as you try to understand its meaning. Finally, you decipher what the Sages intended, as it says, *"To discover useful sayings and record genuinely truthful sayings"* (Mishlei 12:10).

Now study my book, and, with the help of Hashem, you will greatly benefit from it.

TWO KINDS OF PLEASURE

I will now begin to discuss the subject I had in mind at the outset. Just as a blind man cannot perceive colors and a deaf person cannot hear sound and a eunuch cannot feel the desire for marital intercourse, so the human body cannot enjoy spiritual pleasures. And just as the fish do not know the element of fire because they live in the opposite element of water, so are the pleasures of the spiritual world unknown in our physical world. Indeed, we know of no pleasures other than those of the body, the joys we derive from eating, drinking, and marital relations. To us, there is no pleasure aside from these.

---

[6]Since water symbolizes the Torah, David's thirst for water is interpreted to mean that he needed help on a halachic problem. He sought guidance "at the gate," which was the seat of the *Sanhedrin* (*Bava Kamma* 60b).

We do not recognize or understand this concept at first; it comes only after much contemplation. This is to be expected because we live in the physical world and therefore can only experience its inferior and transitory pleasures. Spiritual pleasures, on the other hand, are permanent, everlasting, and uninterrupted. There is no connection or kinship of any kind between these two kinds of pleasure.

It is not proper for those of us who are Torah scholars or theological thinkers to say that the angels, the stars, and the heavenly spheres[7] experience no pleasure. In truth they experience very great pleasure in that they know and grasp the true essence of the Creator, blessed is He. This knowledge provides them constant and uninterrupted pleasure. But they have no physical pleasures, nor can they understand such because they have no senses that would enable them to feel what we feel.

So it is for us; when we become spiritually cleansed and climb to this heavenly level after death, we will no longer relate to bodily pleasures. We will have no craving for ordinary joys, any more than a mighty monarch would want to abdicate his crown and become a child again to play ball with others as he did before he became king. Just as he enjoyed this activity during his childhood when he did not know other pleasure, so we value our present bodily pleasures more than our spiritual pleasures.

And if you reflect on these two kinds of pleasure, you will recognize even here and now the mediocrity of the one and the excellence of the other. This is evident from the way most people inflict unbearable stress on their souls and bodies in order to attain greatness, honor, and prestige, which are spiritual pleasures very unlike the pleasures of eating and drinking. Similarly, many value the satisfaction they derive from getting even with an enemy more than bodily pleasures. Likewise, many people refrain from physical pleasure so as not to be disgraced and embarrassed or because they want to earn a good reputation. If this is true in the physical world,

---

[7] In *Hilchos Yesodei Hatorah*, the Rambam describes nine translucent spheres that are layered in space, one above another, like onion skins. The planets are fastened to the eight lower spheres. The constellations of the zodiac are situated in the ninth, outermost sphere. The Rambam ascribes a soul and understanding to the stars and the spheres. "They are alive and recognize the Creator. Each of them sings Hashem's praises like the angels" (3:9).

then surely it is true in the spiritual world, the World to Come, where our souls will have an understanding of the Creator to match or even exceed the comprehension of higher beings.

Spiritual pleasure cannot be subdivided. It cannot be described or compared to anything. Marveling at the greatness and magnificence of this pleasure, David said, *"How abundant is the good that You have in store for those who fear You"* (Tehillim 31:20). Addressing the same subject, the Sages said, "In the World to Come there will be no eating, drinking, washing, anointing, nor marital intercourse, but the righteous sit there with their crowns on their heads, enjoying the radiance of the *Shechinah* (Divine Presence)" (*Berachos* 17a). The phrase *with their crowns on their heads* symbolizes the immortality of the soul when it gains a comprehension of the Almighty, as the great philosophers explain at length. This statement of the Sages, "enjoying the radiance of the *Shechinah* (Divine Presence)," describes those souls that delight in understanding the essence of the Creator, just as the holy beings and angels enjoy what they understand of His Existence.

You see, the greatest happiness and the ultimate purpose of life is to become part of this elevated group and to share its veneration. The soul that reaches this state, as I have explained, is everlasting, just like the Creator. He is the source of the soul's existence because it recognizes Him, as has been explained by the early philosophers.

This is the great good to which no other good can be compared and which cannot be matched by any other pleasure. For how can something that is everlasting be compared to something that is finite? The Sages derive this thought from the verse, *"You will have it good, and you will live long"* (Devarim 22:7), which they expound as follows, *"You will have it good,"* in the world that is all good, and *"you will live long,"* in the world that is infinitely long.

The retribution for absolute evil is *kares* (excision), whereby the soul is isolated so that it ceases to exist. This is what is mentioned in the Torah in this passage, *"That person shall be utterly cut off"* (Bamidbar 15:31). The Sages interpreted this to mean, "*hikareis* (cut off) in this world and *tikareis* (cut off) in the World to Come." Scripture also says, *"The life of my master will be bound up in the bundle of life in the care of Hashem"* (I Shmuel 25:29). Whoever chooses and indulges in physical pleasures, despises the truth, and loves falsehood is cut off from eternal life. He becomes nothing but a mass of material.

The prophet has already explained that the World to Come cannot be perceived through our physical senses. As he phrased it, *"No eye has seen, O God, but You"* (Yeshayah 64:3). Expounding this passage, the Sages said that all the prophets foretold the Messianic Age, but when it comes to the World to Come, "no eye has seen it, O God, but You" (*Berachos* 34b, *Shabbat* 63a, and *Sanhedrin* 99a).

REWARD IN THIS WORLD

Let me tell you how to view the rewards and punishments that the Torah promises. Hashem is saying, "If you fulfill these mitzvos, I will help you attain perfection through them, and I will remove all hindrances to your achievement." Because it is impossible for a person to perform the mitzvos when he is sick, hungry, or thirsty, or when he is at war or besieged, Hashem promises to remove these impediments and provide health and peace until one achieves perfection of knowledge and becomes deserving of the World to Come, which is the ultimate reward for fulfilling the Torah. And if people transgress the Torah, they will be punished with disaster, such as hunger, thirst, war, and siege, so that they will be unable to fulfill the mitzvos, as it is written, *"Because you did not serve Hashem, your God, in joy and gladness over the abundance of everything, you will serve the enemies loosed against you, suffering hunger and thirst, nakedness, and the loss of all worldly goods; they will place an iron yoke on your neck until they have wiped you out"* (Devarim 28:47,48).

If you give serious thought to this matter, you will see what Hashem is saying, "If you fulfill some of the mitzvos with love and diligence, I will help you perform all of them by eliminating all impediments and hindrances. But if you contemptuously abandon any of the mitzvos, I will inundate you with calamities that will prevent your fulfilling all of them. As a result, you will not be able to attain perfection or life in the World to Come." This is what the Sages had in mind when they said, "The reward of a *mitzvah* is a *mitzvah*, and the reward of a transgression is a transgression" (*Avos* 4:2).

THE GARDEN OF EDEN AND GEHENNA

The Garden of Eden is a fertile place in the best part of our earth, where there are many rivers and fruit trees. At some time in the future, Hashem will reveal its location to man. He will show us how to get there, and we will enjoy ourselves there. In addition to plants that we know, we will also find there many fabulous plants that are highly beneficial and delightful to the palate. All this is not impossible or far-fetched. On the contrary, even if it had not been mentioned in the Torah, it would be fair to assume that such a place exists. But its reality is assured by its being mentioned in the Torah.

Gehenna is a term for the suffering and punishment that will be inflicted on the wicked. The precise nature of this punishment is not explained in the Talmud. Some say that the sun will come close enough to burn (*Nedarim* 8b and *Avodah Zarah* 3b). These Sages find their proof in the verse, *"For lo! That day is at hand, burning like an oven"* (Malachi 3:19). Others say that a strange heat will develop inside the bodies of the wicked and burn them (*Sanhedrin* 108a). These Sages cite the passage, *"Your spirit will devour you like fire"* (Yeshayah 31:11).

RESURRECTION OF THE DEAD

The resurrection of the dead is one of the fundamental principles handed down by Moshe Rabbenu. One who does not believe it cannot be associated with Judaism.

Resurrection will occur only for the righteous as it says, "Rain is for both the wicked and the righteous, but the resurrection is only for the righteous" (*Midrash Rabbah,* Genesis 13:6; see also *Taanis* 7a). It does not make sense for the wicked to be brought back to life, for even when alive they were like the dead, as our Sages said, "The wicked are considered dead, even during their lifetimes. But the righteous are considered alive, even after they die" (*Berachos* 18b). You should realize that all men must die, decompose, and disintegrate into the substances of which man is made.

THE MESSIANIC AGE

The Messianic Age refers to the time when the monarchy will be reestablished and the Jewish people will return to the Land of Israel. The Messiah will be great, and his rule will begin in Zion. His fame will be known throughout the world, and he will be more celebrated than King Solomon. All nations will seek to treat with him, and the world will venerate his righteousness and the miracles he will bring about. Whoever opposes him will be disabled by Hashem and forced to surrender.

The Scripture that speaks of the Messiah predicts his success and our subsequent prosperity. The world as we know it will not alter, but the Jewish nation will regain independence, as the Sages said, "The only difference between this world and the Messianic Age is that our domination by other governments will come to an end" (*Pesachim* 68a, *Sanhedrin* 91a and 99b).

When the Messiah comes, there will still be rich and poor, strong and weak. But it will be easy for people to earn a livelihood and to acquire much profit with little effort. The Sages had this in mind when they said, "In the future, the Land of Israel will produce ready-made loaves of bread and woolen garments" (*Shabbos* 30b). This statement is simply meant to imply an easy life, just like the expression "he has found his bread baked and his meal cooked" shows something that is ready to hand. After all, we know that there will still be sowing and harvesting in messianic times because the verse, *"Aliens shall be your plowmen and vine-trimmers"* (Yeshayah 61:5), tells us so. Rabban Gamliel, who made the above-mentioned statement,[8] became angry at one of his students who misunderstood his statement and interpreted it literally (*Shabbos* 30b). Rabban Gamliel had given the student an answer that was geared to his level of comprehension, but the answer was not meant to be taken literally. We know that this is so because the Talmud uses the incident to illustrate this lesson, *"Do not answer a fool according to his folly"* (Mishlei 26:4).

The most distinctive feature of the Messianic Age will be our freedom from foreign domination, which prevents us from fulfilling all the *mitzvos*. Wisdom will increase, as it says, *"For the land shall be filled with the knowledge of Hashem"* (Yeshayah 11:9). Wars will end, as it is stated, *"Nation shall not take up sword against nation"* (Micah 4:3). Perfection, which grants us the merit of the World to Come, will be commonplace.

The Messiah will then die, and his son will succeed him. He, in turn, will be succeeded by his son. The prophet clearly foretold

---

[8]"In the future, the Land of Israel will produce ready-made loaves of bread and woolen garments" (*Shabbos* 30b).

his death, *"He shall not grow dim or be bruised until he has established the true way on earth"* (Yeshayah 42:4). But his reign will last for a very long time, and people generally will live long because stress and grief will disappear. It should not surprise you that his kingdom will last for thousands of years, because the Sages have said that a union of good people will not easily break up.

We do not anticipate the Messianic Age because of the rich harvests or the affluence it will bring. We do not long for it because we will ride horses and indulge in wine and song, as people with confused ideas believe. Instead, the prophets and pious have yearned for the Days of the Messiah because that is when the righteous will join forces and personal conduct will be guided by morality and wisdom. The Messiah will demonstrate righteousness, integrity, extraordinary wisdom, and a closeness to Hashem, as it says, *"Hashem said, 'You are My son; I have given birth to you this day' "* (Tehillim 2:7).

The prophets have longed for the Messianic Age because it is a time when people will fulfill all the mitzvos of the Torah without negligence or laziness, as it is written, *"No longer will they need to teach one another and say to one another, 'Know Hashem'; for all of them, from the least to the greatest, shall know Me"* (Yirmiyah 31:34), and, *"I will put My Torah into their innermost being"* (Yirmiyah 31:33), and, *"I will remove the heart of stone from your body . . ."* (Yechezkel 36:26).

Many similar passages deal with this theme. It is through these that we will acquire the World to Come.

THE WORLD TO COME

The ultimate goal is the World to Come. It is what we all should strive for, as the Sage[9] who was the authority on the truth recognized when he focused on the single reward that surpasses all else, saying "All Israel have a share in the World to Come" (*Sanhedrin* 10:1).

But although the World to Come is the desired goal, it is not proper for a person who wants to serve Hashem from love to have it in mind, as I explained earlier. Rather, you should serve Him as I

---

[9]Rabbi Yehudah HaNasi, the redactor of the Mishnah, spoke of the World to Come when he began discussing the rewards for performing *mitzvos*.

will tell you. If you believe that there is wisdom and that it is the Torah, which came to the prophets from the exalted Creator, and that He taught them the good traits, the mitzvos, and identified the bad traits, the transgressions, then you will naturally do the good and avoid the evil. By your actions you will perfect yourself and place yourself at a great remove from the animals. And when one has attained such perfection, there is nothing that can prevent his soul from living on. It continues to exist in its natural habitat, which is the World to Come, as I have explained.

The restraint that prevents animals from running wild is external, like a bit and a bridle, as described in this verse, *"Be not like a senseless horse or mule, whose mouth must be curbed by bit and bridle"* (Tehillim 32:9). But man's restraint should come from within, from his humanness. If his soul is perfect, it restrains him from the things that would prevent his achieving perfection—the vices. It encourages him to do those things that will further enhance his perfection—the virtues.

This is what I have come to understand from the sayings of the Sages on this important subject. In the future, I hope to compile everything on this subject in the Talmud and other writings. I will explain and interpret the arguments so as to reflect the truth. I will bring proofs from the Sages, and I will reveal which of their explanations are to be taken literally and which metaphorically. These figurative ideas have their origin in a dream, although they are presented in clear, simple terms as if they were wide awake thoughts. In that treatise I will clarify many tenets of faith and expound on all the things that I have just mentioned here.

Do not criticize me for using certain expressions or making certain assertions that seem unsophisticated. I decided to avoid rhetoric, so that even a person who has no previous training can grasp this difficult subject that not everyone can understand.

Mishnah 1

All of Israel have a share in the World to Come, as it is written, "And your people, all of them righteous, shall possess the land for all time. They are the shoot that I planted, My handiwork in which I glory" (*Yeshayah, 60:21*).

The following do not have a share in the World to Come: Anyone who says that the resurrection of the dead is not alluded to in the Torah, anyone who says the Torah is not from Heaven, and an *apikoros* (one who disbelieves).[10] Rabbi Akiva adds, 'Also a person who reads heretical books, or one who whispers an incantation over a wound,' saying, "I will not strike you with any of the sicknesses that I brought on Egypt, for I am Hashem who heals you" (Shemos 15:26). Abba Shaul says, Also a person who pronounces the divine name the way the letters are written.

---

[10]According to the *Gemara* (*Sanhedrin* 99b), an *apikoros* refers to a person who belittles the Torah and the Sages, and denies the existence and the oneness of Hashem. The Rambam explains that the term *apikoros* is derived from the Aramaic word *hefker,* (loose and immoral), and denotes a person who is contemptuous of the Torah. The word *apikoros* also relates to Epicurus, the Greek philosopher who taught that physical pleasure was the highest good.

Commentary

The word *apikoros* is Aramaic for one who degrades and derides the Torah or Torah scholars. Therefore, this term is applied to anyone who does not believe the fundamental principles of the Torah or to one who insults the Sages or any Torah scholar, or to one who humiliates his teacher (*Sanhedrin* 99b).

"Heretical books" refers to the books of the *minim* (sectarians), and to the book of Ben Sirach, who wrote foolish books about the practice of discerning character in the features of the face, which is a senseless and useless subject. The books are nothing but a waste of time. The Arabs have books like these that tell stories about their past and the lives of their kings, books about genealogies of the Arabs, books of songs, and similar books that contain no wisdom and are of no practical use, but are only a waste of time.

One who whispers an incantation over a wound has no portion in the World to Come. This is true only if he also spits on the wound, because this is an insult to Hashem.

A person who pronounces the divine name has no portion in the World to Come.

The Sages also mentioned other things that cause a person to lose his share in the World to Come: He who publicly embarrasses his neighbor (*Bava Metzia* 58b), he who calls his neighbor by a belittling name, and he who elevates himself by shaming his neighbor. Although the average man deems these minor abuses, only one who has a mediocre, imperfect soul would act this way, and such a person is not worthy of life in the World to Come.

At this point I think it is necessary for me to mention—and this is the most appropriate place for it—that our faith is based on the following thirteen fundamental principles.

Thirteen Principles of Faith

THE FIRST PRINCIPLE

The first principle is belief in the existence of the Creator, blessed is He. There is a Being who is perfect in every possible way, and He is the prime Cause of all existence. The continued existence of the universe depends on Him and flows from Him. It is unthinkable that He not exist because, if such were the case, all things would cease to exist, and nothing would remain. But if we could imagine that nothing else existed, Hashem would not cease to exist. He would not be diminished in any way, for unity and lordship belong only to Him, whose name is Hashem.

His existence is dependent on nothing but Himself, and He does not need any other thing. However, every other being, whether angel, heavenly body, or that which is below, depends on Him for existence. The Torah teaches us this first principle in the first of the Ten Commandments, *"I am Hashem your God"* (Shemos 20:2).

THE SECOND PRINCIPLE

The second principle concerns the unity of Hashem. We believe that He who is the cause of everything, is One. His unity is not, however, like the oneness of a pair (which is a unit that consists of two components), or like the oneness of a species (which is a group made up of many parts). Nor is He like an individual who is made up of many elements. His oneness is not even like that of the simplest physical thing, which can still be divided endlessly. Hashem is One, and His unity is unlike any other. The Torah teaches us this second principle when it says, *"Hear O Israel, Hashem is our God, Hashem is One"* (Devarim 6:4).

THE THIRD PRINCIPLE

The third principle is that Hashem is incorporeal. We believe that
the Being we call Hashem is not a body or a physical force. Because
nothing that can be said about a physical body applies to Him, we
cannot say that Hashem moves, rests, or dwells in a certain place.
Actions such as these can neither be attributed to Him nor be part of
His intrinsic nature. When our Sages speak of Hashem, they teach
that such concepts as joining and separating do not pertain to Him.
They say in the Talmud, "On high, there is neither sitting nor
standing, neither division nor separation" (*Chagigah* 15a). The
prophet says, " *'To whom, then, can you liken Me? To whom can I be
compared?' says the Holy One*" (Yeshayah 40:25), for if Hashem were a
physical being, He would be like other physical things.

In many places, however, our holy Scriptures describe Hashem
in physical terms. Thus, He is portrayed as walking, standing,
sitting, speaking, and the like. In all these cases, Scripture is
speaking figuratively. The Sages, too, teach us, "The Torah speaks
in the language of man" (*Berachos* 31b). Many Sages have also
spoken of this matter extensively.

The Torah teaches us this third principle when it says, *"You
have not seen any image"* (Devarim 4:15). We cannot conceive of
Hashem as having any image or form. This is because He is not a
physical being or force, as discussed earlier.

THE FOURTH PRINCIPLE

The fourth principle is the timelessness of Hashem. We believe that
the One whom we call Hashem is absolutely timeless, and that
nothing else has this attribute. This is discussed many times in
Scripture, and the Torah teaches it when it says, *"The shelter of the
eternal God"* (Devarim 33:27).

THE FIFTH PRINCIPLE

The fifth principle is that Hashem is the only one whom we may
worship and exalt. We may declare only His greatness and obey
only His commandments. We may not direct our prayers toward

anything beneath Him, whether it be an angel, a star, a planet, one of the elements, or any combination of these because they have a predetermined nature and are, therefore, without authority or free will. Since they can only obey the will of Hashem, it is not right to use these things as intermediaries to Hashem. All our thoughts should be directed toward Him alone, and everything else should be put out of mind.

Thus, the fifth principle forbids all forms of idol worship; much of the Torah warns against this transgression.

THE SIXTH PRINCIPLE

The sixth principle deals with prophecy. We must realize that there are individuals who have such outstanding qualities and who have attained such perfection that their souls are ready to receive pure spiritual wisdom. Their human intellects are able to connect with the Creative Mind (*Sechel Hapo'al*) and receive Divine inspiration. These are the prophets, and the inspiration they receive is prophecy.

This is the concept of prophecy. A full explanation would require a more lengthy discussion, but I do not intend to bring proofs for each principle or explain how to understand each because this would include all of wisdom. I only mention these concepts in general terms. There are many verses in the Torah that attest to the prophecy of many different prophets.

THE SEVENTH PRINCIPLE

The seventh principle deals with the prophecy of Moshe Rabbenu. We believe that Moses was the father of all the prophets and that he was superior to all other prophets, whether they preceded or followed him. He was the most magnificent human being who had reached an understanding of Hashem that is greater than that of any man who ever existed or will ever exist. He ascended above the level of mortal man and was included in the category of angels. There was no barrier that he did not breach and penetrate, no physical obstacle that stood in his way. He was not marred by any shortcoming, great or small. Indeed, his imagination, senses, and feelings ceased to exist because his conscious mind was superseded by his spirituality. It is for this reason that we can say he spoke to Hashem without an angel interceding.

I want very much to clarify this mystery and unlock its hidden meanings in the Torah verses. I would like to explain the phrase, *"mouth to mouth I shall speak to him"* (Bamidbar 12:8)[11] and others like it. But I realize that this subject requires a great deal of elaboration. Before delving into it, I would have to bring many proofs, propositions, introductions, and illustrations. I would have to explain the nature of angels and how they differ from the Creator Himself. I would also have to explain the soul and all its powers.[12] The discussion would then have to be expanded to include an exposition of the imagery the prophets used to describe the Creator and the angels. This, in turn, would lead to a discussion of the *Shi'ur Komah*, the Divine Stature, and its meaning.

Even this would not be enough, and no matter how simple my discussion, it would still run to an essay of a hundred pages. Therefore, I will leave these matters for a book of discourses I plan to write. Or I will include it in my book on the prophets that I am currently working on, or in a special volume I will compose to explain these thirteen principles.

Returning to the subject of the seventh principle, let me say that Moses' prophecy differs from that of all other prophets in four ways:

> 1. Hashem spoke to all other prophets only through an intermediary. Moses alone did not need any intermediary. This is indicated in the Torah when it says, *"Mouth to mouth I will speak to Him"* (Bamidbar 12:8).
>
> 2. Every other prophet could receive prophecy only while sleeping. Therefore, Scripture speaks of prophecy as *"a dream at night"* (Bereishis 20:3), *"a vision of night"* (Iyov 33:15), and the like. Even if a prophet receives his vision during the day, it comes only during a deep sleep when all senses are suspended and the mind is blank. This state, which resembles a dream, is a vision or an apparition. Scripture describes it as *"visions of God"* (Yechezkel 8:3). In contrast, the Divine Word came to Moses by day, when he was standing between the two cherubim.[13]

---

[11]This is how Hashem describes Moses' level of prophecy.

[12]The Rambam discusses the soul and its powers in the first part of this volume, *Shemonah Perakim*.

[13]These are on the Ark of Testimony.

Hashem Himself confirmed this, *"I will meet with you there [and I will speak with you, from above the ark cover, from between the two cherubim that are on the ark of testimony]* (Shemos 25:22). Hashem also said, *"If there be a prophet among you, [then I, Hashem, will make Myself known to him in a vision, I will speak to him in a dream]. Not so My servant Moses. Mouth to mouth I will speak to him"* (Bamidbar 12:6–8).

3. Even though other prophets receive their vision as an apparition and may communicate with an angel, the experience saps their strength and unnerves them, causing such overpowering fear that they come close to death. For example, when the angel Gabriel spoke to Daniel in a vision, Daniel said, *"I was drained of strength, my vigor was destroyed, and I could not summon up strength . . . I was overcome by a deep sleep, I lay prostrate on the ground"* (Daniel 10:8). Later he said, *"Because of the vision, I have been seized with pangs and cannot summon strength"* (Daniel 10:16). However, this was not the case with Moses. The Word would come to him directly, and he experienced no terror and trembling at all. This is what the Torah means by the passage, *"Hashem spoke to Moses face to face, as a man speaks to his friend"* (Shemos 33:11). Moses' encounter with Hashem was like that of a casual conversation with a friend, without fear or anxiety. Moses was not paralyzed by the Word, even though it was "face to face," because he was so spiritual a being, as I said earlier.

4. Other prophets receive prophecy only at the will of Hashem, not at their instigation. A prophet might wait days or years without experiencing a prophecy. He might pray that Hashem reveal a prophetic answer to a perplexing matter and then wait for days or months before the prophecy came. Or it might never come at all. There were groups of people who prepared themselves to receive prophecy by purifying their thoughts. Elisha, for example, prepared himself, saying, *"Now bring me a musician"* (II Melachim 3:15), whereupon, the vision came to him. But even with this preparation it was not certain that the prophetic vision would come. Moshe Rabbenu, on the other hand, could attain prophecy at will. He was able to say to a questioner, *"Stand by, and let me hear what instructions Hashem gives regarding your case"* (Bamidbar 9:8). Similarly, Hashem told Moses, *Tell your brother Aaron that he is not to come at all times into the holy place"* (Vayikra 16:2). Our Sages interpret this to mean: Aaron could not approach Hashem at will, but Moses could (Sifrei, Vayikra 16:2).

THE EIGHTH PRINCIPLE

The eighth principle is that the Torah is from Heaven. We believe that the entire Torah that Moses gave to us came from Hashem in a process we metaphorically call *the Word of Hashem*. We do not know how it was transmitted to Moses, but when it was transmitted, Moses wrote it down as a scribe takes dictation. Thus he recorded all the events that occurred in his time, the other stories in the Torah, and the mitzvos. That is why Moses is called a scribe.[14]

All the verses of the Torah have equal sanctity. There is no difference between, *"And the children of Ham were Cush and Mizrayim"* (Berishis 10;6) or *"his wife's name was Mehitabel, the daughter of Matred . . ."* (Berishis 36:39)[15] and *"I am Hashem your God"* (Shemos 20:2) or *"Hear O Israel, Hashem is our God, Hashem is One"* (Devarim 6:4).[16] They all originate from Hashem, and all are part of Hashem's Torah, which is perfect, pure, holy, and true.

Anyone who claims that some verses and stories were written by Moses at his own discretion is considered the most despicable nonbeliever and a perverter of the Torah by our Sages and prophets. Such a person thinks that the Torah must be comprised of an inner kernel and an outer layer, and that the historic stories were made up by Moses and are of no value. Such a person is classified as one who says, "the Torah is not from Heaven" (*Sanhedrin* 90a). Our Sages say that this category includes even a person who believes that the entire Torah was given by Hashem except for one verse that was composed by Moses and not spoken by Hashem (Sanhedrin 99a). The Torah says of such a person, *"He has treated Hashem's word with contempt . . . [his soul shall be utterly cut off]"* (Bamidbar 15:31).

If you understand the Torah, you find that every single word contains wisdom and marvelous insights. But the full depth of its wisdom can never be fathomed — *"Its measure is longer than the earth and broader than the sea"* (Iyov 11:9). Just follow in the footsteps of King David, the anointed of the God of Jacob, who prayed, *"Open my eyes, that I may perceive the wonders of Your Torah"* (Tehillim 119:18).

---

[14]See Numbers 21:18, where Targum Onkelos renders *mechokek* as *safraya* (scribe).

[15]Verses that seem trivial.

[16]Verses that seem important.

The explanation of the Torah[17] that has been handed down to us was also given by Hashem. The specifications for *sukkah, lulav, shofar, tzitzis,* and *tefillin* are exactly as Hashem gave to Moses, and which he faithfully transmitted to us. The Torah teaches us this principle when it says, *"Moses said, 'This shall demonstrate to you that Hashem sent me to do all these deeds, and I did not make up anything myself '"* (Bamidbar 16:28).

THE NINTH PRINCIPLE

The ninth principle concerns the changelessness of the Torah, which was given by Hashem in its present form. No other Torah will be given, and nothing may be added to or eliminated from the Written Torah or the Oral Torah, *"Neither add to it nor take away from it"* (Devarim 13:1).

THE TENTH PRINCIPLE

The tenth principle is that Hashem knows the actions of all men, and He never ceases to observe anyone. This principle counters those who say, *"Hashem has forsaken the world"* (Yechezkel 9:9) and is consistent with the prophet Jeremiah who says, *"Wondrous in purpose and mighty in deed, whose eyes observe all the ways of men"* (Yirmiyah 32:19). The following passages also exemplify this principle, *"Hashem saw that man's wickedness on earth was increasing"* (Bereishis 6:1), and, *"The cry of Sodom and Amorah is great"* (Bereishis 18:20).

THE ELEVENTH PRINCIPLE

The eleventh principle is that Hashem rewards those who observe the mitzvos of the Torah and punishes those who violate its prohibitions.

The greatest reward is the World to Come, and the greatest punishment is *kares,* the disintegration of the soul; I have already said enough about this matter. The Torah presents the principle in this exchange between Moses and Hashem, *"Now, if You would, please forgive their sin, but if not, then erase me from the book You have*

---

[17]This is the *Torah She-be-'al Peh* (the Oral Torah).

written (Shemos 32:33). Hashem replied, *"He who has sinned against Me will I erase from my book"* (Shemos 32:33). Here is proof that Hashem knows both the pious man and the sinner. He rewards the one and punishes the other.

THE TWELFTH PRINCIPLE

The twelfth principle pertains to the Messianic Age. We believe and affirm that Messiah will come. We do not think that he will be late in coming, and *"even if he tarries, we await him"* (Habakkuk 2:3). We should not set a specific time for his coming; neither should we use Scripture to calculate the time of his arrival. Our Sages said about this, "May the people that calculate the time of the final redemption meet with adversity" (*Sanhedrin* 97b).[18]

We believe that the Messiah will be greater and more glorious than any king that has ever lived. This has been predicted by every prophet from Moses to Malachi. If anyone doubts this or downplays the Messiah, it is as if he denies the Torah itself, for the Torah explicitly promises his coming in the story of Balaam[19] and in the Torah portion of Nitzavim (Devarim 29:9–30:30).

Included in this principle is the belief that a Jewish king can come only from the family of David through his son Solomon. One who challenges this dynasty denies Hashem and the words of His prophets.

THE THIRTEENTH PRINCIPLE

The thirteenth principle is the resurrection of the dead, and I have already explained it.

---

[18]Literally, *blasted by the spirit.*

[19]Balaam prophesied, *"When their kingdom is established, their king shall be greater than Agag"* (Bamidbar 24:7). Targum Onkelos translates this, *"A king shall come forth from his children, and he shall rule many nations."* Balaam also said, *"I see him, but not now (King David); I behold him, but not near (Messiah). A star shall come forth from Jacob* (King David); *a scepter shall arise in Israel (Messiah)* (Bamidbar 24:17).

The Basis of Our Faith

When a person believes in these fundamental principles and his faith is based on a clear understanding of them, he becomes part of the community of Israel. It is a mitzvah for us to love such a person, to have compassion on him, and to do for him all that Hashem commanded us to do for one another. We must be kind to him and treat him like a brother, even if he has committed every conceivable sin through unbridled desire and base instinct. He will be punished according to the gravity of his sins, but this sinner in Israel still has a portion in the World to Come.

If a person rejects one of these fundamental principles, he has excluded himself from the community of Israel and denied a basic tenet of the Jewish faith. We call such an individual an *apikoros* (a heretic or unbeliever). He is considered as "one who mutilated the shoots" (one who abandoned Judaism).[20] It is a mitzvah to despise and destroy such a person. Scripture says of such a man, *"O Hashem, You know I hate those who hate You"* (Tehillim 139:21).

I find that I have drawn out my remarks more than I should have, and that I have digressed from the topic of my book. However, I have done so because I saw that it would be helpful to a person's faith. In my work I have compiled useful insights from many great books. If you keep them in mind they will bring you happiness. Review these things many times, and ponder them carefully. And if you make the mistake of thinking that you understand these matters after reading them once or even ten times, God knows that you are fooling yourself. Therefore, do not quickly skim through its pages, because I did not write just what came to mind but only after careful reflection and deep thought. After thorough examination of correct and incorrect opinions, I clarified those that should be believed, and I brought reasons and proofs for each point. I ask Hashem to lead me down the right path.

---

[20]The Talmud in *Chagigah* 14b uses this term to characterize *Acher* (other one), pejoratively referring to Elisha ben Abuya.

Glossary

ADAR—The twelfth Hebrew month
AGGADIC DERASHOS—Homiletic discourses
AL HANISSIM—The prayer of thanksgiving recited on Chanukah
AMAH pl. AMAS—cubit, cubits
ASMACHTA—mnemonic device

B'NEI YISRAEL—Children of Israel
BAMIDBAR—The Book of Numbers
BARAISA pl. BARAISOS—outside text, not included in the Mishnah
BEIS DIN—Jewish court
BEIS HAMIKDASH—Holy Temple
BEN—son of
BERACHAH pl. BERACHOS—blessing
BEREISHIS—The Book of Genesis
BILAM—Balaam
BIRCHAS HAMAZON—Grace after meals
BRIS BEIN HABESARIM—covenant between the halves, a covenant Hashem made with Avraham
BRIS MILAH—covenant of circumcision

CHALITZAH—the ceremony whereby a woman whose husband left no progeny is released from her obligation to marry her deceased husband's brother.

DERASH, DERASHAH—discourse
DEVARIM—The Book of Deuteronomy
DIVREI HAYAMIM—Chronicles

EISAV—Esau
EIVER—a descendant of Noah
ELIYAHU—Elijah

246

ERETZ YISRAEL—The Land of Israel
ESROG—citron

GEMARA—Talmud
GEONIM—Sages who lived after the completion of the Talmud.
GEZEIRAH pl. GEZEIROS—protective measures
GITTIN—divorce

HALACHAH—law
HALACHAH LEMOSHE MISINAI—law handed down from Moses at Sinai
HASHEM—God

IYOV—Job

KARES—punishment of premature death
KESUVAH—marriage contract
KIDDUSH HASHEM—sanctification of the name of Hashem
KOHEIN pl. KOHANIM—Priests, descendants of Aaron
KOHEIN GADOL—High Priest
KOHELES—Ecclesiastes

LEVI'IM—from the tribe of Levi
LULAV—palm branch taken on Sukkos

MA'ASEROS—the tithes
MAMZER—illegitimate child
MASECHES—Tractate of
MASECHTA pl. MASECHTOS—Tractate
MASHIACH—the Messiah
MELACHIM—The Book of Kings
MESUSHELACH—Methuselah
MEZUZAH—parchment scroll containing the Shema that is placed on the doorpost
MIKVEH—ritual immersion pool
MILAH—circumcision
MINHAGIM—customs
MISHLEI—Proverbs
MISHNAH pl. MISHNAYOS—compilation of the oral tradition; it also refers to one paragraph of this compilation

MITZVAH pl. MITZVOS—commandment
MOSHE RABBEINU—Moses our Teacher
MOUNT NEVO—Mount Nebo

NAZIR—nazirite—one who makes a vow to obstain from wine and
   from contact with the dead, he may also not cut his hair
NIDDAH—menstruant woman

ORLAH—fruit of a tree within three years of its planting

PARASHAS—the portion [of the Torah]
PEREK—chapter
PRUZBUL—a document enabling one to collect his loans after the
   sh'mittah year

SEDER—order
SEDER NEZIKIN—the Order of Damages, a portion of the Talmud
   dealing with monetary issues
SH'MITTAH—the sabbatical year when work in the field is
   prohibited
SHABBOS—The day of rest—Saturday
SHAVUOS—Festival of Weeks
SHEM—son of Noah
SHEMOS—The Book of Exodus
SHEVAT—The eleventh Hebrew month
SHIN—a letter of the Hebrew alphabet
SHIR HASHIRIM—Song of Songs
SHLOMOH—Solomon
SHMUEL—The Book of Samuel
SHOFAR—ram's horn blown on Rosh Hashonah
SHOFTIM—The Book of Judges
SIDRAH—portion of the Torah
SUKKAH—hut used on Sukkos
SUKKOS—Festival of Tabernacles

TAHARAH—ritual purity
TAHOR—ritually pure
TAKKANOS—enactments
TAMEI—ritually impure
TEFILLIN—phylacteries

TEHILLIM—Psalms

TERUMAH pl. TERUMOS—contribution to the Kohein

TORAS KOHANIM—a commentary from the Sages on the Book of Vayikra

TOSEFTA—supplement

TUM'AH—ritual impurity

TZITZIS—fringes worn on a four-cornered garment

VAYIKRA—The Book of Leviticus

YAAKOV—Jacob

YECHEZKEL—Ezekiel

YEHOSHUA—Joshua

YEROVAM BEN NEVAT—King of the Ten Tribes who broke off from the Kingdom of Judah after the death of Shlomo; in order to stop the people from going to Jerusalem, he erected golden calves for them to worship

YERUSHALAYIM—Jerusalem

YESHAYAH—Isaiah

YIBBUM—levirate marriage where the wife of one who died without progeny, marries his brother

YIRMIYAH—Jeremiah

YISRAEL—Israel

YOEL—Joel

YOM TOV pl. YAMIM TOVIM—Festivals

Index

Accusations, against Jews, 57–59
Advice, from prophets, 91
Aggados, xix, 81
    derashos, 132–136
    interpretations of, 224–227
Agriculture, mitzvos about, 113–117
Al Dar'i, Rabbi Moshe, 45–46
Alfasi, Rabbi Yitzchak, 145
Allusions. *See also Aggados*
    in Torah, 37, 103
Almohads, invasion by, xii, 6
Analysis
    of laws, 97–98, 101–104
    and ultimate goal of man, 191
Antigonus of Socho, 222, 223
Apikoros, 235–236, 245
Apostates
    behavior of, 53–55
    and Mohammed in Torah,
      20–21
Arabic, Maimonides writing in, xx,
    82
Arabs
    empire of, 36, 43–44
    persecution of Jews by, 42–43
Aristotle, Rambam's differences
    from, xvi, 215
Ashi, Rav, writings of, 131, 132, 144
Astrology, 225
    criticisms of, 31–35, 91–93, 203
    for prediction of Maschiach,
      xvii, 46
Avos (The Tractate of the Fathers),
    167–216

Avrajam
    blessings of, 21–22
    and First Cause of Creation, 33
Azharos, 62

Babylonian Talmud, compiled by
    Rav Ashi, 144
Beis Din, 95
Beis Hillel, 107–108, 147
Beis Shammai, 107–108
Ben Shlomoh, Rabbi Yehudah,
    translation by, xv
Bilam's oracle, 37
"Bimeod meod," 20, 21, 23
Blessings, Yitzchak's and
    Yishmael's, 21–22
B'nei Yisrael. See Jews; Yisrael
Book of Shemos, 114

Cairo, Rambam in, xiii–xiv
Chai Hashem, significance of, 215
Chananiah ben Azur, prophecy of,
    94–95
Character traits
    middle road in, 179–182
    and nature of man, 202, 208,
      213–214
    of prophets, 198–200
Charity, 40
Children, teaching about
    Revelation at Sinai, 16
Chillul Hashem, 67–70
Christianity
    doctrine refuted, xvii–xviii

Christianity *(continued)*
    superiority of Judaism over,
        7–11
Chukkim statutes, 196
Civil laws, mitzvos about, 113,
    121–125
Comfort, and ultimate goal of
    man, 191–192
Commandments. *See also* Mitzvos
    immutability of, 26–27
    leading to moderation, 183–188
    obedience to, 66–67, 203–208
    of true prophets, 89–90, 95–97
Commentary on the *Mishnah*
    Introduction to, xix, 82–164
    reasons for writing, 146–147
    structure of, 147
    writing of, xiv–xv, 81–82
Context, necessity to proofs, 24–25
Conversion, forced, xii, xiii, 12, 59
    behavior after, 53–55, 59,
        63–65, 66–67, 71–73
    prophecy of, 17–18
    in Yemen, xvii, xviii, 6
Covenant, with Yitzchak, 22
Creation, and laws of nature,
    206–208

Daniel
    and arrival of Maschiach,
        29–30
    and persecution by Arabs, 42
    prophecies of, 7, 9, 11–12
David, and persecution by Arabs,
    42–43
Death, 66
    al Kiddush Hashem, 70–73
    for false prophets, 27–28, 39,
        89–90, 97
Derashos
    Aggados, 132–136
    model to understanding,
        136–143

Desires
    as power of the soul, 172,
        174–175
    and self-restraint, 177–185,
        194–196
Devorah, about Revelation at
    Sinai, 23–24
Disasters, as punishment, 93
Discourse on Matyrdom, xviii–xix,
    53–77
Discourse on the World to Come,
    xx, 219–234
Diseases, of the soul, 177–182
Divine foreknowledge, and free
    will, 214–216

Edom
    in prophecy of Maschiach, 36
    rejection of Torah by, 24
Education, 32
    of character, 202
    on commandments, 207–208
    of Maimonides, xii
    necessity of, 133–136, 140
    and ultimate goal of man, 191
Eglon, king of Moab, 63–64
Egypt
    Jews in, 29–30, 208–212
    Rambam in, xiii–xiv
Eight Chapters, The, xix–xx, 167–216
Eisav, 10
    and blessings of Avraham, 22
    relation with Hashem, 64
Elders, and transmission of Torah,
    83, 99
Eliezer, Rabbi, seized by heretics,
    60–61
Eliyahu, criticism of Jews by, 58
Emigration, for religious freedom,
    18–19, 74–76
Empires
    as precursor to Maschiach,
        11–12, 36

response to Maschiach, 41
Encouragement, to Yemenites,
14–15, 35–36
Exile, 35
false Mashiachs in, 47–48
of Jews, in Egypt, 29–30
of Maimon family, xiii
for religious freedom, 18–19,
73–76
Existence, purpose of, 136–143
Ezra, *takkanos* of, 109

Faith
basis of, 16–17, 236–245
encouragement for, 30–31
and persecution, 6–7, 14
rewards for, 235–236
Feeling, as power of the soul, 171,
174–175
Festivals, mitzvos about, 113
First Cause of Creation, 33
Foreign deities, 87
Free will, xvi, 203–212
and Divine foreknowledge,
214–216
Hashem's limits on, 210–213
Future, predicting. *See* Prophecy

Gamliel, Rabban, 232
Gamliel, Rabbi Shimon ben, 195
Gaon, Rabbeinu Saadiah, 29–31
Garden of Eden, as reward,
219–220, 230–231
Gehenna, as punishment, 219–220,
230–231
Gemara
compiled by Rav Ashi, 132, 144
and Mishnah, 146–147
Geonim, 145
Gezeiros, 108–109
Giving of the Torah. *See* Revelation
at Sinai
Goal, of man

to know Hashem, 189–193, 229
the World to Come as, 233–234
Gog and Magog, wars of, 38, 41
Golden Age, of Spanish Jewry,
xi–xii
Greeks, persecution of Jews by, 13,
61
Guide for the Perplexed, The, xi, xvi

Hakadosh, Rabbeinu. *See* HaNasi,
Rabbi Yehudah
Halachah leMoshe miSinai,
101–106
Halachic decisions, 145
disagreements over, 106–107,
147
disagreements recorded in
Mishnah, 101, 111–112
process of making, xix
role of prophets in, 97–98
HaNasi, Rabbi Yehudah, xiv, 100
compiling of Mishnah by, 101,
111–112
Hashem
belief in, 237
desecration of name of,
67–70, 75–77
knowledge of, 189–193, 198,
200–201
nature of, 215–216, 237–238,
243
rewards and punishments
by, 14, 93–94
sanctification of name of,
69–73, 235–236
Hashkafah, influence of
Maimonides on, xi
HaTzaddik, Shimon, Oral Law
traced to, 131
Health
excesses in healing, 177–188
and ultimate goal of man,
189–191

Hoshiah, Rabbi, supplements to
   Mishnah by, 131

Ibn Aryeh, 46–47
Ibn Migash, Rabbi Yosef, 145
Idolatry, 58
   Jews forced into, 12–13, 61, 87
   prohibition against, 66,
      95–96, 123, 238–239
Iggeret Teiman (Letter to Yemen),
   xvii–xviii, 6–49
Imagination, as power of the soul,
   171–172, 174
Incest, prohibition against, 66
Insanity, of false Maschiach, 39–42
Intermediaries, between prophets
   and God, 240–241
Isaiah, prayer of, 213
Islam. *See also* Conversion, forced
   claims of refuted, xvii–xviii,
      20–21, 23–24
   Jewish culture under, xi–xii
   Moslem conquest of
      Cordova, xiii
   prophecy about, 11–12
   superiority of Judaism over,
      7–11

Jerusalem, Jews allowed in, xiv
Jerusalem Talmud, compiled by
   Rabbi Yochanan, 144
Jeshu the Nazerene, 9
   miracles attributed to, 41–42
Jews, 245
   in Messianic Age, 231–233
   Rambam's love for, xviii–xix
   sins of, 57–59
   specialness of, 7–9, 14–16
   Torah taught to, 83–85
   ultimate triumph of, 12–14, 36
Judaism
   principles of, xix–xx, xv–xvi,
      15–16

   superiority of, 10–11, 17–18
   types of attacks on, 7–10
Judges, *masechtos* about, 122–125

Kabbalism, in *Aggadic derashos*,
   133–134
Karaites, xiii–xiv
Kareis, 71, 72
Kares, 229, 243
Kiddush Hashem, 66, 69–70
Kings, response to Maschiach, 41
Knowledge, 200–201, 215–216

Laws. *See also* Commandments;
   Mitzvos
   categories of, 106–110, 195–196
   Halachah leMoshe miSinai,
      101–106
   interpretations of, xv–xvi, 85
   obedience to, 19, 57–58
   origin of, 83–85, 99
   and prophets, 95–96, 99
Laws of nature, and miracles,
   206–208
Letter to Yemen (*Iggeret Teiman*),
   xvii–xviii, 6–49

Maamar Kiddush Hashem (Discourse
   on Matyrdom), xviii–xix, 53–77
Maimonides, life of, xii–xiv
Man
   purpose of, 138–143
   ultimate goal of, 189–193, 229,
      233–234
Manslaughter, prohibition against,
   66
Marriage
   masechtos about, 119–121
   mitzvos about, 113
Mashiach. *See also* Messianic Age,
   calculating arrival of,
      xvii–xviii, 29–31, 36–38
   characteristics of, 39–41, 244

coming of as reward, 75–76,
219–220
false, 9, 39–47
prophecy of, 35–36, 244
Medicine
lessons from, 190
Maimonides as healer, xiii
Meir, Rabbi, 60
Men of the Great Assembly, and
Oral Law, 99
Messianic Age, 231–233. *See also*
Mashiach
belief in, 244
suffering before, 6–7
Metaphysics, and essence of
Hashem, 215–216
Middle road, moderation, 179–188
Milah, 57
Minhagim, and *takkanos*, 109
Miracles
attributed to Jeshu, 41–42
of false Mashiachs, 43–47
and laws of nature, 206–208
and truth of prophecy, 27–28,
86
Mishnah
and Commentary, xiv–xv
compiling of, 101, 111–112
and *Gemara*, 132, 146–147
Sages quoted in, 148–164
structure of, 113–114
Tosefta (Supplement) to, 131
Mishneh Torah, writing of, xv–xvi
Mitzvos
after forced conversion,
66–67, 71–73
importance of, 62–65
influence of prophecy on, 86,
95–98
as *Kiddush Hashem*, 69–70
in Messianic Age, 232–233
perfection through, 11, 230
under persecution, 71–77

punishments for
transgressing, 243–244
rewards for fulfilling,
219–224, 233–234, 243–244
transmission of, 83–84
Moderation, 179–188
Mohammed
attack on Judaism by, 10
claims to be in Torah, 20–21, 23
Jews forced to acknowledge, 53
in prophecy of Maschiach, 36
Moreh Nevuchim. See Guide for the
Perplexed, The
Moshe, Rabbeinu, 187–188
death of, 85
and knowledge of Hashem,
200–201
primacy of among prophets,
15, 26
prophecy of, 14, 239–241
transmission of Torah by,
27–28, 83–85, 88–89, 109

Nachman bar Yitzchak, Rav, 68
Nebuchadnezzar, 12–13, 61, 64
North Africa, Jewish culture in,
xi–xii
Numeric values, xv, 37
Nutritive power of the soul,
170–171, 174

Occult, 25–26. *See also* Astrology
difference from prophecy,
91–93
Oppression. *See also* Persecution
freedom from, in Messianic
Age, 232
Oral affirmation of faith, 73
Oral Law
categories of, 101–110
immutability of, 28, 88–89
transmission of, xix, 83–84,
99–100, 131

Paran, in Moslem claims, 20, 23
Patriarchs, importance of, 33
Perfection
    and Moshe's knowledge of
        Hashem, 200–201
    through mitzvos, 11, 230
    through self-control, 234
    through striving for middle
        course, 183–188
Persecution
    differences in, 73–76
    by Greeks, 13
    mitzvos under, 66–67, 76–77
    by Nebuchadnezzar, 12–13
    ways to endure, 42–43
    in Yemen, xvii–xviii
Personality, of Rambam, xviii–xix
Pharaoh, free will of, 209–212
Philosophy. *See also* Aristotle
    Greek, 203
    in *The Guide for the Perplexed*, xvi
Pleasure, kinds of, 227–230
Powers of souls, 169–173
    control over, 174–176
Predetermination. *See also* Free will
    denial of, 203–208
Prohibitions, leading to
    moderation, 185–188
Proofs
    context and interpretation of
        prophecy, 24–25
    in interpretation of Torah,
        102–104
    lack of, in astrology, 32–34
    refuting foolish, 62
Prophecy, 239
    authenticating, 24–28, 87–91,
        93–95
    of false Mashiachs, 45–46
    importance of, 15, 167
    influence on Torah, 86, 95–98
    of Maschiach, 35–36
    by Moshe, 239–241

and occult, 31–35, 91–93
    of rise of Islam, 11–12
Prophets
    arrival predicted in Torah,
        24–28
    characteristics of, 198–200
    claims of Mohammed to be,
        20–21
    false, 26–27, 39–40, 87–89
    and Oral Law, 99, 109
    primacy of Moshe among, 15,
        240–241
    true, 89–90
Publicness *vs.* privacy
    in sanctification of Hashem's
        name, 70
    in violation of
        commandments, 66–67
Punishments
    for criticism of Jews, 57–59
    for desecration of Hashem's
        name, 69
    disasters as, 34, 93
    and free will, 203, 206–212
    masechtos about, 122
    for sins under persecution,
        71–72, 74
    for transgressions, 223, 230,
        243–244
    in the World to Come,
        219–220, 230–234
Purpose of existence, as model
    derashah, 136–143

Rambam. *See* Maimonides
"Rambam, the." *See Mishneh Torah*
Reasoning, as power of the soul,
    172–175
Religions
    attack on Torah through
        doctrines of, 8–10
    superiority of Judaism, 10–11
Repentance

Hashem withholding power
of, 210–213
power of, 206
Reputation
of judges, 124–125
and use of Hashem's name,
67–69
Restoration of prophecy, as
precursor to Maschiach, 37
Resurrection, of the dead, 244
as reward, 220, 231
Revelation at Sinai
Hashem's arrival at, 23–24
importance of, 16–18, 27–28
Jews as witness of, 15, 16
Rewards
for honoring Hashem, 63–64
for observing mitzvos,
221–224, 230, 243–244
for studying Torah, 221–224
in the World to Come,
219–220, 230–234
Righteousness, and evil, 194
Ritual purity
masechtos about, 128–130
mitzvos about, 113–114

Sacred objects, *masechtos* about,
125–128
Sacrifices
masechtos about, 125–128
mitzvos about, 113–114
Sages, 142–143
and *Aggados*, 132–136, 224–227
on arrival of Maschiach, 30
on behavior after forced
apostasy, 54, 59, 72
and false prophets, 9, 92
and false religions, 11
as healers of the soul, 178–182
interpretations of laws by, 85,
97–98, 106–109, 111–112
masechtos about, 123–124

and persecution, 13, 43
on rewards for honoring
Hashem, 64, 192–193
sayings of, 109, 131, 132,
148–164
and transmission of Oral
Law, 99
Saints, and self-restraint, 194–196
Scholars
behavior befitting, 68–69
and false prophets, 87
interpretations of *Aggados* by,
224–227
under Moslem caliphs, xi–xii
Rebbi HaNasi as, 100
Scrolls, Torah, 85
Seder Kodashim, 125–128
Seder Mo'eid, 117–119
Seder Nashim, 119–121
Seder Nezikin, 121–125
Seder Teharos, 128–130
Seder Zera'im, 115–117
Self-control, 194–197, 234
Sephardic scholarship, xii
Shabbos
desecration of, 77
masechtos about, 117
Shemonah Perakim, xix–xx, 167–216
Shlomoh, King, 17, 63–64
and Mashiach, 35, 47
Shmuel, prophecy of, 91
Shulamis, 17
Sichliyos (rational laws), 195–196
Sihon, King of Heshbon, 211–212
Sinai. *See* Revelation at Sinai
Sins
as barriers to knowledge of
Hashem, 198, 201
and desecration of Hashem's
name, 67
free will for, 194–196, 203–209
of Jews, 57–59
Sins *(continued)*

and prophecy of good
     tidings, 94
repentance for, 210–213
and the World to Come,
     235–236
Solomon, King, on good and evil,
     194
Souls
     diseases of, 177–182
     excision of, 229, 243
     health of, 190–191
     perfection of, 234
     powers of, 169–176
Spain, Jewish culture in, xi–xii
Speech
     conservation of, 53–54
     reviews before publicizing,
          55–56
     and ultimate goal of man, 191
Spiritual pleasures, 227–229
Stand at Sinai. *See* Revelation at
     Sinai
Suffering
     as offering to Hashem, 18
     in persecution by Arabs,
          42–43
     from resisted desires, 195

Takkanos, and *minhagim,* 109
Talmud
     compiled by Rav Ashi, 144
     Mishnah in, xiv
Tanach, on qualities of Maschiach,
     41, 42
Thirteen principles of faith,
     236–244
Tithes and offerings
     masechtos about, 125–128
     mitzvos about, 115–117
Torah. *See also* Revelation at Sinai
     immutability of, 16, 26–28,
          88–89, 243

influence of prophecy on,
     95–98
interpretation of, 101–104
and Islam, 11–12, 20–21
respect for, 24, 235–236
rewards for studying, 221–224
superiority of, 7–11
transmission of, 83–85, 242–243
Tosefta (Supplement) to Mishnah, 131
Tractate Avos, *The Eight Chapters*
     in, 167–216
Traditions
     in interpretation of Torah
          laws, 103
     takkanos and *minhagim,* 109
Translations
     accounts of false Mashiachs
          in, 44
     of Commentary on the
          Mishnah, 82
     of Maimonides's Arabic,
          xiv–xv, xx
     of Torah, 21
Truth, search for, as purpose of
     man, 139

Vices
     as barriers to knowledge of
          Hashem, 201
     and character traits of
          prophets, 198–200
     and powers of the soul,
          175–176
Virtues
     and character traits of
          prophets, 198–200
     as middle road, 179–181
     and powers of the soul,
          175–176
Visions, prophecy through,
     240–241

Wisdom

hidden in *Aggados*, 226–227
search for, as purpose of
  man, 139–141, 189–193
Women
  masechtos about, 119–121
  mitzvos about, 113
World to Come, the. *See also*
  Discourse on the World to Come
  rewards and punishments in,
    210, 229–234
  as ultimate goal, 233–236
Worship
  after forced conversion,
    53–55, 63–67
  under Arab persecution,
    73–76
  rewards for, 219–224

Yaakov
  and blessings of Avraham, 22
  Hashem's promise to, 13
Yad HaChazakah. See Mishneh Torah

Yehoshua bin Nun, 109
  transmission of laws by, 99–100
  use of laws by, 85
Yemen. *See also Iggeret Teiman*
  false Maschiach in, 39–40
Yeshayah, 18
  and advice to abandon
    astrology, 31–32
  on appearance of Maschiach,
    30, 41
  prophecy of, 8, 13
Yirmiyah, prophecy of, 94–95
Yishmael, 24
  and Avraham's blessings,
    21–22
  in prophecy of Maschiach, 36
Yisrael
  appearance of Maschiach in, 40
  Jews return to, 231–233
Yitzchak, as heir to Avraham's
  blessing, 21–22
Yochanan, Rabbi, 68, 144

Avraham Yaakov Finkel

Avraham Yaakov Finkel was born in Basel, Switzerland, and lived in The Hague, The Netherlands, until 1942, when he was deported to Bergen-Belsen by the Nazis. Mr. Finkel is the author of *Contemporary Sages, The Essence of the Holy Days, The Great Chasidic Masters, The Responsa Anthology,* and *The Great Torah Commentators.* He has also translated numerous works, including *Torah Treasures,* autobiographies of the Tosafot Yom Tov and Chatam Sofer, *Dare to Survive, Songs of Hope,* and most recently the biography of Aharon Kotler, founder of the Yeshiva of Lakewood. Mr. Finkel resides in New York with his wife, Suri.